# PERSONALITY AND ADAPTATION

# ADVANCES
# IN
# PSYCHOLOGY

## 2

*Editors*

G. E. STELMACH

P. A. VROON

NORTH-HOLLAND PUBLISHING COMPANY
AMSTERDAM • NEW YORK • OXFORD

# PERSONALITY
# AND ADAPTATION

## P. J. HETTEMA
*Tilburg University*
*Tilburg, The Netherlands*

1979

**NORTH-HOLLAND PUBLISHING COMPANY**
AMSTERDAM • NEW YORK • OXFORD

ISBN: 0 444 85380 4

*Publishers:*
NORTH-HOLLAND PUBLISHING COMPANY
AMSTERDAM • NEW YORK • OXFORD


*Sole distributors for the U.S.A. and Canada:*
ELSEVIER NORTH-HOLLAND, INC.
52 VANDERBILT AVENUE
NEW YORK, N.Y. 10017

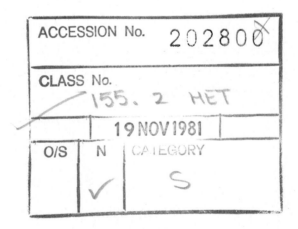
PRINTED IN THE NETHERLANDS

To Paul, to Marc

*Preface*


For every psychologist with an interest in fundamental theory there comes a time when he feels the urge to deliver himself of a major contribution to his field. For me that moment came well over ten years ago. After research in such divergent areas as test development, psychophysics, social perception, information theory as well as in educational and industrial psychology I had become increasingly disenchanted with the overall frames within which research was being conducted. This disenchantment deepened during a one year's stay in the United States on a grant from the Netherlands Organization for the Advancement of Pure Research (ZWO) in 1966. At Stanford University Walter Mischel had by then launched the first of his vigorous attacks on classical personality theory, while Lee Cronbach and Richard Snow were engaged in developing their ATI-paradigm to replace traditional approaches in educational research. In Educational Testing Service at Princeton Samuel Messick and his staff were busily relating test scores to learning parameters in an attempt to transcend classical procedures in selection and placement.

All these endeavors seemed to hold direct or indirect implications for the renovation of personality theory, but their interrelations remained obscure. To me they constituted a challenge to renew my thinking, starting all over by critically examining a number of prominent assumptions, usually held by personality theorists. I intended to write a book that was going to revolutionize theory construction and research in the area of personality. As well as giving a clear and comprehensive exposition of the shortcomings of current theories and mapping out the crucial areas where change was imperative, the book was to formulate postulates and hypotheses in such rigorous terms as to permit testing, preferably in crucial experiments.

Needless to say, that book never materialized, time being a scarce commodity and psychology a complex art. During the years following that first impulse, the field of personality theory turned out to be even more complex than had been expected initially, so that much more time and effort had to be invested. The result of the endeavor as presented here, sets out a number of ideas, some belonging to the established canon of psychological theory construction, others representing recent views that have found some recognition, while yet others are almost entirely speculative. Science being above all a social endeavor, I hesitate to claim that any of the ideas set forth here are strictly original. Whenever possible I have mentioned by name those authors whom I consider to have been the first to express certain conceptions. Among earlier authors I have borrowed ideas from Freud, Allport, Tolman and Brunswik, while among more recent ones I have especially drawn on the work of such divergent authors as Berlyne, Dobzhansky, Hebb, Kelly, Leontiev, Mandler, Simpson and Skinner. Great care has been taken to present these ideas within a comprehensive framework.

The book's overall objective is to contribute to our thinking about personality. While the ideas presented in it are primarily directed to those psychologists who engage in fundamental theory construction, it is hoped that practitioners will also find certain things here that can be usefully applied in their work. Finally, the book is also intended to have some use as a text for advanced students.

If this book succeeds in making a contribution to psychology as a science, this will be due, at least in part, to those who have in the past mustered the patience to take an interest in earlier versions of the text. Among these were the participants in a number of graduate seminars at Tilburg University. I am especially indebted to Jo Vossen of Nijmegen University, who kindly read drafts of Chapters II, III and IV. While disagreeing with me on some core issues, he has forced me to deepen my thinking on those matters, thus making an invaluable contribution to the final result. I am further indebted to Jop Spiekerman of Leiden University, who carefully screened the English text and improved it considerably. Finally, I wish to express my gratitude to Nettie Cools, Ine Maas, Marja Onderwater and Rea Bergmans, who typed the manuscript.

Tilburg, May 1979   Joop Hettema

# TABLE OF CONTENTS

'Personality theorists in their own times have
been rebels. Rebels in medicine and in experimental
science, rebels against conventional ideas and usual
practices, rebels against typical methods and respec-
ted techniques of research, and most of all rebels
against accepted theory and normative problems'. This
statement was made by Hall and Lindzey in the first
edition of their handbook 'Theories of personality'
(1957, p.4). Traditionally, it has always been personality theorists who opened up novel perspectives in
psychology and led the way in new thinking. From
Freud's unconscious mechanisms to Kelly's personal
constructs there stretches a long line of developments
that have had a major impact on psychology as a whole.
But this spearhead function of personality theory appears to have fallen into abeyance in the last two or
three decades. Very recently personality psychologists
have been taken to task by Sechrest in his 1976 annual
review: 'Personality theory is, in my estimation, in
sad shape. When new textbooks come out, whether in
personality or introductory psychology, the discussion
is almost invariably organized around presentations of
Freud, Jung, Adler, the neo-Freudians, etc. with a
usual bow toward the end in the direction of "social
learning theory". In no other field purporting to be
scientific are the current heroes of theory nearly
all dead'. (p. 3).
    This is by no means an isolated statement. It
would not be difficult to cite other comments on the
passivity and downright stagnation of personality
theory in the last twenty years or so. This is not to
say that personality theories have become superfluous. On the contrary, we are today confronted at every turn with individuals caught up in problems with
themselves, with others or with society. What seems
rather more likely therefore is that personality theo-

rists no longer find themselves able to expand new
notions into comprehensive conceptions. A number of
arguments can be adduced to support this view, all of
which concern the nature and functioning of personality theory as such.

At the root of the older, classical theories
there would often be little more than an explicitly
adopted anthropological position, from which deducti-
ons were made that were then examined in the light of
observed facts. Characteristically, the theory itself
would be more or less systematic reflection and speculation on human nature. Links with empirical reality would be established through common sense. But as
various disciplines within psychology matured, personality theory took on a new, integrative and summarizing function. Today, more than ever before, the
personality theorist finds himself confronted with
the task of studying findings in other areas of psychology and integrating them in this theory construction. This development has led to a loss of autonomy
and freedom of the personality theorist, who is now
compelled to examine extensively *all* areas of theory
construction within psychology and subsequently to
select very strictly those topics that he is going to
include in his theoretical endeavors.

The arguments for selection he must derive from
a general position with regard to human functioning,
that is, from a specific anthropology. In choosing
his anthropological stance the theorist is free to
fall in with existing views or, on the contrary, to
repudiate them. So there would seem to be ample scope
for dissidents and rebels, but the consequences of
the theorist's choice, once made, are so all-embracing in terms of the study and research required that
he will think long and hard before committing himself.

For today's personality theorist matters are
further complicated by the requirements imposed on
psychological theory in general. The armchair character of classical personality theory no longer finds
favor with empirically oriented scientists. The de-
mand that concepts should be empirically defined
weighs heavily on the psychologist who engages in integrative theory construction. If he takes the requirement literally his project may well fall by the
wayside long before he has completed its preparatory
stages. Findings that look encouraging under controlled experimental conditions frequently prove untenable when the research venue shifts to a real-world si-

tuation. Carefully contructed assessment techniques
turn out to be poor predictors. Rating outcomes prove
to be specific to the situation in which they are obtained, questionnaires are found to be highly suscep-
tible to response sets. Predictions of individual behavior must allow for moderator and suppressor variables, situational factors, previous behavior and the
like. Even then prediction will rarely be better than
chance. In a wide-scope discipline like personality,
falsification on empirical grounds is not infrequently the fate that befalls a theory.

The growing complexity of the field, coupled
with the absence of spectacular experimental outcomes, tends to make personality theory seem a thank-
less activity making excessive demands on the theorist. As a result, there is a tendency for certain
research themes, traditionally held to be the concern
of personality theorists, to be taken over by researchers in other areas. As Sechrest (1976) has rightly
pointed out, research on emotional behavior is now
widely held to be the province of social psychology,
because of the important contribution made by the social psychologist Schachter. Edward Jones, another
social psychologist, has carried off attribution theory, although much of it is just as relevant to personality as to social psychology. Yet another social
psychologist, Leonard Berkowitz, has for the past
fifteen years dominated research into aggression and
catharsis. Starting out as social psychologists, these researchers were able to specialize in certain
fairly narrow areas, whereas personality theorists
foundered in their efforts to retain a grasp on the
entire field. In the end, a good many of the latter
forsook their old discipline in favor of more abstract areas like methodology or applied areas like
clinical psychology. In view of the manifold problems
besetting personality theory today it would appear
virtually impossible for new theories to be formulated. Any attempt in that direction seems almost bound
to be one-sided or to end up in triviality, if not in
sheer dilettantism.

On the other hand, the importance of integrative
theory construction can hardly be overestimated. Psychology urgently needs wide-scope paradigms to guide
study and research of a more specialized nature. Also, there is a steadily increasing need of theoretical underpinnings for such activities as counseling
or other forms of specialized treatment to deal with
problems of daily life. Personality theory has tra-

ditionally been much to the fore in this type of problem area (cf. Hall-Lindzey, 1970) but seems increasingly unable to sustain that role, as can be seen
from the uncontrolled growth of psychotherapy and
guidance. The last two or three decades have witnes-
sed a considerable shift in the kind of questions
that field workers want answered by personality theory. Where in the past descriptions of 'personality
structure' would mostly suffice, the focus is now on
the investigation of personality in terms of data
that can be used to anticipate decisions with respect to individuals (cf. Cronbach-Gleser, 1957). Interest no longer centers on prediction with regard to
general social notions like leadership and empathy.
Instead, the emphasis is now on prediction in terms
of individual responses to processes and treatment in
education and clinical settings. Tabulation of individual traits or test scores is entirely inadequate
for dealing with this type of problem. In personality
theory a shift from static-structural to dynamic-
functional aspects is clearly called for, but this
shift should not lead us back into the dark years of
psychodynamic speculation. Conceptions of personality development and individual learning processes must
be included in a modern theory of personality, as must
notions concerning the interaction between individual
and environment. This last aspect in particular has
hitherto resisted all attempts at clear conceptualization. Theory and research on the so-called interaction hypothesis are still in their infancy, and
much work remains to be done.

In this book a deliberate effort is made to lay
the foundations of a theory comprising all these elements. Our main concern will be to develop a new paradigm for the study of the individual. This will occupy us most of the time: conclusions pertinent to
personality as traditionally conceived will be drawn
only towards the end. Our concern will primarily be
with such aspects of individual functioning as are
considered important for the relationship between individual and environment. We shall have occasion to
discuss at some length the contributions made by classical theories of personality. On a good many points,
however, we shall deliberately dissociate ourselves
from preoccupations in these theories which have
proved fruitless. Findings from other areas in psychology as well as from other disciplines will be brought
in if they promise to contribute substantially to a
balanced personality theory.

Chapter I discusses existing theories and innovative efforts discernible in the literature. On the
strength of our findings a number of premises will be
formulated on which our theoretical edifice is to be
raised. Chapter II, which is devoted to the biological basis of personality, traces the effects of traditional evolutionary thinking and concludes that
classical personality theories are firmly rooted in
evolutionary thought. But biologists did not stop
thinking a century ago: modern biological conceptions
are therefore considered in terms of their fruitfulness for personality theory. In Chapter III the so-
cio-cultural basis of personality is critically examined and a revision is proposed of the relationship
between personality and culture as usually conceived.
From these analyses a number of principles are derived, which are to serve as elements of a general personality paradigm set forth in Chapter IV. Chapter V,
finally, seeks to formulate a new theory of personality and to examine more closely some of the implications of such a theory for assessment and treatment.

# CHAPTER 1

## *CONCEPTIONS OF PERSONALITY: PROBLEMS AND PERSPECTIVES*

### *1.1 Early developments in personality psychology*

Every science has its classics, i.e. great theories that have been highly influential in the past
and that have set the stage for further developments
in the field. Classical conceptual frameworks appear
to have a major directional function with respect to
theorizing and research, classical formulations have
often served as an issue for ardent disputes between
their adherents. As science develops, particular research findings may suddenly cause a classical position to be revised or to be abandoned altogether.
Research evidence hopefully also indicates new directions to be chosen in order to obtain a better insight into the object of science. Thus, a sound process of scientific evolution will have come about,
resulting in an increase of theoretical clarity and
comprehensiveness.
     Personality psychology has its classics as well,
although there are some doubts whether those classics may as yet be considered to be truly scientific
theories. Sarason (1972), for instance, prefers to
use the term theoretical orientations to indicate the
collections of formulations, hypotheses, and interpretations that are usually called theories of personality. To eventually develop into truly scientific
theories those orientations should be parsimoniously
restated in rigorous terms to allow for empirical ve-
rifications to be made. As long as they are formulated in an ambiguous common sense terminology, over-
loaded with tacit assumption, they may become an obstacle for scientific progress rather than a first
impetus.
     In the present context, a major problem with
respect to classical theories of personality is their
obvious lack of a clear conception of the functional

7

significance of behavior. Classical theorists seem to have been so strongly fascinated by the individual person, that they have largely neglected to take one of the core issues of psychology into account. Of course this statement needs to be clarified and elaborated further. In order to do so, two major traditions may first be discerned which have long dominated the scene and are still widely adhered to today.

The older of the two is the *psychometric* tradition, which has its roots in Darwin's theory of evolution. The fundamental assumption that individual differences are essential for species survival became the starting-point for the work of Galton, who may be considered the father of psychometry. The work of later exponents of the psychometric tradition - Cattell, Guilford, Eysenck, to name but a few - is ultimately rooted in the same differential premise: it is characteristically assumed that differences in overt behavior/*between* individuals directly reflect differences in behavior *within* individuals. Guilford (1959) states unequivocally: 'We can learn much about how individuals function by studying how they differ' (p. 15). This assumption permits evidence on intra-individual structures (traits) to be collected on the basis of interindividual comparison of behavior. Psychometrists tend to look upon individual traits as being to a considerable extent innate and they assume the existence of a high degree of constancy in personality characteristics over time as well as over situations.

The *psychodynamic* tradition is usually assumed to have started with Freud. We can again discern biological insights underlying the conceptualization of personality, but these insights are derived from a quite different area of biology. Freud's early theoretical endeavors may be characterized as neurodynamic and, although he eventually came to adopt psychological concepts, his model has retained a number of characteristics that can be traced back directly to biology. Freud's conception of man is characteristically that of a system in which various processes take place as a consequence of tensions in the organism, their object being to reduce the tensions. Externally observable behavior is the result of these processes and is conceived as multiconditional: the same behavior may be attributed to different processes and different behaviors may be attributed to the same process. The Freudian assumption of multiconditionality of behavior is characteristic of psychodynamic theory in general.

As well as differences, classical personality theories also exhibit similarities. The psychometric as well as the psychodynamic tradition has developed more or less independently of general psychology. Both traditions have made it their task to account for behavior as a function of the individual organism. The existence of effects from other conditions (i.e. situational characteristics) is not denied, but the study of the effects of these conditions is left to other disciplines within psychology. Thus it was possible for a regrettable state of affairs to arise, that was characterized by Cronbach (1957) as 'the two disciplines of scientific psychology'. Cronbach proposed to bring about the integration of the two disciplines by working with interactive designs in which the joint effects of correlational (personality) and experimental (situation) variables are studied. In Cronbach's view, a new 'united discipline' should occupy itself not only with the study of the two approaches separately but also with the 'otherwise neglected interactions between organism and treatment variables' (1957, p. 24).

But the classical personality theories do not lend themselves readily to the study of this type of interaction. The main reason for this must be sought in the reduction that characteristically occurs within the framework of either tradition. Psychometrists as well as psychodynamists have all along been struggling with the problem of the reduction of individual behavior. If one makes observations of a given individual over a longer period of time, a widely varying set of behaviors may be perceived. The attribution of behavior to causes or conditions always occurs against the background of the theoretical posture of the observer, whether explicit or implicit. It is a major characteristic of classical personality theory that behavior is looked upon purely from the perspective of the individual, of his attributes and processes.

With regard to the effects of other factors such as the situation in which the person finds himself and the conditions preceding that situation, psychodynamists and psychometrists adopt different solutions. In the *psychodynamic* approach the origin of behavior is sought in the organism itself (e.g. Freud's instincts), while personality development is ascribed mainly to a built-in plan (e.g. Freud's developmental stages; Rogers' actualization tendency).

The environment is generally held to play a minor role in this process; its impact is restricted to the manner and degree in which environmental events are subjectively interpreted by the individual. *Psychometric* reduction is a direct consequence of an exclusive interest in individual differences. On this score Sechrest (1976) makes the following memorable remarks: 'Ordinary definitions of personality put emphasis on individual differences in a way that has been, I think, detrimental to progress in theory and research...If anatomists had proceeded in the same way as personality psychologists, we would know a great deal about minor variations in the location of the heart without ever realizing that for just about everyone everywhere it is located in the chest just slightly to the left of center. The above is not to deny the importance of individual differences; but until we know more about basic processes of personality, it is difficult to know how to fit the differences in' (p. 4). From a functional point of view, the omission of similarities between individuals is an arbitrary intervention. It may lead to a neglect of essential aspects of the psychological process that must militate decisively against inclusion of the psychometric approach in a so-called united discipline. Interactions between individual and situation can be accounted for neither from a psychometric point of view nor from a psychodynamic point of view. In both traditions behavior is thus deprived of its proper functional significance. For the psychodynamist the significance of behavior is restricted to its reflection of complex internal processes; to the psychometrist, behavior is a personal characteristic that merely allows one individual to be distinguished from another.

The formulation and elaboration of the classical traditions did not of course mark the end of developments in personality psychology. Through the years a gradual rapprochement to general psychology has taken place, which has resulted in new theories that parallel more closely developments in general psychology. Today we can speak of two rival traditions in personality psychology, a cognitive tradition and one grounded in learning theory. In the latter the emphasis is on habit formation through learning processes while in the former cognitive structures, utilized to come to terms with the environment, are stressed. Unlike the classical approaches, these formula-lations are accessible to preceding and actual situations.

Thus learning psychologists of personality like Dollard and Miller (1950) started out from the idea that habits are established on the basis of stimulus aspects (drives, cues, reinforcements) that may be located inside as well as outside the individual. Later authors (Rotter, 1954; Bandura, 1971) have more particularly emphasized social aspects of the learning process. They assume that mere perception of other people's actions and the consequences of these actions is a sufficient condition for learning to occur.

A cognitivist like Kelly (1955) assumes that individuals can be characterized on the basis of conceptions or constructs which they use to anticipate events in their environment. These constructs have a canalizing function with respect to the processes that the individual makes use of in a particular situation. Constructs are maintained in the individual as long as they contribute to an adequate anticipation of events; if that is no longer the case, they are discarded and replaced by new constructs.

Learning theorists as well as cognitive theorists of personality direct themselves to the individual's manner of dealing with the environment, although there is a difference in emphasis. While learning theorists stress the organization of *behavior*, cognitivists place special emphasis on *cognitive* organization. Both priorities are doubtless perfectly legitimate but they also indicate how incomplete either type of theory is. According to an old ideal of personality theory, attempts should be made to integrate them. But that can only be done after a careful coordination of the two traditions has been accomplished so as to allow harmonically integrated personality models to be built.

## 1.2  *Interactionism*

One significant attempt to integrate the two points of view was made by Mischel in his 'cognitive social learning reconceptualization of personality' (1973). The impetus for this undertaking had come five years earlier when Mischel thoroughly criticized classical personality theories in his book *Personality and Assessment* (1968). Theoretically, his criticisms were mainly directed against the adoption of so-called global personality dispositions. This term

is used to indicate broad behavioral dispositions
that manifest themselves stably and more or less independently of stimulus conditions. Mischel made a
distinction between intellectual and cognitive dispositions on the one hand and personality dispositions
on the other. Among the latter, such variables as attitudes, moral behavior, dependency and aggression
were explicitly dealt with to expose the flaws in
traditional personality theory. Mischel clearly demonstrated that global dispositions generally prove
inconsistent as soon as there is a change in the situation in which behavior is being studied. This conclusion holds to some extent for cognitive variables
but pertains particularly to personality variables.

Mischel (1968) extended his criticisms to the
practical use and utility of personality measures in
assessment and prediction. On the basis of a review
of the literature on this area he concluded: 'In sum
the data reviewed on the utility of psychometrically
measured traits, as well as psychodynamic inferences
about states and traits, show that responses have not
served very usefully as indirect signs of internal
predispositions' (p. 145), and: 'These conclusions
for personality measures apply, on the whole, to diverse content areas including the prediction of col-
lege achievement, job and professional success,
treatment outcomes, rehospitalization for psychiatric
patients, parole violations for delinquent children,
and so on. In light of these findings it is not sur-
prising that large-scale applied efforts to predict
behavior from personality inferences have been stri-
kingly and consistently unsuccessful' (p. 145-146).

Mischel's position with respect to classical
personality theory is far from isolated. Hunt (1965),
for instance, stated that traditional personality assessment techniques hardly ever produce reliability
and validity coefficients anywhere near the conventional levels required of a good test. The proportion
of variance attributable to individual effects is only
a fraction of the total amount of behavioral variance
found in research on topics in personality assessment. Petersen (1965) studied the generalizability of
personality traits and concluded that a considerable
modification of existing trait theories is urgently
called for. Wallace (1966) emphasized response factors in the study of personality, but took exception
to a trait conception in which response probabilities are established and used directly to make predictions. Instead, he advocated a skills-conception

of personality which would divorce response assessment from prediction of such responses in future situations. The present author (Hettema, 1967) paid
special attention to the question of how representative the test situation is of real-life situations,
as well as to the problem of generalizability of test
behavior to non-test behavior. He argued that personality tests are usually composed to serve as adequate instruments for measuring one or more traits.
From that point of view, item homogeneity is clearly
the main criterion in test construction. This means
that from the initial item pool those items will usually be selected that virtually replicate one another. In this process, representativeness is sacrificed
in favor of homogeneity. This then leads to a decrease in the generalizability of test scores over
situations. In other words, overemphasis on homogeneity leads to an artificial restriction of the range
of situations for which the test may be used as a
predictor. Hettema concluded by proposing a number of
changes in the personality model underlying test construction, and in particular advocated that environmental variables be represented in personality assessment devices.

   Critical as  all the contributions mentioned
thus far may be, one observation should be made in
defense of the classical position. That observation
has to do with the status of criteria used in personality theorizing. In this context it would be a
gross oversimplification to say that personality psychologists have consistently been barking up the
wrong tree. As long as the theorist's claim does not
go beyond the *description* of personality, the 'language of traits' is as good as any other language. In
concerns of this kind it is of prime importance to
stay as close as possible to everyday usage, and that
is exactly what global dispositionists have done all
along. Problems are only to be expected if one changes his objective from a person-to-be-described to a
person-to-be-treated. That change has come about only
very gradually in psychology and one can at most
fault personality psychology for its failure to create, in good time, appropriate paradigms for dealing
with this larger issue. Mischel (1973) himself ente-
red a qualification to this effect: 'The question becomes not "do traits really exist?" but "when are
trait constructs invoked?" and "what are their uses
and misuses?"'  (p. 262). As long as trait concepts
are only used as a convenient device for describing

other individuals, there can be no objection to admitting them *as such* into a theory of personality.
But that does not imply that traits deserve the
functional significance ascribed to them by many
trait theorists.

In Mischel's view, new theories should renounce the
global disposition approach and concern themselves
primarily with the concrete determinants of individual behavior. His own theoretical efforts are based
mainly on the work of learning theorists like Rotter
(1954) and Bandura (1971) and of cognitive theorists
like Kelly (1955). In his *cognitive social learning
theory*, Mischel (1973) distinguishes five classes of
personality variables which he regards as the products of the total history of the individual:
1. Competencies for the construction of cognitions
   and of behavior;
2. Encoding strategies and personal constructs;
3. Expectations with regard to the outcomes of actions and of stimuli;
4. Subjective evaluations of stimuli and rewards;
5. Systems and plans for self regulation.
   These classes attain an individual mode of re-
alization in the personality and, together, they constitute the key pattern underlying his behavior. Each
of these classes of personality variables may give
rise to individual differences in behavior. At the
same time, such differences will also be determined
by situational parameters. In this context Mischel
distinguishes between powerful and weak situations.
Powerful situations are of a much more compelling
nature than weak situations, and they lead to greater
uniformity of behavior. Individual differences are
particularly liable to arise in weak (ambiguous or
unstructured) situations that leave the individual
more room to make his own interpretations and determine on his own line of action.
   The theoretical formulation  mentioned may be
regarded as a major innovative effort. By distinguishing discrete classes of personality variables,
Mischel has achieved greater precision and differentiation in the description of personality. By further distinguishing between cognitive variables and
behavioral variables he has felicitously eschewed the
bias inherent in either approach. Still the question
must be raised of what will happen to Mischel's reconceptualization as soon as its current format is
reformulated in operational terms and notably when

assessment techniques are based on it and it is used
in applied settings. Judging from the fate of similarly innovative theories in the past, it is to be
feared that, before long, a process of reification
will set in analogous to that which has overtaken
other personality theories. In the first fine flush
of theory construction, the personality description
is couched in action terms but quite soon adjectives
appear on the scene and, finally, the system petri-
fies under the sheer weight of substantives with a
trait character (cf. Carr and Kingsbury, 1938). In
this respect, the vicissitudes of Rotter's concept
'control of reinforcement' (1966) are highly illu-
strative: though explicitly presented as a process
concept, it has only a few years since its introduction become invested with all the characteristics of
a personality trait. In personality, theoretical formulation in process terms is apparently not enough:
the theorist must also state how the processes which
he hypothesizes are to be *measured*.

Apart from this possible reformulation in psychometric terms, there is a risk that Mischel's theory will be converted to psychodynamic uses. Essentially, its formulation treats personality variables as
highly individualized data: in principle, each individual has his own construction competencies, his own
encoding strategies, his own outcome expectations,
his own subjective values and his own plans and systems. In fact, no such high degree of individuality
need be postulated for the conceptualization and prediction of person-situation specific behavior. On
this score Mischel has allowed himself to be (unduly)
swayed by the psychodynamic tradition in its most
phenomenological guise as well as by Kelly's most individualized conception of personal constructs. As a
result, the theory has become unnecessarily unecono-
mical in the number of assumptions made, while the
burden of proof is assigned to verbal, that is, by
their very nature, weak measures.

Downright disappointing is an aspect of Mischel'
s proposition that has to do with the core of his argument. Mischel has not tired of insisting that the
external situation is of crucial importance for the
investigation of personality, but his own theoretical
contribution does not as yet extend beyond the distinction, mentioned before, of weak versus powerful
situations. Relevant in this connection is a statement made by Gordon Allport, the classical personality theorist *par excellence,* in reply to criticisms of

his position: 'I have learned that my earlier views
seemed to neglect the variability induced by ecological, social and situational factors. This oversight
needs to be repaired through an adequate theory that
will relate the inside and outside systems more accurately'.  (Allport, 1966). At this late date,
Mischel's theory is still a long way from adequate
conceptualization of relations between the external
and internal systems.

At this point the question arises which personality aspects should attract the most attention and
emphasis in the interaction model. An overview of the
determinants of behavior from this perspective is given by Endler and Magnusson (1976). Characteristically, neither the situation as such nor the organism in
itself but, instead, a continuous process of interaction between the two is seen to underlie behavior.
Interactionists will thus attach great importance to
the study of situational factors. They tend to favor
analyzing situations in subjective terms, that is, as
perceived by the individual. The psychological meaning of the environment thus becomes an essential de-
terminant of behavior. The personality is conceived
as intentional and active; cognitive factors play a
major part in the interaction process. A pivotal concept is reciprocal causation: just as environmental
events determine individual behavior, so the individual determines his environment. Reciprocal causation
implies that feedback processes are a part of behavi-
or.

Where psychodynamists conceive of behavior as
the expression of complex internal processes, and
psychometrists see it as a distinctive feature of the
individual, the interactionist regards behavior primarily as a *relationship* between the individual and
his environment whose nature is fundamentally determined by its two poles. The relationship develops in
its own specific mode, attains a certain degree of
continuity and comes to a natural end. This model,
which envisages behavior as completing a full cycle,
is sometimes labeled *organismic*. In this conception
the situation does not constitute an obstacle as it
does to global dispositionists, but has become a
well-matched concomitant to the individual. The situation is neither a permanent backdrop to behavior
nor an isolated causal stimulus, but a specific phe-
nomenal field with which the individual relates
through his behavior.

The interaction paradigm comprises a number of
elements of great importance to personality psycholo-

gy. For one thing, the situation is, much more explicitly than elsewhere, included in the theoretical
framework. The way is thereby cleared for an open-
system conception of personality, whose greater lati-
tude promises well for the study of personality.
Mischel's (1973) distinction between processes on the
one hand, and their products in the individual on the
other, is of prime importance for personality theory.
Regrettably, the processes themselves have scarcely
been specified yet. The inclusion of notions from
both learning theories and cognitive theories would
have considerably gained in interest if the processes
and their interrelations could have been more specifically defined in the theory. Finally, it is a matter for regret that interactionists are so much given
to attributing a highly individualistic nature to the
variables they discern. This posture can hardly be
fruitful for the empirical definition  of concepts
and, eventually, research. This must be considered
one of the main reasons why interactionism in its
present form cannot be said to have advanced beyond
the heuristic stage of theory construction.

## 1.3  *Personality as process*

A completely different approach to the personality problem has its origins in developments within
the study of information processing, artificial intelligence and the neurophysiological basis of psychological functioning. Founded on notions derived
from information theory and cybernetics, this approach reached its zenith in the early sixties with
the work of authors like Newell, Shaw, Simon, Miller,
Galanter, Pribram, Reitman, Abelson and Uhr. Processes in areas such as problem solving, learning, concept formation, pattern recognition and thinking were
described, translated into programs and prepared for
computer simulation. The main purpose of these attempts was to describe the processes in a more formal
and rigorous terminology than before and to work out
the implications of pertinent theoretical models.
These developments enabled personality psychologists to reflect in greater depth on the complex processes occurring in the functioning individual as
well as on the key patterns peculiar to individuals.
Unlike the interaction model, this approach is of a
predominantly nomothetic nature. Starting out from
general process notions, certain process parameters
are assumed to differ from individual to individual
and the differences are held to account for indivi-

dual differences in overt behavior. Great importance
has all along been attached to the possibility of si-
mulating processes regarded as of crucial importance
for individual functioning, such as simulation of
affective processes (Abelson, 1963), simulation of
neurotic processes (Colby, 1963; Moser et al., 1970)
and simulation of the personality as a whole (Loehlin,
1968).

All these activities may be seen as endeavors to
formalize more or less speculative notions about personality functioning. Gradually, however, the results
of empirical research and the simulation of processes
have drawn closer together. Thus, more recently,
Messick (1972) has formulated a number of principles
for translating empirical results into process terms.
In his conception, complex personality processes can
be divided into sequential activities arranged in line with a particular strategy. In behavioral sequences a number of sub-processes can be distinguished,
resulting from frequently recurring activities elici-
ted by environmental demands. Through repeated confrontations with identical environmental events these
sub-processes will gradually stabilize, with the result that they eventually assume the character of
traits. Conversely, if one wishes to predict the outcomes of complex processes, the obvious policy is to
make use of information about the sub-processes. In
Messick's view, this information can be obtained from
test scores particularly where cognitive abilities
are concerned. Depending on the nature of the complex
task, some cognitive abilities will be more and others less relevant.

Empirically, Messick's approach is to a large
extent built on the results of factor-analytical research, but he does not join the ranks of those who
simply translate the factors obtained into process
units. Inferences in terms of common processes made
on the basis of empirical factors have a precarious
status, Messick holds: at best, they represent possible processes that may have produced the correlated
results. Factors are to be considered structural variables, some of which stand for important latent
constructs, but they do not furnish the functional
linkages among those constructs. To trace such links,
Messick (1972) advocates 'augmenting the ubiquitous
factor analysis of concurrent covariation by the experimental methods of the laboratory and the comparative and inductive methods of naturalistic and clinical field study' (p. 358). The approach whereby,
within a theoretical functional network, factors are

related to one another as well as to situational and
test variables is called the *multivariate experimental approach*. Messick regards this approach as an indispensable prerequisite for inferences in terms of
personality processes. This type of research strategy has produced a number of successful investigations
into, for instance, complex motor learning (Fleishman
*et al.*, 1955), transfer of learning (Ferguson, 1956),
concept learning (Bunderson, 1967; Frederiksen, 1969)
and problem solving (Hunt, 1961).

An offshoot of the approach advocated by Messick
is multivariate analysis of the activities that make
up sub-processes. Basically, this operation amounts
to construct validation, in terms of information processing, of tests and factors representing cognitive
variables. In this line of research French (1955) was
able to demonstrate that the factor structure of
tests for cognitive variables varies as a function of
the particular problem-solving strategy adopted by
the subject. Hettema (1968) analyzed a number of
tests for cognitive abilities with respect to their
process characteristics and found specific factors of
cognitive anchoring and information transmission in
different subsets.

It seems  worthwhile to proceed along these lines,
particularly in cases where indications are sought
for treatment. Here process models have definite advantages over the classical personality models. Notably, they are more flexible and adaptive than the
psychometric model and at the same time more rational, not least in terms of testability, than the
psychodynamic model. What is more, process models
leave room for the inclusion of ideas and findings
from cognitive and learning theories. On the other
hand, process models have certain disadvantages, a
major one being that the models are esentially of a
*reactive* nature. While feedback provisions can indeed
be built in, the reciprocal action of the environment
on the organism *and* of the organism on the environment is very difficult to realize in these models. No
matter how complex an actual behavioral sequence may
be, the process model always envisages the subject
as reacting to given environmental events without being able to actively restructure the situation. We
have seen that the organism as an active agent produ-
cing an impact on events in his environment is a pivotal element in the interaction approach. If this
notion is to be retained in a model of personality
functioning, situational parameters will somehow have

to be accommodated in the process chain.

## 1.4  *Outline of an open-system conception of persona-lity*

There can be no doubt that interactionism as well as the process approach are significant innovative approaches to personality. Both build on to developments in general psychology. Interactionism is based mainly on cognitive theory and on notions derived from learning theory while, also, certain notions from social psychology and environmental psychology play an important part. The process approach likewise rests on findings in cognitive psychology and learning theory but, in addition, incorporates conceptions derived from cybernetics and systems theory. As to their utility for practical purposes, both approaches appear to offer links with specific treatment strategies pursued, for instance, in psychotherapy and education. As regards their applicability to problems in daily life, one may cherish a hope that both formulations have something to offer, albeit at different levels. The interactionist tends to go in for comparative analysis of situations with an eye to establishing situation taxonomies; the process theorist is interested in forms of simulation based on rigorous selection of aspects of the situation in the form of specific stimuli.

Assumptions from the classical global dispositional approach that have proved less fruitful are not adopted by either. Thus, individual differences are acknowledged by both, but they do not constitute the foundation of theory construction; in both approaches they appear in specific circumstances in the guise of hypotheses but they do not acquire the status of basic assumptions.

If both types of theory therefore satisfy the conditions of modern theory construction, each has its characteristic priorities. Interactionism emphasizes more in particular the study of molar behavior in molar settings, favors real-life studies, focuses in the main on cognition and perception, permits subjective interpretations and, methodologically, frequently uses analysis of variance. The process approach, on the other hand, stresses the study of more molecular behavior in molecular settings, shows some preference for artificial conditions (tests, experimental situations), concentrates on performance as measured in objective ways and favors factor analysis as a method.

In terms of Brunswik's (1969) 'conceptual framework of Psychology' we can say that the interactionist emphasizes the central and distal layers of the
behavioral system whereas the process theorist stresses its proximal and peripheral layers. In other
words, the interactionist is primarily interested in
the more remote, broad causes and effects of behavior
in the 'real world', as governed by central cognitive
considerations. In contrast, the process theorist's
main objective is to study the way in which more specific segments of the environment are perceived and
elicit specific products of action. In this latter
approach the organism is often conceived as an infor-
mation-processing system controlled by psychophysical
laws and physiological mechanisms.


The two conceptions may be regarded as comple-
mentary, and the similarities as well as the differences between them seem to warrant the view that
they can be integrated into a single conceptual
framework. Such an integration is possible only if,
in the first instance, a highly formal language is
used which permits the essentials of the two conceptions to be formulated in neutral terms and subsequently amalgamated. *General systems theory* provides
such a language and an attempt will therefore be made
to formulate a number of basic premises for a personality theory in system-theoretical terms. These premises will be developed in subsequent chapters and
eventually reformulated in psychological terms. Before an integrative system-theoretical model can be attempted, however, a number of decisions must be made.
The need for these decisions arises primarily from
differences in the basic assumptions underlying the
two formulations that are to be amalgamated. For the
present, three problem areas are considered crucial,
each of which will be dealt with in a separate section: the boundary problem, the problem of individuality and the problem of personality constants.

1.4.1 *The boundary issue*

Most traditional personality models are basically
closed systems, which means that the models envisage
personality as not essentially affected by the environment and the environment as not essentially affected by the individual. As we have seen, the interac-

tionist assumes an altogether different theoretical
stance, so that for a system-theoretical formulation
the personality will have to be provided with an environment. In this context environment is defined as
whatever has an impact on the system as well as whatever is in its turn affected by the system (cf. Von
Bertalanffy, 1958; Klabbers, 1972). If the first requirement alone held, all past environmental events
would qualify no less than the environment in which
the organism actually finds itself at present. But
the second requirement restricts the environment of
the personality system to the situation actually obtaining. The effects of earlier situations are conceived as parts of the system itself and will manifest themselves as the effects of memory content on
present behavior. From an interactionist's point of
view, inclusion of the prevailing situation in the
system's environment must be considered a mandatory
requirement. From the definition of the personality
system's environment it follows that inclusion of the
actual situation is not only necessary but sufficient
as well. Inclusion of the environment qualifies the
personality system to be built as an *open system*.

For the process approach, openness of the system
is not strictly required. Owing to the proximal-peri-
pheral posture assumed, the global situation in which
the individual is seen to behave is seldom taken into
account. Rather, the process theorist occupies himself with questions concerning specific aspects of
the situation, such as its information content, or
the effects of discrete stimuli upon behavior. On the
other hand, the inclusion of the actually prevailing
situation in the personality system is certainly not
incompatible with the process approach, as will be demonstrated later.

The decision to include the environment in the
personality system holds some interesting theoretical
implications. In making this decision, the theorist
recognizes that any attempt at theorizing about personality without the environment is meaningless or,
in other words, that individual behavior can only be
understood in the light of the situation actually obtaining. At the same time, adoption of this principle
means that the fundamental relationship between individual and environment will have to be explicitly defined, notably in terms of the individual's *adaptation*. Adaptation thus enters our personality theory
as an axiomatic construct which is held to be at the
root of all individual functioning.

We shall see later how the environment is to be
conceived in this context and, also, what rules govern the reciprocity of organism and environment. At
this early stage we must content ourselves with pointing out, by way of illustration, that artificial e-
limination of important situational aspects - as, for
instance, in experiments on sensory deprivation -
will lead to depersonalization in the most literal
sense. Again, at the risk of laboring the obvious we
must make the point here that strict personalogism -
the study of personality in isolation from the environment - is regarded as an inadmissible reduction,
not only as a theoretical position with respect to
personality, but also as an approach to psychology in
general.

## 1.4.2  *The individuality issue*

In traditional personality psychology the unicity of personality has been especially emphasized in
the work of George Allport, who, next to general
traits, was always careful to leave room for individual or morphogenic traits, that is, traits peculiar
to one individual. That position is hard to maintain
conceptually as well as scientifically, as Allport
(1963) was the first to admit. It is interesting
therefore to see how the unicity issue reappears on
the scene, no whit diminished, with the interaction
model, a point, incidentally, which was already adum-
brated in our discussion of Mischel's work. Endler
and Magnusson likewise take the view that the individual maintains strictly individualistic relations
with his environment. In their conception, this relationship primarily revolves around the meaning of
environmental events, which they regard as to a high
degree individualized. It would seem as if for these
authors recognition of cognitive mediation automatically leads to individualization. But that step presupposes that an individual's cognitive structures
are all individualized to the same degree. It remains
to be seen whether such an assumption is in fact in-
escapable.
It is not hard to find arguments for the unicity
of the individual. One only has to think of his physical appearance, physiological and biochemical processes (Williams, 1956), fingerprints and so on. But
as soon as the human personality is defined on the
basis of the organism's characteristic relations with
the environment, his unicity should equally be defined as a function of these relations. In fact, there

appears to be no *prima facie* evidence for such an assumption of unicity except in respect of the environmental events which the subject confronts, or has confronted. Of these events one can rightly say that they are unique. But that does not necessarily mean that every individual derives unicity from the situations that he has confronted. With the interactionist we must say that the *manner in which* he deals with situational parameters determines the individual. Now, the number of ways in which situations are dealt with is finite, so that it becomes pertinent to ask whether we can somehow arrive at a *general* description of modes of dealing with situational factors, unique though the latter may be in themselves. On this score, the process approach to personality has yielded a number of suggestions that deserve further study. But even if one arrives, along these lines, at a general description, the person's unicity is not negated. Only, it will be seen to reside, not in structural attributes, but in the functional relations that the individual maintains with his environment.

### 1.4.3  *The issue of personality constants*

The search for structural elements that are crucial for individual functioning has long been a favorite occupation of personality theorists. Allport (1958), who gives an overview of the more important ones, lists a respectable number of elements. Two questions are of prime importance with respect to personality constants:

What is their origin?    and
What is their function?

In interactionism as well as in the process conception, cognitive variables are stressed as personality constants. But as regards their *origin*, the two models emphasize different aspects. In the most fully worked out version of the interaction conception (Mischel, 1973), social learning processes are much to the fore. Genetic dispositions are not explicitly excluded: they are simply not mentioned. In the process approach as advocated by Messick (1972), the innate aspect of behavior is emphasized. It is held to manifest itself in such second-order factors as fluid intelligence. Acquired characteristics, like crystallized intelligence, are supposed to become manifest

in more specific stimulus settings. The learning process is individualized by the trait equipment of the
individual and leads to the formation of stable habits through overlearning.

The two conceptions also differ with respect to
the *function* of personality constants.Interactionists
emphasize the interpretation of the environment and
decisions concerning the most desirable behavior.
Process theorists see constants functioning mainly in
internal processes, particularly in sequences of *mini-decisions* that have to be made there. All this can
be summed up by saying that the more molar personality processes are the purview of interactionists, who
preferably theorize in terms of social learning processes, whereas the more molecular processes are the
concern of process theorists, who tend to emphasize
innate determinants of personality as well as acquired determinants.

From our review of the three problem areas these
three conclusions can be drawn:
- With respect to the *boundaries* of the personality
  system, inclusion of the situation actually obtaining as the system's environment is considered essential.
- With respect to the problem of *individuality*, a general process description is chosen that leads to
  individualized relationships only in confrontations
  with actually prevailing situations.
- With respect to personality *constants*, innate as
  well as acquired characteristics are considered acceptable, with the proviso that a functional distinction between the two classes must in principle
  be considered possible.

In conclusion, the main issues that have been raised
in this chapter can be briefly summarized as follows.
Classical personality theories have been examined and
some criticism reviewed. It has been pointed out that
these classical theories developed largely in isolation from general psychology, which is considered a
disadvantage for integrative theory construction as
well as for the progress of personality psychology.
Later developments reveal some rapprochement to more
general disciplines like learning theory and cognitive theory.

In recent years two new theoretical trends have
become discernible that promise well for the renovation of personality theory. An analysis of these

trends shows that it is possible to draw together a
number of strands from either conception into a single conceptual framework. To this end, a formal language must be devised, the elements of which can, in a
more or less ready-made form, be derived from systems
theory.

Personality is provisionally defined within the
present framework as a system of interacting biological and culturally determined elements, which maintains an open relation with the environment actually
obtaining. An initial confrontation of interactionism
and process theory leads to the formulation of a number of basic premises which, in a way, mark new de-
partures. They will be worked out and refined in subsequent chapters.

For the present they may be conceptualized as
follows:

(1) Personality is an *open system*.
(2) The *relations between organism and environment*
are at the root of the personality conception to
be developed here. An explicit conception of adaptation will be one of the mainstays of the argument.
(3) *Processes of adaptation* are conceived as *general*
processes in which feedback plays a major part;
within these general processes, *individual* parameters are assumed to work.
(4) In the personality model a distinction is made
between *processes* on the one hand and *process results* on the other.
(5) *Individual differences* in overt behavior do not
constitute an assumption in this model, but their
occurrence may be hypothesized within a specific
environment.

# CHAPTER II

## ADAPTATION

### 2.1 Personality and adaptation: the classical conceptions

There are few concepts in psychology which are used in as many different ways, and are therefore as vague and ambiguous, as the concept of adaptation. It has been applied to the adjustment of sense organs to incoming stimulation, but also to the acceptance of societal and interpersonal demands; to structural change in an organism to meet environmental conditions, but to mastering reality by means of innate protective mechanisms as well; to the elimination of irrelevant behavior in the course of learning processes, but equally to any beneficial modification that is necessary to meet environmental demands;to upward adjustment and compensation for innate deficiencies, but also to modifications in drives, attitudes and motives (cf. Wolman, 1978). In many personality theories, one or more of these notions play an important part.

Psychometric as well as psychodynamic theory is firmly rooted in the classical concept of adaptation derived from evolutionary biology as has been habitual since the days of Darwin. In summary,Darwin held that evolution is achieved by means of natural selection, favoring congenital modifications with the highest chance of survival in the environment in which the organism is living. The underlying process basically consists of two components: variation and selective retention. The variation component rests on the occurrence of variations within a species, that cause individual organisms to differ from one another, on a genetic basis, in structural and functional characteristics (morphology and physiology). Selective retention means that, in an environment making specific demands with respect to the survival of its

27

inhabitants, some organisms have a better chance to
survive than others. Which organisms will survive depends upon the individual properties that are pertinent to that particular environment. Through selective breeding, gradually more specialized organisms
originate, that are better equiped to cope with the
problems; the other organisms become extinct. Thus,
*adaptation* comes into existence as a permanent morphophysiological correlation between the properties of
plant and animal species, on the one hand, and the
environment in which they live on the other.

Adaptation is a concept pertaining to *species*,
but it functions through (and at the expense of) individual organisms. These organisms constitute the
elements through which evolution occurs; within the
framework of evolution theory, individual organisms
are conceived as elementary collections of stable,
hereditary properties. To speak of a more or less
adequate adaptation with respect to individual organisms is meaningless. Evolution is an opportunistic
process, so that adaptation can only be defined
against the background of the environment in which
the species lives. In classical evolutionary thought,
adaptation does not refer to some form of exchange
between organism and environment. The organism is
seen solely as a closed system with properties that
more or less match the environment in which it finds
itself and that are crucial for survival.

Man was seen by Darwin as an animal with superior intelligence and provided with social instincts.
The capacity to remember past experiences and to anticipate future events, significantly contributes to
survival of the human species in divergent circumstances. Several authors have borrowed principles
from evolution theory to apply them to human and societal functioning. The relationship between environment and species, as revealed by evolution theory,
served as a model for Spencer's social darwinism. On
the basis of natural selection, society was to develop into a better world than before. Haeckel's so-
called biogenetic law, according to which the embryonic and later development of an organism was seen as
a reflection of the phylogenetic development of the
species, was adopted by G.S. Hall to be applied to
human mental development. The evolutionary conception
of heredity of physical properties was extended to
the development of mental properties by Francis Galton. That author established a eugenetic program, intended to create a human super race by way of selec-

tive breeding. Thus, Darwin's ideas have been of major influence in the prime of behavioral sciences. It is obvious that they have affected classical personality theories as well.

The concept of adaptation as used by Freud was the classical biological concept of adaptation. As Freud has emphasized repeatedly, for the individual organism instinct behavior does *not* serve any adaptive function. But in the population things are quite different; the very fact that some organisms perish and that others are not capable of reproduction should, in Freud's view, be seen as part of our all-embracing biological adaptation, directed at survival of the species as a whole (cf. Bowlby, 1971). The distinction made by Freud between life instincts and death instincts derives its significance from this conception of adaptation. This view has been elaborated very concretely in the aggression phenomenon. In *Totem and Taboo* (1955) Freud describes how the aggression of sons against their fathers in primitive communities serves to eliminate weak individuals in favor of the defensibility of the group as a whole (cf. Spitz, 1969).

With respect to the smallest unit of adaptation, the individual, Freud had a clear preference for arguing in physiological terms. Personality was conceived after the model of a closed physiological system. In this system a finite amount of energy is available and this energy can manifest itself in different forms. But once it is accepted that the organism is a closed system, the total amount of energy can never be changed (the first law of thermodynamics only holds within closed systems). Thus, psychic energy can in principle always be transformed into physiological energy and vice versa, without any exchange between organism and environment taking place (cf. Hall & Lindzey, 1970).

Whereas Freud's theory was modeled primarily on the prevailing fashion of biological adaptation through physiology, morphology has especially been the model for psychometric thinking and theory. In the early days of evolution theory, Francis Galton already attempted to distinguish between a number of elementary properties of psychic functioning, which he called mental faculties. The isolation of distinct psychological attributes has been pursued until today and has resulted in a vast number of traits that are assumed to determine individual behavior. This behavior is conceived (once more) against the background

of the view of species adaptation derived from classical biology.

Several elements from this view can be recognized, for instance, in the modern trait theory of
Cattell. Human properties or traits are seen as stable structural elements of personality. In the population they show a large amount of variation (the variation principle from evolutionary thinking). In a
particular environment, each trait makes its own contribution to behavior as a whole, according to the
so-called specification equation (cf. Cattell, 1956).
Thus, properties with positive effects in one environment, may have neutral or negative effects in another
environment. In a given environment the predictive
validity of a particular trait with respect to behavior is fixed. Granted the variation principle, this
means that individuals are predestined by their properties to behave in a particular way in that environment. If one attaches a certain value to behavior
with respect to individual survival, the principle of
selective retention is represented in the theory as
well. Cattell distinguishes between innate traits and
environmental-mold traits, thus reissuing the biological distinction between genotype and phenotype. He has
also made important contributions to behavior genetics, methodologically (the MAVA-method) as well as
empirically by investigating the effects of hereditary factors upon individual functioning (Hundleby,
Pawlik and Cattell, 1965).

In summary, it can be observed that classical
personality theories have leaned heavily upon a conception of adaptation derived from 19th century biology. Personality is primarily conceived as an element in the species, equipped with a set of properties, largely determined by hereditary factors. It is
a closed system with stable elements that predispose
the organism to particular forms of behavior.

Objections to this view can be raised from psychology, which in its development has gradually attained a different relationship with biology. But, in
the first place, a number of observations have to be
made with respect to the biological background as
such, which must be considered obsolete nowadays. Biologists' conceptions of evolution, its connections
with adaptation and the position of behavior in that
context, have changed considerably during the last
few decades. Thus, first of all, attention will be
directed towards recent developments in evolutionary
thinking.

## 2.2  *Synthetic evolution theory and adaptation*

In the thirties, an innovative movement started
in biology that has had far-reaching consequences
for evolutionary thought. For decades there had been
a running battle between Darwinists and Lamarckists
over the issue of whether natural selection or transformation had to be taken to be the cause of evolution. The controversy was further complicated by the
rise of mutationism and developments in heredity
thinking since Mendel. The situation that had come
into existence has been described by Simpson (1964)
as follows: 'The neo-Lamarckians knew and overemphasized the fact that adaptation is pervasive in nature
and essentially purposeful in aspect, as if the environment had forced and the organism had sought a-
daptation. The neo-Darwinians knew and overemphasized
the fact that the more or less adaptive status of variations is influential in determining the parentage
of a following generation. The geneticists knew and
overemphasized the fact that new hereditary variants
arise abruptly and, as far as we know and as far as
adaptive status is concerned, at random....What was
necessary was synthesis, bringing together the facts
and theories of all the schools, accepting those mutually consistent and reciprocally reinforcing'.
     Synthetic theory of evolution, usually associa-
ted with names like Dobzhansky, Simpson, Mayr and
Huxley, is built upon three main foundations, i.e.
genetic mechanisms, random processes and oriented
processes. The following description of the foundations of synthetic theory is adopted from Simpson
(1969). *Genetic mechanisms* are concerned with the population as the actual object of evolution. Individual organisms in the population exhibit interactions
between heredity and environment, in their first development as well as later on. Chromosomes and genes
define the range within which individual properties
vary. Within that range the environment determines
the actual result. But the latter is not inherited;
only the range has been genetically determined. The
genetic structure of the population is almost entirely defined by type, number and combination of chromosomes and genes, that are available in the total population. Mutations may cause slow alterations to occur in the gene pool of the population. But, on sta-
tistical grounds it has been ascertained that no
drastic change of genetic factors can occur in the
gene pool (Hardy & Weinberg's law). Even mutations

are eventually balanced out by countermutations. What
does occur are random fluctuations around the mean in
different subsequent generations. These *random processes* may lead to evolution on strictly fortuitous
grounds. If for instance a sample from the population
is isolated in a new environment, on the basis of
sampling errors a new adapted species may originate
(genetic drift). But, generally speaking, the effects
of random evolution are negligible as compared with
the effects of non-random evolution. The latter can
take place only through the process of reproduction,
being the only genetic process not necessarily occurring at random. *Oriented processes* have their course
through differential reproduction that leads to an
increase or decrease of genetic material. A number of
conditions may be pointed out that intensify sexual
reproduction, such as the nearness of male and female
organisms, sexual attraction, actual impregnation,
genetically compatible gametes, normal embryonic development, survival of offspring, etc. Darwin himself
placed great emphasis on the latter condition, but it
is only one out of a complex whole of conditions.
     Synthetic theory has broken away from the clas-
sical conception, whereby evolution was seen as pure
ectogenesis, imposed and dictated by the environment.
Furthermore, the endogenetic view, in which evolution
is completely determined by forces that are available
within the species, is rejected by that theory. Evolution is characterized as a process of challenge and
response (Toynbee). Simpson (1965) has defined adaptation in this context as 'a complex of processes
(and results of processes) bringing about and maintaining an organism-environment relationship useful
to individual organisms and populations' (p. 523).
The core of that definition is the notion that adaptation should be seen as a *relational* concept, in
which both the organism (or the species) as well as
the environment are always involved. Both elements of
adaptation will be discussed in greater depth.
     In the *species*, adaptation can become manifest
in widely divergent ways. Thus, warm-blooded animals
that during winter are exposed to severe cold, can
arm themselves through evolutionary processes by for-
ming a fur, but also by hibernating, by emigrating to
warmer areas or by the use of fire in their habita-
tions. Animal species that are continually threatened
by predators can arm themselves by improving alert-
ness, or protect themselves by mimicry; they may
start to produce poison, to show aggressive behavior

or escape behavior by increasing their speed. In addition they can unite and form groups, or develop a reproduction rate so high that the population's survival is guaranteed. All these so-called adaptive strategies (Dobzhansky, 1974) may be classified according to three basic categories, the *adaptive modalities*, i.e. morphology, physiology and behavior. Each of these modalities determines a connection between the species (or the organism) on the one hand, and the environment or ecological niche on the other hand. But each modality locates that connection at a different level.

*Morphology* determines the sort of environments in which the species can survive and also the sort of environments in which it cannot survive. Thus, the whale's morphology is suitable to his ecology, the ocean, but unsuitable in a number of other environments. The cow's digestive system predestines that animal to live in a vegetable environment. In general, species-specific morphological equipment leads to double selection. On the basis of its morphology the species selects a particular kind of environment, i.e. the species restricts itself to the ecological niche to which it is suited. On the other hand, the environment selects species and organisms that can survive in it. The latter type of selection forms part of the process of natural selection as described by Darwin.

Within a given ecological niche fluctuations may occur in the prevailing conditions. Very often it is of vital interest for the organism to adjust to these fluctuations. This sort of adjustment is frequently acquired through *physiology*, providing external physiological adaptation. In this connection it is usually important to keep particular internal states constant under varying external conditions. This phenomenon, that is characteristic of external physiological adaptation, is designated as steady state. Furthermore, physiology provides for the mutual adjustment of organ systems within the organism according to the principle of negative feedback (internal physiological adaptation). In general, it can be stated that the criterion for physiological adaptation is equilibrium between organism and environment, as well as within the organism.

A further distinction may be made, within an ecological niche, between biologically useful and biologically harmful environments or aspects of environments. *Behavior* enables the organism to take up an active and selective position with respect to those aspects. Locomotion provides the opportunity to go to useful environments and to escape from or avoid harmful environments. Manipulation is a powerful aspect of behavior by which the organism may alter prevalent biologically non-useful or harmful aspects of the environment into useful aspects. Behavior assumes a high degree of integration of subsystems in the organism; each behavior presupposes the cooperation of sensory, motor and integrative subsystems (Nissen, 1969). Furthermore, behavior is characterized by a large amount of variation and exchangeability of means. Thus, the same muscular group may contribute to foodfinding, flight from danger, mating behavior and carrying the young. In behavior flexibility of means is coupled with constancy and specificity of goals. This very combination makes behavior a perfect modality for altering direct environmental aspects in a given direction that enhances biological utility to the organism.

Adaptation is complicated, viewed from the organismic side of the process, but the effects of the environment upon adaptation are at least as intricate. *Environments* can be divided into innumerable different kinds, with respect to the demands they impose upon species. They may be homogeneous or heterogeneous, they may be stable or subject to enormous alterations. On the basis of this type of distinctions, different forms of natural selection can be distinguished (cf. Stebbins, 1974).

The first form is relatively trivial. It occurs whenever a population stays in a stable environment consisting of so-called closed ecological niches. The population is not subject to evolutionary change and *stabilizing selection* takes place, so that only the best organisms survive. Thus, certain species which are throwbacks from times long gone by, have managed to survive until today; they are designated as living fossiles, like, for instance, the horse shoe crab and the opossum.

When radical environmental changes occur, continuously working in the same direction, *directed selection* will take place. Evolution will work along the lines pointed out before and lead to a species with new characteristics and specialized in surviving in the new environment.

A third possibility presents itself when an existing homogeneous ecological niche falls apart into a number of heterogeneous niches. In this case, the population reacts with so-called *adaptive shifts*

in different directions. These shifts cause adaptive
radiation to occur and this finally leads to an increase in heterozygotism in the population. Generally
speaking, it may be said that heterozygotism protects
the population by decreasing its vulnerability to divergent threats to survival.

Finally, the population may be exposed to a number of successive threats that are differentially directed. In such a case, there is great danger of the
population being extinguished altogether. The reason
is that those organisms that survive one threat are
not very likely to survive the others. But according
to evolution theorists, there is a possibility of
survival, if the population manages to reach an essentially higher level of functioning. In that case
*evolutionary progress* has become manifest. In table 1
the effects of the environment upon the course of e-
volution have been summarized.

Evolutionary progress must not be seen as a universal characteristic of evolution. It only consists
of a specific increase in the level of organization
of the population in response to extraordinary external circumstances. Stebbins (1974), who has described
this phenomenon, has estimated that the number of major instances of evolutionary progress throughout natural history does not exceed seventy. Among them are
the transition of unicellar to multicellular organisms, the origin of limbs and a nervous system in
vertebrates, the origin of social behavior, and so
on. Modern evolutionary biologists consider as a major form of evolutionary progress the capacity to
gather information on the environment, to process the
information, and to control the environment with the
help of that information (Dobzhansky *et al*, 1977).
They also recognize that this capacity has culminated
in the human species. Thus, the view intuitively held
by many (notably cognitive) psychologists that information can be used for the purpose of environmental control, seems to be confirmed by recent insights
in evolutionary biology.

As regards the study of behavior, evolution theorists  have always had difficulties. The main source
of knowledge concerning morphology and physiology has
always been the study of fossils. But behavior does
not fossilize (Mayr, 1966). Thus, a phylogenetic psychology in the strict sense is impossible. Students
of behavior in an evolutionary perspective are forced
to fall back upon other sources of knowledge, as, for
instance, behavior genetics. But in that area, few

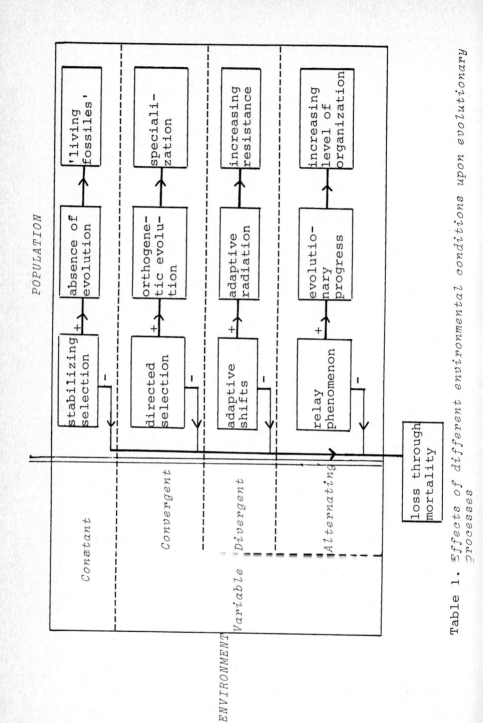

Table 1. *Effects of different environmental conditions upon evolutionary processes*

unambiguous results have as yet been provided. True,
Tryon (1942) accomplished a clear improvement in rat
maze learning through inbreeding. But several later
investigations have revealed that not behavior as
such, but behavioral components of a physiological
and temperamental nature had been inherited (Caspari,
1969).

Attempts to connect evolution theory and the
study of behavior are of relatively recent date: they
have not been very successful as yet. Roe and Simpson (1969) have characterized that area as follows:
'The evolutionary study of behavior and the behavioral study of evolution, although not wholly neglected, have comparatively little literature and few
triumphs. It is true that the label "evolutionary"
has been attached to a number of studies in comparative psychology, but all too often a student of biological (other than psychological) evolution found
this to be a misnomer. Use of evolutionary theory and
concepts in such work was frequently naïve or badly
outdated, when it was not downright wrong' (p. 1).

The data we have at our disposal at the moment
and that are pertinent to the evolution of behavior,
mainly come from comparative psychological and comparative neuro-anatomical research. On the basis of
these data several authors assume that behavior in
many respects does *not* change with the phylogenetic
level of the species. The differences that do occur
between different levels, have become manifest especially on the *receptor* side of behavior. Thus, Pribram (1969) concluded on neuro-anatomical grounds
that the evolution of behavior does *not* consist of
the extension of the behavioral repertoire. Nor does
it express itself in the ratio of learned and innate
behavior, but merely in an increase in the diverse
sensory and motivational determinants of behavior. In
Harlow's (1969) view, the increase in learning ability in higher animals is closely related to the evolution of receptors, enabling those animals to make
better discriminations in their environments. Skinner (1966) has pointed out that there is not much
difference in the appearance of phylogenetic (in-
stinctual) and ontogenetic (learned) behavior. According to this author, differences have to be looked for
in the stimulus variables that control both types of
behavior.

Taken together, all these comments point in the
same direction, i.e. that with respect to behavior as
a modality of adaptation, a form of evolutionary pro-

gress has occurred. That progress has led to the general possibility of connecting *existing* forms of behavior, occurring as such at different evolutionary
levels, to *new* areas of stimulation. Hence, it becomes increasingly possible to handle the environment
by special forms of selection, transformation, and,
finally, control. Thus the adaptation problem in
particular animal species and especially in humans,
becomes of quite a different order compared with the
strictly morphophysiological adaptation  described by
Darwin and his successors. For personality psychology
this conclusion has some far-reaching consequences,
that will be elaborated in the course of this book.

To conclude this section, some insights adopted
from recent developments in the synthetic theory of
evolution will be summarized. This theory has managed
to integrate a number of prevalent views on evolution; it has also rejected a number of other insights
as being one-sided. Thus, on the one hand, the idea
is rejected that species adaptation is brought about
by means of pure ectogenesis, on the other hand the
idea is rejected that adaptation is the result of
pure endogenesis. Synthetic theory conceives of the
process of adaptation as a *relation* between the species (or the organism) and the environment on the basis of challenge and response. That relation may take
several forms, that can be categorized according to
different modalities of adaptation, one of which is
behavior.

Evolution is no longer seen as a process of *general* progress with man as its highest form. On the
contrary, it is stressed that there is a great di-
versity of ways along which to proceed, whereas only
in extraordinary circumstances specific forms of
evolutionary progress will occur. One of these forms
of evolutionary progress is closely connected with
behavior as a modality of adaptation, since it refers to a definite increase in the capacity to gather and process information regarding the environment. That capacity holds out a prospect that control of the environment in which the organisms lives
is enhanced.

## 2.3   *Psychological adaptation*

The relationships between organisms and environments are studied by biologists from the point of
view of survival of species and of individual organisms. To the biologist, behavior is a modality like

any number of other modalities that may contribute
to survival. Psychology, on the other hand, has as
its object behavior *per se:* it does not primarily
occupy itself with survival. A psychological concept
of adaptation can therefore never be based on the
life or death paradigm of biology. But even in biology the ties between adaptation and survival have gradually been loosened, notably in the synthetic theory of evolution. On that subject, Meyer (1967) has
commented as follows: 'La théorie synthétique de l'e-
volution...établit que la sélection adaptive, liée
dans les formes inférieures et dans les étapes primi-
tives de l'évolution à l'élimination physique brutale
par tout ou rien, prend progressivement des formes
moins draconiennes et plus subtiles:à la selection
létale succède progressivement une sélection concur-
rentielle qui laisse se multiplier, se diversifier et
se hiérarchiser des modes d'adaptation. Chez l'homme,
ce processus atteint son maximum. Sans doute la forme
catégorique de l'inadaptation est-elle la mort, mais
en deçà ae ce cas limite, il y a mille nuances de
l'adaptation: nombreuses sont, devant les agressions
du milieu, les adaptations par acceptation d'un sta-
tut non létal mais dégradé à tous les degrés possi-
bles de l'efficacité' (1) (p. 10,11).

Synthetic theory explicitly leaves room for
forms of adaptation that operate less drastically
than by elimination. The room that is left open by
synthetic theory will be filled up here with the help
of the concept of *psychological adaptation*. This concept is not intended, as it frequently has been in
the past, whether explicitly or implicitly, as a wa-
tered down version of biological adaptation. It is,
on the contrary, seen as a life modality in its own
right that is definitely distinct from biological
adaptation, with which it can indeed even come into
conflict.

The definition of the notion of psychological
adaptation conceives of behavior as an adaptive modality with the specific function outlined in 2.2.,
where it was described as transformation or alteration of the environment. Now,first of all the question must be asked how that function can be consistent with biological adaptation. If environments can
supposedly be transformed at the whim of an organism,
they no longer impose stringent demands upon this organism, so that the basis for biological adaption is
removed. In the context of biological adaptation,
Bowlby (1971) has used the term 'environment of evo-

lutionary adaptedness', to indicate those segments of
the ambient world with which a species has achieved a
stable relationship. But that term would lose its
meaning if transformation of the environment were to
become predominant. Naturally, however, there are limits to the possibility of transforming environments
through behavior. As long as these limits can be ascertained, there is no problem with respect to behavior as a modality of biological adaptation.

If, for convenience, it is assumed that the results of environmental transformation are always directly to the organism's benefit in terms of nourish-
ment, shelter, propagation, etc., then the take-off
points of such transformations define the contribution of behavior to adaptation. If the collection of
directly biologically useful environments is represented by a circle, then the other environments together constitute a wider circle that encloses the
first one. That wider circle comprises those environments that are of direct biological use as well as
those environments that can be transformed into useful environments. This means that the wider circle
also represents the environment of evolutionary a-
daptedness, because all environments within it in
fact offer possibilities of survival, either directly or indirectly. This conception implies that there
are also environments in which the organism can neither perform its biological functions nor transform
through behavior into those where indeed it can. Thus
far, the function of behavior has been described in
terms of current conceptions of biological adaptation.
But as soon as the number of environments that can be
transformed in a biologically useful way is taken to
be in principle unlimited, the bounds of biological
adaptation are transcended.

In the light of the possibilities held out by
behavioral adaptation, the entire ecology may be
divided into three concentric areas. At the centre
there is an innermost domain in which biological functioning is directly guaranteed. Around that
area there is a second domain, where transformation
to the first area is possible through evolutionarily
determined behavior. These two areas together constitute the environment of evolutionary adaptedness.
Outside that environment a third area is seen to
exist that could, in principle, be transformed into
area I or II, but not by means of mechanisms determined by common evolutionary processes. The argument

presented thus far is summed up in fig. 1.

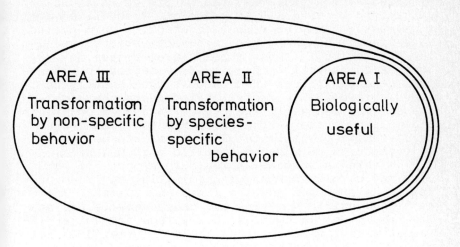

Fig.1. Environmental classification on the basis of adaptive behavior.

Transformations within area II, as well as from area II to area I, are studied by a special branch of biology, *ethology*. Ethology differs mainly from psychology in that, in the former, environments that are transformed by the organism can be strictly defined and must satisfy fixed conditions. As a matter of fact, one of the main tasks of ethology is to track down environmental elements that are necessary conditions for the occurrence of species-specific behavior. The very fact that such environmental elements can generally be described accurately in terms of so-called sign stimuli, demonstrates that the boundaries of area II are fixed. The effectiveness of sign stimuli upon behavior is affected by the motivational state of the organisms (Hinde, 1970). That evidence fits in with the conception developed here because, whether or not transformations will actually occur,will depend upon the biological need state of the organism.
        Transformations as such are part of species-specific behavior, i.e. a collection of behaviors that nearly all organisms in the species have at their disposal, and that develop independently of the particular environment in which they grow up. In this

connection Hinde (1970) has used the term *environmental stable behavior*. This behavior comprises a number of fixed action patterns, the nature of which is not determined by external stimulation. These fixed action patterns may be strung together to form chains, each element of which has to be activated by specific sign stimuli. Thus, a behavioral system is brought about that is particularly suited to transform defined initial environments into equally defined, biologically useful environments, by highly stereotyped means. If the system is not effective in accomplishing the latter environments, goal corrections remain possible to allow a certain degree of adjustment to be made to specific circumstances.

Within this scope, three main aspects of behavior may be distinguished: the initial environment, the transformation and the final environment. In species-specific behavior all these aspects are stably rooted in the species. But things are quite different with transformational behavior that does not belong to the species-specific equipment. Hinde (1970) has qualified that kind of behavior as *environmental labile* to indicate that it develops in individual organisms dependent on the environment in which they are raised. The environment to which environmental labile behavior is applied does not form part of the environment of evolutionary adaptedness; in the present terminology it belongs to area III. If the organism wants to survive there, it has to develop behaviors that transform the environment in such a manner that it finally belongs to area II, or area I. That is possible only if in new and unknown environments behavior can be developed that leads to directed transformations. Crucial for that development is the capacity to connect *existing* elements of behavior with *new* stimulus environments. The capacity for transforming environments in such ways that they become biologically more useful, is designated here as *environmental control*.

As we have noticed before, evolutionary biologists regard the gathering of information on the environment to obtain environmental control, as a major form of evolutionary progress. This progress only occurs in particular lines of phylogenetic development, whereas in others it is almost or entirely absent. It is a major contention of this book that psychology should especially occupy itself with the study of behavior pertaining to transformations in area III. In this connection, environmental control and the acti-

vities that are involved in it, are designated here
as *psychological adaptation*. Psychological adaptation
is not conceived as independence of the environment,
but as the capacity to transform new environments into biologically useful environments (area I), or into any other environment that can in turn be transformed into a biologically useful environment (area
II). Psychological adaptation has the important function of enlarging the range within which the organism
can act, of enlarging the ecological niche determined
by biological adaptation: the environment of evolutionary adaptedness.

In the following pages an endeavor will be made
to describe in greater detail how psychological adaptation functions. Several psychologists have made attempts in that direction and they have made use of
divergent terminologies. Thus, Fullan and Loubser
(1972) have described the process analogously to
Darwin's conception of evolution. If an individual is
confronted with a problematic situation, he will scan
his behavioral repertoire to find the best way to behave in that situation. He has at his disposal a certain range of variations and the versatility that allows him to respond variously in the form of alternative behaviors. He also has a certain retention capacity manifesting itself in the ability to evaluate,
select and apply a particular course of action, to
the exclusion of other behaviors. Through analysis he
arrives at the selection of the most appropriate response for that particular situation. In Fullan and
Loubser's conception, adaptation essentially comes
down to the selection of the 'right behavior'.

A similar line of reasoning is pursued by Berlyne (1965) in his exploitation of the notion of 'optimal response'. In that author's view, adaptation
consists of the transformation of actual responses into optimal responses, for example through the process
of directed thinking.

Skinner (1973) does not make use of the concept
of psychological adaptation, but he must have had in
mind something like it  when he spoke of the effectiveness of behavior. That effectiveness can be optima-
lized through increasing behavioral control by environmental reinforcement contingencies.

The problem with all the conceptions mentioned
thus far is that they all start out from the assumption that, basically, optimal behavior can be defined. Laws outside the organism are seen as decisive
for answering the question as to which behavior or
behaviors are optimal in which conditions. The fact

that the authors cited study behavior in highly controlled environments (experimental laboratory,
school) is probably not unrelated to that assumption.
But the issue is whether such optimality can in fact
be defined, quite aside from the bias toward such
overly controlled environments. Generally speaking,
this will not be the case in real-life situations. As
has been pointed out before, the main function of
psychological adaptation is to transform new or unknown environments. That is to say that, by definition, in such environments optimal behavior cannot be
defined beforehand.

An author who showed awareness of this problem
was Egon Brunswik  (1943), who conceived of adaptation as a process leading to a compromise between two
systems: the organism and the environment. Precisely
because the environment can only be represented par-
tially and inadequately by the organism with the aid
of proximal cues, our knowledge of the environment is
of a probabilistic nature. Actions that are based on
that knowledge can never be better than 'the best bet
on the basis of all the probabilities' (p. 258).

Piaget (1967) speaks of cognitive adaptation,
which he sees as a special case of biological adaptation. To Piaget, cognitive adaptation is a stream
of active and new states of equilibrium. These states
are established as re-adaptations after initial states of disequilibrium. The adaptive organism shows
endogenous activities but these are being continually
corrected on the basis of environmental feedback. Also in Piaget's work, uncertainty with respect to the
real character of the environment is considered a
main characteristic of adaptive behavior.

Environmental uncertainty and, as a consequence, the provisional nature of adaptive behavior are
likewise at the basis of the position taken here.
Environmental uncertainty not only refers to the response, but also to the initial environment in which
behavior occurs, as well as to the final environment
resulting from it. The initial environment of the
process of psychological adaptation is not defined
by a fixed combination of sign stimuli. Rather than
being defined by species-specific effective stimuli
as studied by ethologists, the initial environment of
psychologically adaptive behavior is to a certain degree always marked by novelty and unfamiliarity. The
capacity of some animal species to deal adaptively
with new stimulus areas is interpreted here as an increase in psychological adaptation.

A first characteristic of psychological adaptation is an increase in discriminative capacity. Furthermore, there is an increased sensitivity to new *combinations* of stimuli as well as the capacity to integrate them. In view of the uncertainty manifesting itself in the perception of new environments, integration is completed there according to a so-called uncertainty-geared strategy, for instance the principle of vicarious functioning (Brunswik, 1943).

The final environment of the process of psychological adaptation will at first belong to the environment of evolutionary adaptedness and can as such be defined with the help of sign stimuli. But eventually, when transformations from specific environments in area III to area II have frequently occurred, the initial environment (from area III) can take the role of a final environment in new transformations. The argument here is that the organism 'knows' that from that environment transformations to area II are always possible. In this way, transformational *chains* may develop according to the principle of 're-cursive anchoring' (Berlyne, 1965). This principle implies that a series of useful points of support for behavior are developed ontogenetically, of which only the terminal point is established by evolutionary means (a major difference between the present use of recursive anchoring and Berlyne's conception of the term is that the fixed point is situated here at the end of the chain but at the start with Berlyne). Developments as outlined above show how psychological adaptation finally leads to a real increase in an organism's radius of action.

The operations that have to be performed to accomplish transformations require no other motor patterns than the fixed action patterns described by ethology. But an important change occurs in the *organization* of behavior. As soon as an organism has experienced that it is possible to arrive from different initial environments at the same final environment, changes in route become, in principle, possible. The stable chains that ethologists were able to point out in species-specific behavior, are interrupted, and a much larger degree of means flexibility is established in behavior. Instead of chaining, causal hierarchies (Tinbergen, 1969) and plan hierarchies (Miller, *et al*, 1960) become possible. Thus, the process of transformation has gained flexibility in such a way that new environments may be approached and will be approached more frequently with a fair chance of success.

After this description of the process of psycho-

logical adaptation, the connection between biological
adaptation and psychological adaptation can be further explicated. Biological adaptation determines an
environment of evolutionary adaptedness, psychological adaptation enlarges that environment and allows
for survival outside that environment as well. Biologically adaptive behavior is environmentally stable
behavior: essentially, it develops in all organisms
that belong to the species, no matter in which environment they grow up. Psychologically adaptive behavior, on the other hand, is environmentally labile;
it develops depending on the particular environment
in which the organisms are raised. One important implication is that psychological adaptation is not to
be seen as a *species concept*, but has to be defined
at an individual level, as it is closely connected
with ontogenetic experiences of individual organisms.
For that reason, psychological adaptation constitutes a major foundation for the psychology of personality. Finally, biological adaptation directly relates
to survival of individuals and species, psychological
adaptation merely has survival value in threatening,
novel or changing environments. In more familiar environments it leads to an increase in flexibility and
efficiency of behavior.

If both types of adaptation are directly interrelated, the following conclusions can be drawn. In a
general sense, psychological adaptation amounts to an
extension of biological adaptation: it furnishes a
supplement and, if necessary, a compensation for the
species-specific equipment of the organism. But in
the long run, biological adaptation may even be over-
ruled by psychological adaptation. In systematically
expanding the ecological niche, the environment can
no longer function properly as an executioner in the
process of natural selection. It is assumed here that
this process reaches a climax in the human species
and we agree with a statement made by Mayr (1950):
'If the single species man occupies succesfully all
the niches that are open for a *Homo*-like creature, it
is obvious that he cannot speciate'.

Generally, adaptation can be viewed as a process
of transmission of information from the environment
to the species. This process utilizes the structure
of genes in biological adaptation (Dobzhansky, 1974,
Lorenz, 1965, Thorpe, 1963). In psychological adaptation, information is transmitted as well, but here
transmission proceeds directly through learning processes, starting as soon as organisms are confronted
with new environments.

## 2.4   *The continuity of behavior*

In the preceding sections doubt has been cast on
the fruitfulness of the classical evolutionary conception as the background of personality, and finally
that conception has been rejected. Personality is no
longer seen as an element in the species that is determined by its gene structure (endogenesis) or as an
exclusive result of environmental influences (ectogenesis). Furthermore, the view that personality should
be seen as an autonomous agent, functioning separately from the environment, is not shared here. As an
extension of modern conceptions of biological adaptation, in which the *relation* between organism and environment has become a core element, the concept of
psychological adaptation has been defined, and this
concept will serve as the main background for the
description of personality. Psychological adaptation
refers to the relations between organisms and environment; personality is seen as an individual appearance, concretizing that principle. A consequence of
this point of view is that personality must not be
seen as a vital phenomenon that as such is decisive
for survival of the individual. The manner in which
the relations between organism and environment are
arranged by the organism is the object of personality
psychology. Termination of all relations by death
must be considered a marginal given from that point
of view.
    If biological adaptation with its mechanisms of
variation and selective retention is abandoned, behavior can no longer be described in terms of genetic
structures and selection pressure. The major structural aspects of behavior will have to be revised to
match the principle of psychological adaptation. Notably, it must be considered at what level of functioning the more dominant process aspects of behavior
will have to be located. And, closely related to this
question, it must be asked at what level the more
continuous aspects of behavior are to be looked for.
    Psychological adaptation has been globally des-
cribed as directed transformation of the environment.
The processess involved in this activity are of a
complex character: in the personality system they
presuppose activities of various levels and natures.
To speculate somewhat further on these activities, it
is convenient to recapitulate the main elements that
have been distinguished in defining psychological a-
daptation. This concept then refers to behavior in

new environments, consisting of directed transformation of these environments. In the preceding chapter provisions have already been made for the inclusion of the actual environment by introducing the
open-system approach. The other element, directed
transformation, presupposes other structural provisions to be made in the system. To allow for directed
transformations, in the system a clear distinction
must be made between internal and external activities. Internal activities are necessary as a basis
for the directional aspect of psychological adaptation. It is hard to conceive of purposive behavior
without assuming the occurrence of some form of internal activity. External activities are a necessary
condition for actual transformations to take place
in the environment. Behavior as a whole comprises
both aspects.

Now the important question has to be asked at
what level of functioning the continuity of behavior
has to be located. That question refers to the nature
of the behavioral model in terms of which personality
will be defined eventually. The answer to that question is decisive for the basic psychological position that will be taken in this book.

A first possibility is to decide in favor of
continuity at the level of *internal* activity. In that
case the organism is primarily seen as a cognitive
system in which cognition processes, memory contents,
motives, expectations, intentions, etc. determine the
functioning as a whole. Information processing and
transformation *within* the organism are emphasized and
new information especially is seen as something to be
integrated within existing information structures.
Continuity of cognitive processes is premised, external activity is seen as a derivative of internal activity (see figure 2).

Cognitive psychologists in particular cherish
such a view, which seems at least to a considerable
degree to be shared by interactionists (Endler &
Magnusson, 1976, pp. 12-13). But in the framework of
psychological adaptation this conception leads to
serious problems. Actual transformation of the environment requires more than a cognitive system. Cognitions have to be translated into actions in the first
place, as has for instance been pointed out by Miller,
Galanter and Pribram (1960). In turn, actions must
lead to environmental changes that satisfy the requirements of the organism. A personality system in
which continuity is located at the cognitive-symbolic

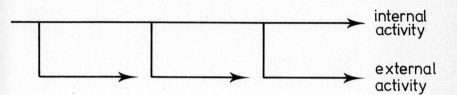

Fig. 2. Continuity at the cognitive-symbolic level.

level does not seem capable of performing these operations.

The second possibility is to choose for continuity of behavior at the level of *external* activity.
In that case, behavior is not regulated 'from inside'
but governed by rules in the environment. Overt actions and environmental changes occurring as a consequence are the focus of attention. This approach is
primarily concerned with what Skinner has called the
public domain: only those activities are studied that
can immediately be perceived by observers. Internal
processes are left out of account (empty organism
approach) or are indicated only briefly. This approach, of which Skinner's operant conditioning is
the classical example, is chosen in this chapter to
provide a rough outline of psychological adaptation.
In terms of the system, continuity is located here in
the external environment, the state of which can be
accounted for at any moment. On this view, activities
within the organism are at most considered to be a
derivative of external activities. Relations between
organism  and environment change only as a function
of environmental conditions. This type of continuity
is called sensomotor-operational continuity. It can
be represented diagrammatically in fig. 3.

But sensomotor-operational continuity no more
than cognitive-symbolic continuity provides a basis
for behavior as a means of psychological adaptation.
External activities have to be directed towards the

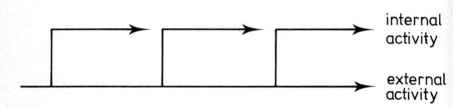

Fig. 3. Continuity at the sensomotor-operational level.

goals of the organism to be effective. If the organism's behavior were to be completely determined by
external continuity, each environmental change, however miniscule, would lead to disturbances that would
have to be corrected. The organism would for ever be
chasing after the facts, find itself in a state of
continual restlessness, and would be obliged to ac-
commodate again and again.
      Psychological adaptation, as defined before, re-
quires a third level of functioning that is located
in between the internal and external activities of
the organism. This third level of functioning is indicated here as the *control level*. Continuity of behavior must be sought at this level, the reason being
that here connections between the other two can always
be established. At this level it can be ascertained
whether actions correspond with intentions and also
whether these actions lead to the intended results,
the intended transformations. The level of control is
determined by the relations actually obtaining between organism and environment. The basic idea is that
it is precisely in these relations that the more du-
rable aspects of adaptation are shaped. Adaptation is
seen as a fundamental given, the input of which is
provided by the organism as well as the environment,
whereas on the other hand both are affected by its
output as well.
      Continuity at the control level implies relative
discontinuity in the internal as well as the external

activities of the organism. Thought processes are interrupted if they do not work out, actions are stopped if the results do not agree with previous intentions. It is precisely the discontinuity at both levels that allows for the connection *between* those
levels to be maintained. By contrast, it is because
of the continuity at the level of control that the
relationship between two isolated systems, organism
and environment (cf. Brunswik, 1943; Allport, 1966)
can be maintained (cf. fig. 4).

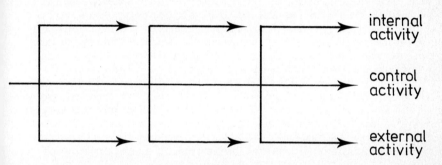

internal
activity

control
activity

external
activity

Fig. 4. Continuity at the control level.

The view that in behavior a third level of organization has to be distinguished is shared by Leontiev (1977), who concluded an analysis of behavior in
a personality perspective by stating: 'Um das in der
Psychologie vorherrschende dyadische Schema zu über-
winden, musste man vor allem das "Mittlere Glied" er-
mitteln, das die Beziehungen des Subjectes mit der
realen Welt vermittelt' (2) (p. 62).
Furthermore, Piaget's views on the subject of

adaptation do not substantially differ from the i-
deas developed here. In his theory construction
Piaget has always stressed the concepts of assimilation and accommodation, that are successively related with cognitive and operational continuity as defined here. The connection between assimilation and
accommodation has frequently been the cause of mis-
understanding, as, for instance, appeared at a symposium on adaptation in Marseilles, 1967 . One of the
speakers, Meyer, there proposed to utilize the dominance of assimilation over accommodation as an index
of successful adaptation. But Piaget did not agree and
reacted by stating that dominance of assimilation
would not improve adaptation, but lead to autism instead. The *balance* between the two processes is especially emphasized by Piaget, as an essential element
in his conception by successful adaptation. Regulation
of that balance would in our conception fall to the
control level. At that level transactions occur between organism and environment, that finally determine the way they relate to each other, the so-called
individual-environment fit (Pervin, 1968).

The control level is also the level at which a
number of major elements of the open system of personality are established. An open system may be defined
mathematically as a set of non-homogeneous differential
equations (Rapoport, 1972). It is capable of striving
for a definite purpose, relatively independent of its
initial state (equifinality).
Furthermore, in an open system a dynamic equilibrium
with the environment may be established. Both properties of equifinality and dynamic equilibrium make
the open system particularly suitable to serve as a
model for psychological adaptation. They are viewed
here as established primarily at the control level,
from which also their effects on the other levels are
determined. For further elaboration of the model the
reader is referred to Chapter IV. In the meantime
it is stated here that the way in which psychological
adaptation is seen to affect behavior will be based
on the view that behavior may be divided according to
three levels: the cognitive-symbolic level, the control and the sensomotor-operational level. Of these
three levels, the middle one, control, determines continuity of the system as a whole. The other two levels
are considered to function in a relatively discontinuous way.

The system will comprise those aspects and processes that may contribute to the explanation of
directed transformation of the environment. In this

context, from the side of the organism one could think
of data on perception, motor behavior, language,
thinking, learning, memory, emotional behavior and
external physiological adaptation. From the side of
the environment only ecological aspects of the environment merit consideration, viz. those aspects that
can be perceived and/or manipulated. Left out of the
system are data on the organism's morphology and internal physiology, as well as physical and geographi-
cal aspects of the environment. With respect to the
environment it has been pointed out before that the
environment that is actually present is always taken
into consideration. The non-actual environment, preceding and future environments are left out. These
environments may affect the system in an indirect way
via the individual who can represent the environments
by means of his memory or his expectations with respect to the future.

*Footnotes*

1. 'Synthetic theory of evolution...shows that adaptive selection - in inferior forms and in primitive stages of evolution connected with brutal
   physical all-or-none elimination - has progressi-
   vely adopted less radical and more subtle forms:
   lethal selection is increasingly succeeded by
   competitive selection diversified into several
   modes of adaptation. In man this process has
   reached its maximum. Categorical non-adaptation
   no doubt means death, but in addition to that li-
   miting case there are many shades of adaptation:
   many different kinds of adaptation, none of them
   lethal but  all involving some kind of reduction
   in all possible degrees of efficacy, may occur
   under environmental aggression'. (translation by
   the author).

2. 'In order to surmount the diadic model, which is
   so prominent in psychology, one should above all
   direct attention to the "central link", maintaining the relationship between the subject and the
   real world'. (translation by the author).

# CHAPTER III

*INFORMATION*

## 3.1  *Culture and personality: a critical review*

Psychological adaptation is based on the assumption that the organism has the capacity to gather and process information with respect to the environment and to perform directed actions on the basis of that information. In this chapter the question will be discussed as to how the individual can manage to obtain information on the complex world he lives in as well as the question  of how he is able to make effective use of that information. In terms of the three levels of adaptive functioning distinguished in the previous chapter, the discussion will be carried on mainly at the cognitive-symbolic level. With respect to the acquisition of information the important assumption is made here that the individual is not left entirely to his own resources, but can to a considerable degree fall back on the culture of the community in which he lives. Culture provides information on the strength of which man can map out and manipulate his environment. This information is taken in by the individual, it is processed and applied in everyday life.

However, there remain certain questions concerning the nature of these processes and the part they play in establishing individual behavior which need further consideration. In older conceptions, usually closely connected with classical evolutionary thought, the view can be observed that transfer of culture occurs in a very direct way and almost completely determines individual functioning. Some theorists have taken the position that cultural information is transferred hereditarily, and that for the individual it is among the constituents of his innate equipment. Others have assumed that the information has causal-deterministic effects upon behavior and al-

so that it directly determines the course of processes like perception and thinking. On the basis of a
critical review of these theories we shall attempt
to formulate a view with respect to the impact of
culture upon individual functioning.

A specific conception concerning the *transfer*
of cultural information can be found in the work of
Jung, who assumes that a major part of that information is transferred through heredity. The information
is cast in the mold of so-called archetypes, universal phenomena which are part and parcel of the make-up
of mankind as a whole. Archetypes are conceived as
products gradually shaped by evolutionary processes
in the remote past, and setting up a predisposition
to particular perceptions, intentions, expressions
and the like. In Jung's view the human psyche must be
seen primarily as a historical given: 'The psyche is
not of today: its ancestry goes back many millions of
years. Individual conscience is only the flower and
the fruit of a season, sprung from the perennial rhi-
zome beneath the earth...' (1956). The actual information that the individual derives from his culture
during his life  merely has the function to stimulate
unconscious archetypical activity and to structure it
symbolically. A major part of cultural information is
thus seen as pre-established and congenital. Therefore, Jung's theory is a theory of the cultural inhe-
ritance of mankind in the most literal sense.

But, at present, that conception is no longer
widely subscribed to. In particular the view that
cultural data are determined and passed on by evolutionary processes, has been rejected by evolution
theorists. Thus, Huxley (1969) regards culture as an
extension of biological evolution, having its roots
in man's biological evolution, but not established by
the mechanisms of natural selection. Archetypes such
as birth, death, child, mother, old man, animal, and
so on, are closely connected with *general biological*
phenomena; the fact that they manifest themselves
within every culture does not need to be explained on
the basis of specific hereditary structures.

The distinction between evolution and culture is
particularly emphasized in the work of Russian behavioral scientists from the so-called cultural-histo-
rical school, such as Vygotsky, Luria, Galperin and
Leontiev. These authors consider the acquisition
*(Aneignung)* of cultural elements to be a social process of a completely ontogenetic nature. The difference between these processes and evolutionary pro-

cesses is indicated by Leontiev (1973) as follows:
'Zwischen den Anpassungsprozessen im Eigentlichen
Sinne des Wortes und den Aneignungsprozessen gibt es
folgenden prinzipiellen Unterschied: Bei der biolo-
gische Anpassung *verändern sich* die Arteigenschaften
und das Artverhalten des Individuums. Beim Aneig-
nungsprozess reproduziert dagegen das Individuum die
historisch gebildeten Fähigkeiten und Funktionen.
Durch diesen Prozess wird in der Ontogenese des Menschen das erzielt, was beim Tier durch die Vererbung
erreicht wird: Die Entwicklungsergebnisse der Art
werden in den Eigenschaften des Individuums verkör-
pert' (1) (p. 283). That conclusion is endorsed here,
so that henceforth we will take the position that
cultural information is not inherited but is, on the
contrary, acquired during life.

Given the point of view  just mentioned, the question
becomes of interest whether the process of culture
acquisition should be located at the level of a culture as a whole, or at the level of the individuals
participating in that culture. The former opinion is
held especially by anthropologists, who have introduced the concept of *group character*, to indicate
differences between ethnic and national groups. In
that connection they also speak of the ethnic character or the national character. On the basis of these
notions cross-cultural psychologists have attempted
to create a 'modal personality' that is typical of a
particular culture. Thus, Kardiner (1939,1945) uses
the concept of *basic personality*, by which is meant
a specific psychological configuration, peculiar to
all members of a society. The origin of the basic
personality first and foremost rests on the primary
institutions that can be discerned in the culture of
the community in question. Primary institutions constitute the social and technological environment to
which each individual has to adjust. For the individual they must be considered to be the hard and rigid
environmental conditions he has to find ways to cope
with.
    According to Kardiner, culture provides support
for individual adaptation by offering individual safety systems, suitable to deal with specific problems that are bound to occur, and also capable of
reducing the anxiety aroused by these problems. Together, these safety systems belong to the so-called
secondary institutions of the culture in question.
On that basis, specific dispositions, temperament and

value structures are implanted in each individual during childhood, constituting a stable matrix within
which individual traits may develop. It is this matrix, common to all members of the society, that
tells us why all the Comanches are Comanche, why all
the British are British and, for that matter, why all
the Dutch are Dutch.

The basic personality may be explored empirically by means of comparative cross-cultural studies.
Kardiner has performed some studies of this type and
he reached different conclusions with respect to the
basic personality in different societies. Thus, for
example, the basic personality of the inhabitants of
the Marquise Isles is characterized by very little
overt hostility. The basic personality of the American Comanches is characterized by uncomplicatedness
and courage; the Alorese (inhabitants of Alor, one of
the Sunda Isles) are fearful and suspicious, and so
on.

Attractive as the theory of basic personality
may be in its simplicity, a problem arises if one
tries to answer the question where precisely the basic personality ends and the individual personality
begins. Kardiner (1939) himself has called attention
to this problem and he admits that the relationship
between the two concepts is as yet not quite clear.
The notion of basic personality indicates that the
individual will behave in a particular way, within
the limits imposed by his culture. But within these
limits considerable differences remain possible that
have to be accounted for by individuality.

Kardiner's theory has been profoundly analyzed
by Dufrenne (1953) who arrived at the conclusion that
the conception of the basic personality as a veridical part of the total personality is untenable. The
basic personality must primarily be seen as a scientific abstraction that has subsequently been generalized to all members of the community. Personality as
it functions in daily life is not built up out of a
general part and an individual part; to the individual the basic personality has the function of a
*norm*. In actual behavior that norm is confronted with
a real environment, resulting in a unique confrontation of nature and culture. The conclusion to be
drawn here is that the individual does not exist to
realize the norm, but that the norm is 'for the individual' (cf. Dufrenne, 1953, p. 220). An implication
of that conclusion is that individual behavior can
neither as a whole, nor in part, be directly explai-

ned on the basis of culture.

As Sapir (1970) has noted, anthropologists tend to look upon culture too easily as a 'given', merely to be adopted by the individual, but 'culture is... not something given, but something to be gradually and gropingly discovered. We then see at once that elements of culture that come well within the horizon of awareness of one individual are entirely absent in another individual's landscape' (Sapir, 1970 p. 25). Culture only provides an 'assembly or mass of loosely overlapping idea and action systems which, through verbal habit, can be made to assume the appearance of a closed system' but it is not adopted *as such* by the individual members of society. Rather, the system should be seen as a reference system that opens up a number of different possibilities of action for the individual.

Doubtlessly, one of the major vehicles for the transfer of culture is *language*. Of the different aspects that may be discerned in culture, language is probably the first to develop. A high degree of language perfection is required for culture as a whole to develop. Therefore, language may be regarded as more characteristic of a culture, as compared with behaviors and habits of the members of the community: 'Language is the symbolic guide to culture', as Sapir (1970) has stated. Within a culture the statement could be made that 'every experience is saturated with verbalism'.

Language constitutes culture but, on the other hand, language is also of prime importance where distribution and transfer of culture are concerned. Instruction and education are inconceivable without language: language has a communicative function. But an even more fundamental function of language is to symbolize reality. Therefore language is not only of interest in processes of communication, but it also has an impact on our conception of reality as such. The expectation that there exists a close connection between language and thought seems to be very obvious.

Hypotheses about the way in which, and the degree to which, language determines our conceptions of reality, have been formulated by linguists as well as anthropologists. Von Humboldt (1836) still conceived of language as a spontaneous product of the mind, that determines our knowledge of reality. But since de Saussure (1915) such a close connection between

language and reality is no longer assumed. In that
author's view, linguistic signs are arbitrary and do
not bear intrinsic relationships with reality. Language is a product of convention, originating from intersubjective agreement.

Interest in the relationship between language
and reality has been revived by the work of anthropologists, who started to compare languages in different cultures. They generally concluded that verbal
classifications of natural phenomena show considerable differences in different cultures. But not only
concepts and classification systems are different,
also grammatical structures, representing relations
between classes, diverge substantially.

Whorf (1956) for example, who studied American
Indian languages (Hopi, Navajo, Apache), noticed that
some tribes do not distinguish between subject and
predicate. With regard to thought processes in different cultures, Whorf drew far-reaching conclusions
from findings of this type. Not only the *content* of
thought, but also formal dimensions like time, space,
matter and logic supposedly differ profoundly on the
basis of language.

The so-called Whorfian hypothesis is very important, not only for comparative anthropology, but
also for the psychology of thinking as well as for
psycholinguistics. However, attempts to test this
hypothesis have produced many problems, because it is
very complicated to start with. Miller and McNeill
(1969) have called it a 'formidable thicket of inter-
twined propositions'. These authors have reviewed a
number of empirical investigations that are relevant
to the Whorfian hypothesis.

Among these investigations were codability studies, i.e. investigations testing the effect of the
availability of certain verbal categories upon results in a number of cognitive tasks. The problems
consisted of recognition and memorization of colors
that were offered to the subjects. Miller and McNeil
classified these studies according to the evidence
they supplied with respect to the Whorfian hypothesis and they reached a differentiated conclusion. As
long as in the experiments a direct reaction is required to concrete stimuli (perception), no effect of
verbal categories materializes. But as soon as storage of information in memory is called for, linguistic coding turns out to be important. Miller and
McNeil concluded that the Whorfian hypothesis is confirmed by empirical evidence, provided that it is

restricted to *memory*.

Recent memory studies have shown that semantic memory is not restricted to word definitions and simple lexical rules. According to Norman (1973), memory in addition at least includes a deeper insight into the way linguistic concepts operate in real environments. Thus, the Whorfian hypothesis seems to be reduced to realistic proportions: language teaches the individual to categorize his environment in a particular way, and, by doing so, it also induces a particular course of action in that environment. But that does not imply that the individual's thought processes are formally determined by language as well.

To summarize this section, it can be stated that different theories have centered upon different aspects of the relationship between culture and personality. In these theories the individual person is predominantly viewed as a product of heredity, historical background and environment. The criticisms that were raised against those conceptions mainly concerned the minor role that was left for the individual's activities, individual aspects of behavior being unduly attributed to broad cultural influences.

It was concluded, then, that cultural information is not tranferred by means of innate structures but by means of an ontogenetic process of acquisition. In that process language plays an important part with respect to communication as well as with respect to problems of application in dealing with the environment.

Cultural information is concerned primarily with the environment: assimilation of information provides the individual with a normative system of reference that he can use to deal with the environment. It is assumed here that this information has radical effects upon the individual's relation with the environment, and thus becomes of prime importance for an interactionistic conception of personality.

## 3.2   *The interior of personality*

With respect to psychological adaptation as defined earlier, information *on the environment* is necessary and also sufficient. But that does not hold for the classical global disposition theories of personality, which have generally attempted to gain insight into man's *interior*, apart from his environment. One of the most prominent ways to obtain such insight has been through language. A particular jargon is included in language, that seems peculiarly suited to describe internal processes and states. In that connection Klages (1932) has stated: 'Language excels in unconscious insight the acumen of the most talented thinker, and we contend that whoever, having the right talent, should do nothing but examine the words and phrases which deal with the human soul, would know more about it than all the sages who omitted to do so, and would know perhaps a thousand times more than has ever been discovered by observation, apparatus, and experiment upon man'.

Granted that language comprises a great deal of wisdom, the question is to which ends that wisdom may be adequately used and to which ends it may not. More specifically, the question is whether language can tell us anything about processes and states that are connected with forms of internal psychic functioning. The problem introduced here is well known to psychologists as the problem of introspection. Criticisms of introspection are as old as the method itself and have lately been reformulated by Nisbett and DeCamp Wilson (1977). A review of a large number of pertinent investigations led these authors to conclude that man has little or no access to higher cognitive processes through introspection.

A recent study of personality descriptions by young children has revealed that development in that area typically evolves from short, simple descriptions of overt characteristics to longer and more complex descriptions of covert characteristics (Bromley, 1977). In addition, in children a conception of *other* people typically precedes the development of a conception of self. Self-concepts seem to be based on a comparison in overt behavior between self and the other. These findings point to the fact that self-insight is primarily a derivative of the conceptions we have of others and that it does not rest on some form of direct accessibility of our own internal structure.

In this section we shall try to demonstrate that the specifically human way of gathering and transferring information by verbal means does not lend itself to application to 'the interior'. Many psychologists, notably personality theorists, have started from the assumption that it does. Within personality psychology this has given rise to a 'cultivation of the interior' that has taken different shapes in different traditional approaches to personality. We shall re-

strict ourselves to three major approaches, i.e. the
psychoanalytic approach, the cognitive-phenomenological approach and the trait-theoretical approach of
the interior, each of which has produced its own core
concept, viz. the symbol, the self and the trait.

In Freud's early work the concept of *symbol* en-
tered the scene as a substantial element of the theory. In Freud's conception symbolization consists of
an indirect representation of repressed contents of
consciousness, by means of neutral symbols of a re-
presentational character. The relation between the
repressed content and the symbol is of a superindividual nature, so that interpretation of the content
with the aid of the symbol is essentially possible.
In the original statement of symbolization theory the
unconscious was seen as the active given,'releasing'
its contents, after which they were assimilated by
the conscious ego and provided with a new form. Symbolization itself was characterized as a coupling of
two elements, one of which was always unconscious.
Activities occurring in the symbolization process were seen as examples of primary-process thinking of a
primitive nature.

Later authors (cf. Lorenzer, 1972) have pointed
out inconsistencies in the original symbolization
theory, notably stating that the unconsious id is in-
capable of introducing structure as is assumed by the
process of symbolization. They see the process as a
product of the ego, the only entity that can handle
images as well as symbols. Symbols are not merely
functions of the ego, but they also constitute a necessary condition for secondary-process thinking.

Lorenzer (1972) conceives of symbols as psychic
products, that can represent objects and events, are
dissoluble from these in the process of thinking, and
are also capable of being made substantive objects of
thinking in turn. Symbolization of repressed contents,
according to Lorenzer, is nothing but a deficient
form of symbolization, a regression of the process of
knowledge into the direction of *cliché:* repression is
de-symbolization.

Since, generally, the symbol gives access to
communication with the speech community, repression
consequently means exclusion of certain individual
experiences from the speech community. In the terminology used here, repression means secluding oneself
from cultural information with respect to the event
that is being'repressed!.

Lorenzer's analysis makes it perfectly clear
that no particular significance has to be attached to

symbolization in the Freudian sense, with respect to
internal processes that determine behavior. That conclusion has been generalized by Lorenzer (1971) to
psychoanalysis as a whole, on the basis of considerations derived from philosophy of language: psychoanalysis should be considered primarily as a theory of
*interaction* instead of a theory of *behavior*. 'Das,
was in der Psychoanalyse erfasst wird, sind nicht in
erste Linie Verhaltensweisen eines Handelenden, son-
dern zugleich und vor allem Interaktionsstrukturen,
die im Medium der berichtenden Subjekte begriffen
werden' (2) , states Lorenzer (1971, p. 43).

With this conclusion he joins the famous philosopher of language, Wittgenstein, who has repeatedly
cautioned against the confusion of verbal interaction
with other forms of behavior. According to that author, interaction  has its own course and its own
special laws: no other reality needs to be assumed to
coincide with elements of interaction through language.

In this context, Wittgenstein has wondered:
'What do psychologists record? - What do they obser-
ve? Isn't it the behavior of human beings, in particular their utterances? But *these* are not about behavior' (Wittgenstein, 1968). Those utterances might serve several functions within the context
of the interaction process. However, a particular intention being communicated should not be confused with a *description* of an internal event. For,
as Wittgenstein has stated: 'I reveal to him something of myself when I tell him what I was going to
do. - Not, however, on the grounds of self-observa-
tion, but by way of a response (it might also be called an intuition)' (p. 167).

Psychoanalytic symbolization has not been the only
attempt to cultivate the interior by means of language. A second form is the concept of *self*. That concept is generally used to describe and interpret
one's own behavior. Usually the self-concept is not
primarily concerned with overt activities, but rather
with ideas, feelings and internal states. Ever since
the days of William James the self has been viewed by
psychologists as the source of psychic activities that
determine behavior. As an object of study the self is
primarily accessible by means of consciousness or
self-reflection. Theorists like Symonds, Snygg and
Combs, Lundholm, Bertocci, Chein and Rogers assume
forms of self-experience or self-awareness to be the

primary source of knowledge about the self.

Hall and Lindzey (1970), who have summarized the
most important theories of self, made a distinction
between the *self as object* and the *self as process*.
The first of these concepts refers to the self as it
is known by the individual, the way he thinks about
himself. The second self concept describes the self
in the way it constitutes the basis of his psychic
activities.

The major issue in the framework of self-theory
is, whether, besides the self as object, another self
might and should be distinguished. Cautious self-the-
orists speak of an'inferred self'to indicate that the
second type of self is assumed to exist in so-called
naive psychology, but that this assumption can never
be tested directly. Hilgard (1949), for instance,
primarily sees the use of the self-concept in that
sense as an emphasis on responsibility for his own
behavior by the'man in the street'.

The social philosopher George Herbert Mead (1934)
can only accept the self as object. In his view there
is no reason to accept a self as process, because man
does not have direct access to his own experience.
Initially, man sees other men as objects, and it is
only on the basis of other men's reactions that he
*learns* to conceive of himself in the same way.

Views that are in agreement with Mead's can be
found in the work of psychologists like Stephenson
(1953), Skinner (1973) and Kouwer (1973). These authors show a marked reluctance to conceive of self as
*the* basis of behavior, as well as of consciousness as
the source of knowledge concerning that basis. Thus,
Skinner does not see consciousness as a reality in
its own right but as a social product. It owes its
existence to the interaction of the individual with
his social environment, it is a derivative of social
behavior. Once established, consciousness does not
play an initiating but a mediating part. In his own
words: 'Without the help of verbal community all behavior would be unconscious. Consciousness is a social product. It is not only *not* the special field of
autonomous man, it is not within range of a solitary
man'. (Skinner, 1973, pp. 187-188).

A similar conception of consciousness is held by
Russian psychologists working in the cultural-histo-
rical tradition. That view can be traced back to Karl
Marx, who seems to have stated as early as 1845 that
'consciousness is therefore from the very beginning
a social product, and remains so as long as men exist

at all' (cf. Bottomore 1964, pp. 19-20).

The clearest statement in this vein may well be imputed to Leontiev (1977): 'Das individuelle Bewusstsein als spezifisch menschliche Form der subjektiven Widerspiegelung der objektiven Realität kann also nur als Produkt jener Beziehungen und Vermittlungen verstanden werden, die mit der Gesellschaft entstehen. Ausserhalb des Systems dieser Beziehungen (und ausserhalb des Gesellschaftlichen Bewusstseins) kann es keine individuelle Psyche in Form des Bewusstseins geben' (3) (p. 46). With respect to the self-concept this position has extreme consequences. Instead of the *object* of consciousness the self becomes a *product* of consciousness and, finally, of our social environment.

The self is not a natural given, but something we receive, notably from others. An illustration of the latter may be found in the early development of speech. Children usually start to indicate themselves by their names and only later in development they begin to use terms like I and self (Menyuk, 1969). The self-concept has a definite function in interaction processes, as, for instance, in psychotherapy where the client himself is the main theme of the conversation. It enables people to exchange views on their own behavior. In addition the self-concept has a control function with respect to social relations, where a certain amount of 'person constancy' is a fundamental condition for interaction and cooperation (cf. Goffman, 1967; Hettema, 1972; Kouwer, 1973).

The self as object seems to be completely explainable from social relations and there does not appear to be any reason to postulate a self as process. Yet, although the primary function of self is a social one, it may also serve to control individual behavior. However, in that case, the self should not be seen as a process, but as a norm next to the many other norms that the individual uses to guide his behavior.

The third concept that is widely used to account for individual behavior, is the conception of *trait*. Trait concepts have been used since antiquity and they have remained *in vogue* until today. In the course of time the preference for the utilization of particular trait concepts has changed, but the trait phenomenon as such has been very stable in our culture. Gordon Allport (1937) has given the trait the status of a veridical inner psychic structure, the 'ultimate reality of psychological organization'.

Cattell has further elaborated trait theory and provided it with a firm empirical foundation. His theory is based on trait names that were borrowed from the famous linguistic study of Allport and Odbert (1936). Cattell had a large number of subjects indicate how well people they knew could be characterized with the aid of these trait names. The data thus obtained were called L-(life history) data. The results of this study were then reduced to a limited number of factors through factor analysis. These factors were assumed to constitute important basic dimensions of personality , and Cattell hypothesized that they might be identified by other methods as well. The factors were then compared with other factors, obtained from self-descriptions by means of questionnaires (the latter data were called Q-data). The results showed that factors from L- and Q-data are to a fair extent comparable.

Subsequently an additional comparison was made with factors derived from objective test scores, the so-called T-data. It turned out that factors from T-data did not show much similarity with factors from L- and Q-data (cf. Hall & Lindzey, 1970).Cattell has suggested that this lack of correspondence merely means that the different measurement approaches sample data at different levels of generality. An argument for that point of view is that some T-data factors later turned out to correspond to *second-order* factors derived from L- and Q-data.

But that argument seems at variance with the notion that descriptions and self-descriptions are more abstract by nature than the scores of specific objective tests. A much simpler explanation of the lack of correspondence between T-factors on the one hand and L- and Q-factors on the other is that the use of verbal descriptions in both L- and Q-data has been the critical issue for the establishment of corresponding factors. Verbal descriptions give access to preconceptions about personality that are culturally determined, so that factors derived from verbal descriptions are not primarily concerned with behavior itself but with *opinions about behavior*.

That those opinions do play some part in behavior is not denied here, but the hypothesis that they play a *causal* role seems highly improbable. In this connection Mischel (1973) has stated: 'Thus while the traditional personality paradigm views traits as the intrapsychic *causes* of behavioral consistency, the present position sees them as the *summary terms* (labels, codes, organizing constructs) applied to observed behavior' (p. 264).

Arguments in favor of this position may be obtained by a closer inspection of results within the domain of verbal measurement of traits. In that area some striking differences have been found between trait ratings and trait self-ratings. As is well known to those who have ever filled out a personality questionnaire, subjects are usually reluctant to describe themselves in trait terms. If they do so at all, they first seem to imagine how others would describe them, and only later on to complete the questionnaire.

Mischel (1973) has proposed the view that subjects do not attribute their own behavior to traits but to situational factors instead. This hypothesis was put to test by van Heck and Van der Leeuw (1975), who asked 98 subjects to rate the probability of aggressive behavior to occur in a number of situations, for themselves as well as for their best friend. Through analysis of variance they were able to show clearly that ratings have much more cross-situational consistency than self-ratings. These authors concluded that the trait model is preferred only when judging others, but not in judgement of self.

The issue of consistency in ratings and self-rating was further pursued by the present author. In a recent study (Hettema, 1979) he compared the internal consistencies of self-rating scales and rating scales. Self-ratings were significantly less consistent while in the construction of self-rating scales much more items (up to 70 %) had to be eliminated to obtain a tolerable amount of consistency.

It seems that traits are used to describe people, but only *other* people. This is a peculiar finding if one really views traits as the ultimate reality of psychological organization. Our conclusion is that traits cannot be seen as causal factors determining individual behavior, but should rather be conceived as verbal expedients which primarily aim to bring order into the social ecology man lives in. As such they might be very useful to social psychology, but they can never constitute the basis of a scientific conception of personality.

To summarize this section, it can be stated that a number of personality theorists (probably the vast majority) have founded their work on concepts derived from everyday usage. The theories that they have developed belong to our culture, and as such they essentially form part of the information that individuals have at their disposal. Individuals may or may not utilise that information in dealing with other people. Thus, classical theories may have heuristic significance to guide behavior in social situations.

However, as a critical examination has demonstrated, there does not seem to be much reason to attach great value to global-dispositional theories of personality, where insight into internal psychic processes is concerned. Classical theories have generally laid such claims, but the question remains on what grounds they are built.

Presumably one of the assumptions made by the classical theories has been a conception of language that must nowadays be considered obsolete. Formerly the view was widely accepted that linguistic elements like words and phrases always refer to real or possible objects in the world. But nowadays linguistic elements are primarily considered meaningful on the basis of convention and usage.

For instance, Wittgenstein (1968) admits meaning to terms referring to internal states only as a function of the setting in which those terms are *used*. Reference to 'real' inner states is no longer assumed: 'The criteria for the truth of the *confession* that I thought such-and-such are not the criteria for a true *description* of a process. And the importance of the true confession does not reside in its being a correct and certain report of a process. It resides rather in the special consequences which can be drawn from a confession whose truth is guaranteed by the special criteria of truthfulness' (Wittgenstein, 1968).

In 'reporting' on his inner state, the reporter turns himself into a particular element of the environment for the receiver of the report. However, the reporter can only be blamed if his subsequent behavior does not agree with his earlier statement. Whether or not that statement was correct as such, is of little consequence for the receiver and cannot be verified anyway.

In this respect there is an important discrepancy between statements concerning inner states and statements concerning the environment. The description of inner states and processes lacks the basis that is necessary for a meaningful statement, i.e. intersubjective reference. Yet, of course, it cannot be denied that communication and language are of major re-

levance with respect to individual functioning, even
where inner states are concerned. But the relevance
of that kind of communication must primarily be seen
within the framework of reciprocal relations *between*
individuals.

In this section some prominent core concepts from
classical personality theories have been critically
examined. A number of arguments have been put forward
to demonstrate that inclusion of these concepts in
personality theories purporting to refer to internal
processes, is unjustified. Concepts adopted from everyday usage are no more than elements of the culture
and cannot be taken to refer to any real psychological states or processes. Thus, unlike in the previous
section, we have stated here that elements of culture
have wrongly been included in the individual personality.

The conclusions of sections 3.1 and 3.2 taken together  lead us to an altogether different conception
of the relationship between culture and personality.
In this conception, culture is primarily seen as a
source of information, which the individual may utilize in the interest of his psychological adaptation.
That information is to be characterized as to its
origin as *social* instead of individual, it is concerned with the *environment* (social as well as physical) instead of with the organism and, finally, it
*accompanies* individual behavior, instead of causing
individual behavior. In the following sections the
different parts of this proposition will be elaborated further.

*3.3  Language, culture and information transmission*

     In order to gather information on the environ-
ment, man, as well as animals, can turn to the environment in question, explore it, and acquire knowledge from experience while acting in that environment.
This way of acquiring information is fundamental in
the sense that it determines man's primary information on the environment, constituting the basis for
other forms of knowledge. However, if man's information were to be restricted to direct experience,
psychological adaptation would proceed at a rudimen-
tary level. The acquisition of knowledge from personal
experience is a slow process which is hazardous as
well because of the dangers and uncertainties immi-

nent in unknown environments.

A second strategy that can be used to acquire
information is based on direct communication with
congeners, possessing the information wanted. This
communication proceeds by way of signs, indicating
how the state of affairs is in the situation in question. The science that directs itself to communication through signs is called semiotics. Transmission of
information by means of signs occurs in divergent
animal species as a part of the species-specific behavioral equipment. In this connection one could
think of the mating call of grey-hens, the triumphal
cry of geese, the tail movements of wolves, the dance
of bees, the zigzag move of sticklebacks. Communication by means of signs provides information on concrete situations and is of major immediate interest
for activities in these situations.

As well as through natural signs, man may also
communicate through artificial signs or symbols. The
efficacy of symbols is not based on a natural relationship with environmental aspects but on agreement
and convention. Symbols also lend themselves to the
conveyance of information on environments and states
of environments that are not actually present, as
well as on situations that have not been encountered
before.

As has been pointed out earlier, the main symbol
system man has at his disposal  is language. The major significance of language with respect to adaptation is that at any given moment, by means of language, information can be conveyed on circumstances
that will be actually present only in the future. The
nature and amount of information is thus disconnected
from individual experience: essentially it concerns
the accumulated knowledge and experience of large
groups of men. Not only does it concern the experience of living members of society, but also the knowledge of those that died in the remote past.

This complex of knowledge is to be reckoned a-
mong the culture of a society; therefore culture may
be viewed as the means *par excellence* for psychological adaptation in man. In this connection Kluckhohn
and Murray (1971) have defined culture as 'a great
storehouse of ready-made solutions to problems which
human animals are wont to encounter' (p. 54). Thus
they have indicated that culture essentially has pre-
ventive effects with respect to individual problems
of adaptation. To have these effects, culture is
first to be transferred to individual members of so-

ciety.

The transfer of culture is closely related to
and dependent on the development of the symbolic function. As has been pointed out before, man as a species does not have available precoded information
processing mechanisms, such as in animals form part
of species-specific behavior. Instead of phylogenetic transmission of information, man is almost entirely dependent upon ontogenetic transmission.

The latter type of transmission is assumed to be
rooted in the individual's experience. Therefore in a
child's cognitive development exploration of and interaction with the environment plays a crucial part.
In environments rich in stimulation there is more opportunity for exploration as compared with environments with poor stimulation. Research has indeed
shown that cognitive development is established faster and better in the first type of environments (La
Crosse *et al*, 1969).

Processes of cognitive development in connection
with the environment have been described by Piaget
(1951). Varied and repeated experiences with stimuli
and objects like fingers, the bottle, the mother,
toys, and so on, lead the young child to develop object schemas. They are brought about through abstraction from a large number of sensomotor experiences.
Initially the schemas merely comprise scattered experiences, but later on they become coordinated to
form new schemas in which veridical knowledge of objects is represented. On that basis the child dis-
criminates permanent objects like fingers, bottles,
and so on. Prolonged experience with objects leads to
the development of a complex of schemas, enabling the
child to maintain a well-balanced relationship with
the environment at the level of sensations and actions.

During the next stage the development of the
symbolic function is actually started. Instead of
dealing with real objects, the child learns to use
mental representations, so that it becomes increasingly capable of dealing with objects without their
actual presence and without direct actions being involved. In the very development of the symbolic function, language development plays an important role,
a fact that finds general acceptance. But with respect to the precise nature and the sequence of developments there is considerable room for debate.

According to Piaget, actual symbol formation is
preceded by another phase, one in which objects are

imitated by imitative gestures. These gestures are subsequently internalized in the form of images, and only after that are they provided with symbolic labels derived from language. Thus, a development takes place from an individualized language to a general language. Chomsky (1965), on the other hand, assumes that man has available an innate, precoded mechanism of information, the so-called universal grammar. This mechanism supposedly determines the form of his knowledge in advance, and leaves limited room for subsequent increases of knowledge. Chomsky states that: 'the general features of language structure reflect, not so much the course of one's experience, but rather the general character of one's innate capacity to acquire knowledge'...(Chomsky, 1965).

Clearly, it is assumed here that a basic set of concepts can be found from which all others can be derived. However, as Shotter (1970) has pointed out 'In psychology we have distinguished between the "knowledge" which we derive from our actions and the schemas of organization, derived from social interaction, which we can impose on it'...'a description is only of such use if it relates in some way to the methods that people have available for taking some sort of action in the world, that is, relates to their "knowledge" derived from bodily activity' (p. 251).

A position, diametrically opposed to Chomsky's view as well as Piaget's, is taken by Vygotsky (1962). Instead of Chomsky's innate structures and Piaget's development from egocentric to socialized language, this author stresses the primacy of social interaction. An organized pattern of interaction between the child and others enables the child to organize its own behavior *at a later moment*. Linguistic symbols acquire their meaning in the process of communication and only afterwards can they carry out their function in individual behavior. On this view languages are not built on concepts existing before language development, but concepts are the *result* of the process of language development. Once they are established, concepts may be connected with knowledge that the individual has acquired on the basis of his sensomotor relations with the environment.

Clearly, Vygotsky's conception of development of the symbolic function is much in line with the idea of psychological adaptation and the thoughts developed here with respect to the acquisition of information from culture.

Symbolization through language gives access to generalizations and discriminations of a type that is
considered relevant in culture. These generalizations
and discrimations can be utilized by the individual
to raise behavioral effectiveness.

Next to language development information is ab-
sorbed by the child; educational practices contribute
a great deal to that process. Thus, parents teach
their children the names of objects, they explain
when certain descriptions are to be applied and when
not, on the basis of which data distinctions are
to be made, and which explanations may be given for
the events in their environment. Children are corrected when they infringe the rules of logic or when
they deviate from current usage. Very soon they are
urged to 'think first' before acting, and they are
criticized if their actions are impulsive, thought-
less or too hasty. Education through language is primarily directed towards a correct use of elements of
culture (Dollard  &  Miller, 1950).

Psycholinguists assume that linguistic concepts
are interrelated on the basis of their semantic
structure or meaning. Thus, Collins and Quillian
(1969) have suggested a conception of semantic memory
as an associative network in which semantic relations
between concepts are represented.

According to Katz (1972), a concept may be defined on the basis of so-called semantic markers, by
means of which the concept can be distinguished from
other concepts. These markers are viewed as properties of the concept. They are not necessarily represented in single words. Katz (1972) defines the semantic marker  as: '...a theoretical construct which
is intended to represent a concept that is part of
the sense of morphemes and other constituents of natural language...'. Concepts in turn are described as:
'...abstract entities. They do not belong to the experience of anyone, though they may be thought about,
as in thinking about the concept of a circle. They
are not individuated by persons: you and I may think
about the same concept' (p. 38).

Concepts are normative in the sense that they
prescribe the conditions that have to be met,
in order  that the concept may be used. Meaning in
terms of semantic markers defines the empirical re-
ferents of the concept. But that does not imply that
a concept can be described exhaustively in terms of
*perceptual* attributes. In addition to those, it has
to be indicated to what ends objects and events, des-

cribed with the concept, may be used, and also what
their prospects are (cf. Miller & Johnson Laird,
1976, p. 267).

Summarizing, we reach the conclusion that with
semantic memory individuals have available a behavioral reference system of an intersubjective nature.
That system on the one hand allows application of
cultural achievements to individual behavior, on the
other hand communication with others about private
experiences. Essentially, it enables the individual
to tackle his psychological adaptation problems with
the aid of a superindividual system. The conceptual
structure included in semantic memory  provides him
with the opportunity to segregate meaningful units in
his environment, and to react with appropriate behavior, even if he has never been there before.

In the previous chapter psychological adaptation was
defined as directed transformation of the environment. Problems with respect to psychological adaptation were to be expected because of a fundamental
uncertainty regarding the initial and the final situation, as well as transformational behavior itself.
We can now see how that uncertainty may be reduced
by bringing in information that is available in culture and precipitated in language.

First of all cultural information is concerned
with the segregation of environmental segments  that
will be indicated here as *situations*. Kluckhohn and
Kelly (1952) have pointed out this important function
of culture by stating: 'Culture is - among other
things - a set of readymade definitions of the situation which each participant only slightly retailors
in his own idiomatic way' (p. 91). These authors assume that each culture, in its own way, provides
classifications of the environment in the interest of
behavioral effectiveness of its participants. In these classifications indications are given as to which
aspects of the environments are to be given special
attention, which environments are to be considered
dangerous and which environmental aspects may serve
as starting-points for behavior.

Vast differences exist between cultures with
respect to definitions of situations, in turn manifesting themselves in language. Thus, Eskimos distinguish between several kinds of snow, whereas a
general term for that phenomenon does not exist in
their language (Boas, 1911). The Bororos, a tribe in
the Amazone region, use different terms for a number

of parrot varieties, but do not use a general term to
describe the parrot genus as a whole (Levy-Brühl,
1912). The Trobrianders have a separate term for an
uncle on the father's side (Malinowski, 1927).

The significance of distinctions of this kind
must be seen in the functional importance they have
in the cultures in question. They refer to different
ways of dealing with the environment, that may or may
not be based on differences existing in natural ecology. For the individual the significance of culture
first and foremost must be seen in ordering and eva-
luating the world: 'cultivating' the environment is
one of the major functions of culture.

However, such cultivation does not restrict itself to defining and classifying. Defining situations
can only be of interest with respect to individual
adaptation if definitions have consequences for behavior. The recognition of a particular situation first
of all has to allow for prediction of the future developments of that situation. In that case the individual may take measures on the basis of his expectations. Thus, for example, in traffic we frequently
enter situations that have been defined and marked
according to a particular code. Each traffic sign
leads to a particular pattern of expectations: up-
turned triangles indicate that traffic coming from
either side has (and usually takes) right of way.

Besides patterns of expectation, culture also
provides means to transform situations. With the aid
of these the individual may transform situations in
such manner that his private aims are realized better. In this connection, Murdock (1945) has characterized adaptive behavior as the transformation of
'situations evoking drives into those bringing about
their reduction' (p. 130). Directed transformations
require behaviors leading to results specified in advance, and those behaviors are specified and transferred by culture. According to Murdock (1945) each
culture comprises 'a number of so-called instrumental
responses which of themselves reduce no basic drives
but merely pave the way for other acts which have re-
warding results' (p. 132).

From this perspective culture has also been defined as a collection of traditional ways to solve
problems: 'It is as though the culture gives instructions: "This is the way we meet this problem" (Hamburg, et al, 1974, p. 410). Problem solving is conceived here as the resolution of a conflict between
an actual and a desired state of affairs. 'Man's abi-

lities to cope with the environment depend on the efficacy of the solutions his culture provides', states
Mechanic (1974). In that process use can be made of
contingencies that have been established by others
(Skinner, 1973), of pragmatic-axiological information
existing in culture (Van Peursen *et al*, 1968). Henceforth that information will thus be indicated as
*pragmatic information*.

First of all it must be stated that solutions
for problematic situations as they exist in culture
are far from always being effective. Practices that
have been used in the past to fight diseases are now
being designated as quackery and actions for improving the harvest  by sacrifices to the weather-gods
are now seen as examples of magic belief. Thus, in
pragmatic information, a distinction might be introduced with respect to the degree of certainty of effectiveness. In some cases pragmatic information does
have an algorithmic status with regard to the problem,
but not infrequently it merely has heuristic value.

Examples of pragmatic information are not hard
to think of: all kinds of prescriptions and recipes
belong to it, as, for instance, cookery-books, medical encyclopedias, traffic instructions, Spock's ba-
by-care, and so on. Prescriptions as meant here are
usually directed at concrete, recognizable situations
in daily life and they provide  lines of action to
deal with them.  Altogether they presumably have an
enormous impact upon the things people do most of the
time, because, as Campbell (1975) recently put it:
'On purely scientific grounds, these recipes for living might be regarded as better tested than the best
of psychology's and psychiatry's speculations on how
lives should be lived' (p. 1103).

Pragmatic information is usually adopted from
people who have thoroughly explored particular situations and who have recorded their experiences. Utilization of that information has the effect that inex-
perienced followers avoid classical mistakes, and that
they are enabled to change more easily a certain state of affairs to their advantage. Thus, Machiavelli,
second to none in being abreast of the political ma-
chinations of his day, described preferable modes of
consolidating power. In doing so, he made a distinction between power acquired on the basis of law, of
personal courage, of financial resources, of criminal
actions, and so on. Also, it is a matter of interest
to Machiavelli whether one has been elected a ruler,
one has conquered a state, reconquered a state after

a revolt, and so on (cf. Machiavelli, 1974). This
example also indicates that pragmatic information
(what is to be done?) always presupposes semantic information (in what circumstances?). Both types of information taken together, constitute the so-called
*exploitative system* (Waddington, 1960), that enables
man to directedly select his life environment and to
directedly transform that environment.

In the remainder of this section an attempt will be
made to further formalize the exploitative system. To
do this, some concepts have to be defined first. One
of these concepts is the *situation-concept* $S_y$. A concept is called a situation-concept if it relates to
the environment (in its broadest sense) and if its
properties or semantic markers may be referred to intersubjectively. It is a concept meant to be applied
to concrete environments, in such a way that consensus remains possible on the question whether that application was justified (concrete environments as referred to in the last sentence will later be indicated with the symbol $S_x$).

A single situation concept may be defined by
means of one or more aspects, it may be more or less
abstract, its range of convenience may be large or
small. Situation concepts are defined in terms of semantic markers: in language there is a variety of
possibilities to represent them. Thus, situation concepts may be described in terms of verbs, nouns, ad-
verbs, adjectives, and so on. The concepts have a normative character: they point out a number of conditions that have to be met in the real environment to
allow their use.

The $S_y$ is seen here as a further specification of
the contribution that culture makes towards an effective categorization of the ecology by the members of
the community. The situation concept may be seen as
a direct extension of the ideas developed before,
concerning the partitioning of the natural ecology
into the areas I, II and III. Situation concepts may
essentially be applied to all these areas, but their
main function with respect to psychological adaptation is connected with area III. In this area individuals must be considered helpless and extremely vul-
nerable unless they are supported by their culture.

The idea of partitioning natural ecologies deserves some further explanation. Basically, the human
ecology may be divided according to an infinite num-

ber of aspects. All objects and qualities that are
discriminable in ecology may in principle be used as
discriminative cues. The first interest of situation
concepts is to reduce environmental uncertainty by
categorizing an infinite number of environments ($S_x$)
according to a limited number of $S_y$'s.

But uncertainty reduction as such is not sufficient. Categorization according to $S_y$'s is effective
only if it is based on situation transformability. To
distinguish between two initial situations that may
be transformed into the same final situation by the
same means, does not make sense. The effectiveness of
an $S_y$-taxonomy rests on the degree to which it is discriminative with regard to behavioral consequences in
the situations that are being distinguished. Therefore, in addition to situation  concepts there must be
a provision for *transformation rules* ($R_y$), specifying the behaviors that are considered to be effective in the different situations.

These transformation rules are conceived here in
much the same way as situation concepts, i.e. they
have a bearing upon environmental change and they may
be referred to intersubjectively. They may be defined
by semantic markers that will by nature demonstrate
a different emphasis as compared to the markers used
to define situation  concepts.

Both conceptual elements - situation concepts and
transformation rules - together are assumed here to
constitute the exploitative system, a gigantic conceptual structure that characterizes a particular
culture. Schematically that structure may be presented in the form of a transition matrix (Table 2).

The $S_y$'s located in the left margin of the matrix represent the initial situations, whereas the
$S_y$'s in the top margin represent the situations  obtained after transformation of the initial situations.
The entire set of final situations is conceived to be
identical to the set of initial situations. Each of
the situation concepts is defined by a number of semantic markers that are represented in the column and
row next to the situation concepts. The body of the
matrix contains actions in the form of transformation
rules, to bring about transformations from initial to
final situations.

Clearly, many cells in the matrix have to be
left blank, because the particular transformation

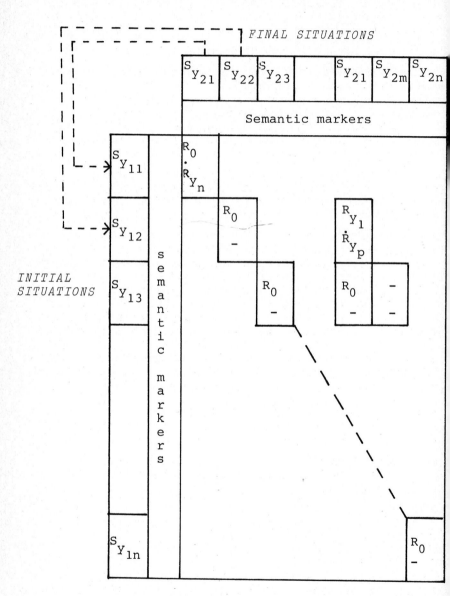

**Table 2.** *The exploitative system represented as an SRS transition matrix*

from initial to final situation cannot be accomplished by any means. Other cells may be filled up with a
great number of $R_y$'s indicating that there are many
ways to accomplish that transformation. In those cases a hierarchy is assumed to exist between different
$R_y$'s in the sense that some activities are considered
to be more effective than others to carry out the
transformation in question.

　　Thus far we have concerned ourselves mainly with
the activities of individuals and their effects. However, transformations may well occur without any interference on the part of the individual. In that case, there is a question of expectations with respect
to autonomous developments of situations. In the matrix, provisions have been made to account for this
type of transformation by inserting the term $R_o$ in
the cells that are concerned with 'autonomous' change. $R_o$ means that particular transformations are to
be expected even if the individual does not act himself. Whether these transformations are due to 'natural' developments or to the activities of other individuals is left out of consideration here.

　　A special problem concerns the main diagonal of
the matrix. Since the matrix is considered to be sym-
metrical, the cells on that diagonal refer to transformations of particular situations into themselves.
At first sight it seems reasonable to leave these
cells blank, indicating that there is no activity at
all. But since previously $R_o$ was defined to indicate
the absence of activity, it seems logical to insert
$R_o$ in each cell on the diagonal as well. In addition
to $R_o$, in these cells all kinds of transformations
may be included that do not essentially affect the
character of the initial situation.

　　A structure as outlined here provides an opportunity to transform all kinds of discrete situations into
other situations. But it does more than that. Because
the set of initial situations is considered to be i-
dentical with the set of final situations, they may
be seen as interchangeable. In other words, each final situation may be conceived as an initial situation
as well. Thus, instead of single transformations,
chains of variable length may be built, conformable
to the principles outlined in chapter II.

　　The SRS-transition matrix described here is assumed to be intersubjective. It represents the entire

experiental knowledge of a culture in so far as it
has been endorsed by its members. It may be transmitted by instruction to the individual members for the
benefit of their psychological adaptation. Individuals may or may not take in that knowledge. It is assumed, finally, that adoption of the exploitative
system constitutes an important condition for the effectiveness of an individual's interaction with his
environment, or, in other words, his competence (cf.
White, 1959).

## 3.4  *The situation*

Situation concepts may be defined with the aid
of semantic markers. Thus, for example, the concept
of school may be defined as a situation with a number
of properties that are essential for the school situation and distinguish it from other situations. The
concept may be described as a location where young
people gather to learn. The location shows a number
of characteristics of a spatial nature, such as the
schoolbuilding, classrooms, seats, and the like. In
that building there are teachers and auxiliary staff.
A stable temporal structure may be noticed with fixed lectures, interspersed with breaks, and so on.
Each new specification introduced in the definition
further distinguishes the concept of school from other concepts. Increasing the number of semantic markers makes the concept shed ambiguity.

There are other situations that are defined much
more ambiguously than the school situation. Thus, we
may indicate situations as a working situation, playing situation or social situation without indicating
precisely what their properties are. However, even in
those situations it remains possible to name semantic
markers which find intersubjective agreement. The
latter element vanishes as soon as situations are being qualified instead of being defined. What constitutes a painful, happy, precarious or dangerous situation for one individual does not necessarily do so
for another individual. The distinction meant here is
akin to the semantic distinction into denotation and
connotation, as well as to the distinction between
reference and meaning.

Even if we restrict ourselves to denotation it
must be stated that large differences exist with respect to the amount of ambiguity of situation concepts.
As has been noticed before, Mischel (1973) speaks of
a *powerful* situation if that situation is perceived

in the same way by a large number of people, and he
speaks of a *weak* situation if only a small number of
people agree on it. Powerful situations induce uni-
form expectations, and they are very explicit with
respect to behavior that is considered to be appropriate. Ambiguity, however, is not only a function of
existing situational definitions, but of the degree
to which individuals have assimilated these definitions as well. Thus, a child entering school for the
first time  has little notion of what lies ahead. He
is placed amidst a number of unknown children of his
own age, and is made to engage in new activities by
an adult who is equally unknown to him. Some activities are rewarded, others are punished, and initially
the why is not always clear. The situation is unknown, not organized ecologically. Similar experiences are well-known to those who have ever visited
foreign countries, without being familiar with the
prevailing customs. Knowledge of relevant environmental contingencies is lacking.
      In non-social environments an analogous argument
is valid. A division of environments into dangerous
and harmless situations is possible only if one is
aware of the situational aspects that have to be attended to. In western countries traffic signs are of
vital importance, but in less cultivated regions
footprints, pawmarks and sounds of wild animals, as
well as signs of floods and storms must be heeded.
The environment must be assessed continually, to be
sure that behavior is appropriate to its demands. But
even after careful assessment one can never be completely sure of the events to be expected in that
situation, or the consequences of one's own behavior.
That more basic uncertainty is due to the fact that
each new environment has its own idiosyncracies.
Schools do not always satisfy the requirements of the
standard school situation and not every highway is
provided with traffic signs in agreement with standard
traffic situations. The general question that should
be asked here is: 'What is the relationship between
situation concepts and natural environments?' The
simplest answer to this question is: 'They coincide'.
      Among those who give such an answer are theorists
stating that human situations are essentially to be
viewed as *biologically pre-established* environmental
segments. One of these is Roger Barker. In his 1963
address, called 'On the nature of the environment',
he distinguished between a number of molar behavioral

fields within human ecology, called behavior settings.
These are considered to be self-regulating units in
the environment determining behavior within them to a
high degree. Molar behavior that is demonstrated in a
behavior setting does not depend on the particular individuals finding themselves in that setting. The
settings are characterized by Barker as biophysical
units that regulate behavioral episodes within them,
in a way that is comparable with the regulating effects of molecules with respect to atoms, of organs
with respect to cells, and of structures with respect
to the elements they are built of. As examples of behavior settings Barker mentions the church ceremony,
the court session, the baseball-game, the traffic
road, the rotary club, the doctor's parlor, the gara-
ge, the bridge club, and so on.

These examples (all powerful situations in the
sense of Mischel) clearly show  that 'natural' units
as conceived by Barker, are highly determined by a-
greements, conventions and institutionalization, in
a word by culture. Thus, 'on the *culture* of the environment' would have been a more appropriate term,
to indicate how culture distinguishes between areas
in the environment, provides them with identification
marks, and indicates the correct or permitted behavior within them.

As well as investigators like Barker, holding a
largely biological view of the situation, there are
others - notably sociologists - who prefer to define
the situation on the basis of its *social meaning*.
Thus, for instance, McHugh (1968) has developed a situation conception in terms of two parameters that
are considered typical of the social order of cohe-
rent human knowledge. These parameters are connected
with the spatio-temporal aspects of the environment.
*'Emergence'* constitutes one dimension, in which the
past, the present and the future are discriminated
analytically, but also coincide, because their behavioral effects cannot be discriminated in the same
way. *'Relativity'*, on the other hand, is a dimension
in which an event is seen against the background of
other events in terms of space. According to McHugh,
each situation may be described in terms of both
points of view.

Social interaction can only be expected to follow an orderly course, if the interaction participants define the situation in the same way. In
McHugh's conception, the meaning of the situation is
not based on the content of object descriptions but

on the rule or agreement, the content of which is
used to describe it. Thus, culture provides norms
that may be shared by members of the community, and
that determine the meaning of the environment.

Although this view is largely subscribed to here
in so far as the *origin* of situation conceptions is
concerned, it is considered too narrow when it comes
to *application* of these conceptions. Notably, to restrict the meaning of the situation concept to social
interaction insufficiently brings out the general
biological significance of the concept for the individual. The situation concept is conceived here as
an aid to categorize and transform physical as well
as social environments. Thus, a complete coincidence
of the situation concept and the natural environment
does not have to be assumed.

Norm situations, distinguished by culture in terms of
$S_y$'s, constitute a finite collection, but in nature
many more distinctions are possible. They constitute
an infinite collection of 'potential situations'. If
these potential situations are labeled $S_x$, the following relationship between $S_y$ and $S_x$ may be formulated. Not a single $S_x$ usually satisfies the situation
definition given by means of $S_y$ completely: the relation between $S_x$ and $S_y$ is probabilistic. A particular
$S_x$ is connected closer with some $S_y$'s as compared
with others. The amount of agreement is determined by
the semantic markers defining the $S_y$'s. In the $S_x$ e-
lements are present that may or may not agree with
the markers. With Brunswik (1952) we conceive of these elements as *cues*, i.e. spatio-temporal sensory data functioning as local representatives of a distal
object or a distal variable.

In Brunswik's conception cues have a definite
validity with respect to the object. That object
exists in the subject's distal environment and, as it
were, scatters its cues that are collected and processed by the individual. In the words of Hammond
(1966, p. 37): 'The distal cause in the environment
scatters its effects and the organism "recombines"
them'. That process has been represented by Brunswik
in his lens model (cf. fig. 5). In this model two
processes are actually represented. The first process is connected with the way cues are spread by

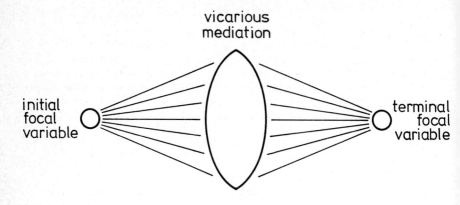

Fig. 5. Lens model (after Brunswik)

the object, viz.the initial focal variable. That process can be assessed objectively in terms of the ecological validity of the cues. The second process is
connected with the subjective combination of cues to
deliver the response or terminal focal variable. Unlike Brunswik's model the first process is considered
here not as an objective process, but as an *intersubjective* process instead. Ultimately the process is
based on the experiences of the community and precipitated in culture. Ecological validity in our terms
may only be determined if consensus exists with respect to the object, in this case the situation.

The situation is not conceived here as a natural
phenomenon, but it has emerged on the grounds of recognition and definition by the community. An important consequence of this position is that even less
'graspable' situations are essentially open to definition. In addition, extension and alteration of the
$S_y$ collection always remains possible. *The situation,*
then, is defined here as a *culturally specified cue
structure of a spatio-temporal nature, that has been
provided with a particular meaning.*

Our position does not require strong assumptions
with respect to the distal ecology as made by Brunswik. Whereas that author assumes a 'well-organized

independent ecology' to exist, we merely assume the
ecology to be an independent furnisher of proximal
feedback to our actions. With this position, we join
for example Piaget (1960), who assumes assimilation
of the environment to occur in schemas, thereby defining the environment subjectively. With respect to
the objective external environment Piaget has pointed
out the relativity and continual development of our
joint notions of reality. All we have at our disposal
is an increasingly complex system of interpretations:
the *Ding an sich* will never be attained.

Even more restraint is demonstrated in the conception of Kelly (1955). In his view, man creates
constructs, he builds a fictitious world that only
lasts as long as man may utilize it for his benefit.
Relationships between that world and the real world
are ruled out completely. The $S_y$'s as defined before and used in the way as proposed here, show some
resemblance with Kelly's constructs.  In both instances one may speak of constructive units of a pragmatic nature, that play a decisive role in behavior,
but that may as well be replaced by others. In Kelly's conception however, the *personal* character of
constructs is emphasized, whereas here they are conceived as *general* cultural constructs. The unique situation of the individual is as such not communicable,
and it does not provide access to directed transformations. This is not meant to imply  that they may
not play an important part in the individual's life:
later on (in Chapter V) we shall return to this issue, and try to connect that type of situations with
the $S_y$'s as described here in general terms.

The definition of the situation  given here
rests on two main elements, i.e. sensory cues and
culturally determined situation concepts. No particular resemblance has been assumed between the environmental *structure* and the conceptual *structure*. However, in this connection one might raise the objection that the environment has a structure of its own,
and that, furthermore, man has provided access to
that structure,through physics, chemistry and biology. The question could be raised why we should not
simply adopt the conceptual frameworks of physics and
chemistry, in order to relate them to the definition
of situations as meant here. Brunswik (1947) has
dealt with this possibility and he came to the following conclusion:

'Many of the environmental stimulus variables
mentioned by psychologists, such as "physical size"

or "physical color", seem at first glance simply to
be taken over from physics or chemistry. Others, such
as "food", "sit-uponableness" (William James), "lika-
bility of a person", and so forth, are obviously conceived with an eye to potential effects upon organisms. In both cases the "dispositional" character
of the definition (Carnap) is maintained, the psychological slant of the latter type of variables notwith-
standing. Upon closer inspection, however, even the
former often reveal psychological entanglement when
they appear in the context of a psychological experiment. For example, the "size" of physical objects
(more precisely, of physicists' objects) figuring as
one of the major stimulus variables in the statisti-
cal survey of size constancy...are in fact to be specified as "size of objects of attention, that is, of
potential manipulation or locomotion, of a certain
human being"...It is the type of organism-centered
specifying redefinition mentioned above which may be
summarized by saying that *stimulus variables are "e-
cological"* rather than purely "physical" or "geogra-
phic" in character'.
    Human ecology may be defined in terms of diver-
gent conceptual frameworks, including those derived
from different sciences. But even if the latter were
adopted, we should have to speak of a redefinition of
ecology for the benefit of man and his opportunities
to act. That kind of redefinition would, depending on
the state of affairs in that particular science, simply lead to another definition of the situation in
which other cue-elements are emphasized. However, it
can never be stated that the very definition of the
situation structurally comes closer to 'reality'. At
the utmost, such redefinition increases the behavioral
effectiveness of those making use of it.

## 3.5  *Information processing*

    Utilizing information on behalf of psychological
adaptation calls for specific types of information
processing in the individual. In the framework outlined here, these processes occur within the boundaries
of situation concepts ($S_y$) and transformation rules
($R_y$), on the one hand, and of the actual environment
($S_x$) on the other. The function of the processes is
to promote psychological adaptation, which here again
is briefly designated as directed transformation of
the environment. A core element in directed transfor-

mation is the notion that a given initial situation
is altered into a final situation, that is *specified
in advance*. In addition, the means whereby the transformation may be accomplished, should equally be
specified in advance. *Directed action presupposes directed thought*.

In directed thought, symbolic structures and
symbolic elements are utilized that have been transmitted by means of language. Symbols may be used for
communication purposes as well as for representatio-
nal purposes. In the case of communication, symbols
are generated by subject A and intended to influence
subject B's behavior. In the case of representation
one might say that symbols are generated to influence
one's own behavior. This type of influence is not accomplished through communication but by way of thinking. In the discussion to come, we will restrict ourselves to information processing activities that are
related to the latter purpose, while admitting at the
same time that communication is a very important behavioral process that deserves extended study in its
own right.

Symbolic mediation through thinking then depri-
ves activity of its spontaneous character. Or, as
Shotter (1970) has pointed out, inclusion of language in behavior has the effect of transforming spontaneous activities into deliberate activities. The
activities that occur in thinking, as well as the symbolic structures involved in it, have been described
by psychologists of thinking. Some of these explicitly
conceived of thinking in an adaptation frame of
reference and, clearly, they are of prime importance
in the present context. One of them is Berlyne (1965),
who completed a study of thinking as an adaptive process some time ago. This author has also attempted
to integrate a number of current theories with respect to thinking processes, notably the work of Hull,
of Piaget and several Russian investigators. Berlyne
conceives of the thought process as passing through
a series of symbolic structures that represent stimulus situations which differ from the situation in
which the subject actually finds himself (Berlyne,
1965, p. 107).

In his theory, Berlyne makes an important distinction between *directed* thought and *autistic*
thought. Directed thought typically consists of so-
called transformational thoughts, operations that
transform an existing thought content into a new
thought content. This conception of directed thought

is based on the classical work of the Russian theorist Sechenow (cf. Berlyne, 1965, p. 111), who considered three successive elements to be essential
for the process of thinking. The first element is
the representation of a stimulus situation. The second element is a process, corresponding to a response serving to adjust a receptor. And the third element of thinking is the representation of the stimulus
situation that would have emerged if the subject had
given the response (represented by element 2) to the
initial situation (represented by element 1). The re-
ceptor-adjusting response determines the relationship in thinking between the initial and the final
situation. In Berlyne's theory transformational
thoughts constitute the connecting links between so-
called situational thoughts. Thinking can be called
*directed* thinking only if these links are present.
Directed thought is not led by external simuli, but
is essentially based on the information available in
the symbolic structures of the individual.

Sechenow's triad as well as Berlyne's elaboration of that structure fit in very well with the exploitative system described in this chapter. Processes of directed thought would have to include at
least three elements in our conception as well. Initially there would have to be a situation concept
($S_{y_1}$), subsequently a transformation rule ($R_y$) would
have to be applied, and finally there should be another situation concept ($S_{y_2}$) at the end. The choice
of $S_y$'s, as well as the sequence they adopt and the
direction they take, can obviously not be arbitrari-
ly determined. Transformations obey certain rules.
Berlyne (1965) speaks of legitimate transformations
in directed thought  and mentions examples like the
rules of the chess game, the rules of mathematics
and logic. In a practical situation those tranforma-
tions may be considered legitimate that are known to
be able to transform particular elements of the situation into new elements. Directed thought is regulated and is basically subjected to social control.
The rules may be broken: rational discussion on this
type of thinking  is possible.

As stated before,Berlyne has made use of the notion of legitimate transformation to indicate the essence of directed thought. Similarly one can speak
of the legitimacy of the symbolic elements that are
the components of directed thought. As we have pointed out before, each culture recognizes a number of

symbols to represent reality. Those symbols are connected with the legitimacy of the thought process,
and they may be used to see whether in the course of
the process unlawful elements have managed to slip
in. A test procedure based on this principle is for
instance applied in testing theorems in mathematics.
If the correct derivation fails to be found, it may
be checked whether or not transformational errors were made, by testing the intermediate products.

Apart from these specific and highly disciplined
activities, directed thought has a large number of
additional functions. Berlyne (1965) for instance
mentions gathering and rejecting information, generating internal stimuli through transformation, prepa-
ring information for memory storage, abstraction from
concrete material by insertion in so-called equiva-
lence classes, and the reduction of incoming information by recognition of redundancy and triviality. All
these functions of thought have a bearing upon the
significance of incoming information with respect to
behavior. For behavior in more practical situations
directed thought is especially important to determine the aims of behavior and the means that are going
to be used to achieve these aims. In those situations
legitimacy of directed thought acquires a different
nature as compared to situations in which theoretical
problems are to be solved. The most legitimate transformations are those with the highest probability of
successfully changing a given $S_{y_1}$ into an intended $S_{y_2}$

Another aspect distinguishing practically directed thought from theoretical thought concerns the value
attached to the result of thinking as such. Utility
in that sense usually does not play a part in theoretical thought, but is of major significance in
practical thought. In the view of decision theorists
(e.g. Edwards, 1954), the utility of a particular
outcome, together with the probability of that outcome,
determines expected utility:

$$U_E = f\ p\ (y_2/y_1),\ U_{y_2}$$

in which $U_E$ = the expected utility;
$P(y_2/y_1)$ = the probability of obtaining $S_{y_2}$ from $S_{y_1}$;
and $U_{y_2}$ = the utility of $S_{y_2}$.

It is assumed here that expected utility usually sets the course that the thought process takes in a

practical situation. In that respect a connection
exists between the present formulation and Rotter's
(1954) social learning theory, in which the decision
paradigm was initially utilized to theorize about
personality.

   But there are differences as well. In Rotter's
conception the choice of *behavior* is under discussion,
rather than the choice of the $S_y$. In the original
formulation of social learning theory, the choice of
behavior is a direct function of chance and utility
considerations. Here only the direction of *thought* is
considered to be determined by these considerations.
The extent to which the thinking result will demonstrate itself in behavior as well, depends upon processes at the control level which, as has been pointed out, ultimately determine behavioral continuity.
(Incidentally, Rotter extended his theory in 1966 by
introducing the concept of locus of control, so that
behavior is no longer exclusively determined by chance and utility. Especially the *subjective* probability
of the effect of behavior is thus codetermined by the
question whether the individual believes in internal
vs. external control of reinforcement).

   Thought in the sense of directed thought does
have the important adaptive function of transforming
an initial $S_y$ in such a way that directed actions become possible. These transformations may be represented as chains in which $S_y$ and $R_y$ alternate:

$$S_{y_1} \rightarrow R_{y_a} \rightarrow S_{y_2} \rightarrow R_{y_b} \rightarrow S_{y_3} \cdots \rightarrow S_{y_n}.$$

Thinking originates with an $S_y$, hence it will from
now on be designated as $S_y$-*thinking*. This kind of
thinking is abstract in the sense that the real situation concerned does not have to be actually present.
The highly regulated nature of $S_y$-thinking makes it
look like a type of thinking that was described already by Freud (1966) and called secondary-process
thinking.

   However, in addition another type of thinking
may well be distinguished. The process of thinking
is much more concrete there, because it is directly
connected with the environment in which the individual finds himself. In Berlyne's (1965) conception,
thought processes that are connected purely with the
actual situation, are called *autistic* thoughts. In
that type of thought the individual is not restricted

by transformation rules: he symbolizes via simple combinations of prevalent internal and external stimuli. Autistic thought becomes manifest in a typical way of dealing with the environment by means of a peculiar form of exploratory behavior, called diversive exploration. The function of this type of behavior is the introduction of interesting, amusing or dispersing simuli, that may lead to widely divergent esthetic experiences. In autistic thought, transitions from one thought to the other do not cause any problem at all. Day dreaming and free association are examples of this type of thinking.

It is not difficult to detect similarities with primary-process thinking as described by Freud, the function of which may be described briefly as 'presentational symbolization ' (cf. Lorenzer, 1972). Primary-process thinking is a less disciplined way of thinking, that is not primarily led by reality and logic, but in which impulses act freely. The primary process is usually corrected by the secondary process, which is characterized by a strict application of reality indices.

Authors like Brenner (1967) and Rapaport (cf. Gill, 1967) have pointed out that the primary process should not be conceived as a childish form of thinking that will eventually disappear, but rather as a mode of thinking that develops earlier than the secondary process. In adults primary-process thinking is still available, but is generally dominated by the secondary process. According to Brenner it is easier to talk about the secondary process, merely because it is regulated by a clear set of rules. The primary process, on the contrary, frequently gives the impression of being incomprehensible, illogical, idiosyncratic and uninhibited. It is characterized by free associations, the use of analogies and metaphors, sensory impressions instead of verbal categories, and by a complete neglect of temporal order. This type of thinking shows a striking mobility: switching over to another object does not seem to cause any trouble at all.

The process'directedness towards immediate rewards, its egocentrism, its capricious course, but especially its lack of realism and rationality, in the first instance lead to the conclusion that, in primary-process thinking, we have to do with a not very adaptive way of thinking of doubtful functionality. Yet, it is assumed here that this kind of thinking has a very important function, because it is

indispensable as an impetus to symbolic transformations of the situation in which the individual actually finds himself. If the individual were to operate
purely according to processes of directed thought,
perfect transformations would emerge responding each
to Berlyne's principle of legitimacy. Yet, these
transformations would not be adaptive because the
main assumption - connection with the prevailing situation - would not be satisfied. Another process
seems to be required to establish that connection.
That this process is characterized by free associations, a high degree of mobility and a lack of inhi-
bition, only seems to be advantageous for finding an
$S_y$ that fits the prevailing environment. However,
what is to be said with respect to the irrealistic
nature and the irrational course of the primary process?

Realism has been specially emphasized by Freud
as the cornerstone of adaptation. Shortages in that
area were seen as an indication of psychopathology.
Pierre Janet even considered the *'fonction du reel'*
to be the highest level of human functioning. However, in our conception concerning the role of information in the process of psychological adaptation,
the term 'reality' as such would not appear. What is
usually conceived as reality in daily speech is to
be seen as no more than a social construction with
a certain amount of plausibility for society. To symbolize an actual $S_x$ by means of an $S_y$ may be done more or less adequately, but even in the latter case
the symbolization could be useful for the individual.
In the framework of psychological adaptation legitimacy is only one among several criteria.

The irrationality of primary thought, finally,
would lead to an inaccurate, biased picture of reality.
According to Freud (1966) the purpose of all thought
processes is 'to bring about a state of identity, the
conveying of a cathexis emanating from outside, into
a neurone cathected from the ego' (p. 332). In that
conception a reconstruction of reality of the utmost
accuracy would be required to provide the organism
with enough certainty to constitute the basis for directed action. But Brunswik (1954) has rightly pointed
out, that such a view is founded on an incorrect conception of the proximal environment, in which behavior takes place. That environment is erroneously
conceived as lawful and determinate. In Brunswik's
view the most effective way to act in such a lawful

environment would be to make use of a so-called cer-
tainty-geared strategy as for instance, directed
thought. But in an uncertain environment where laws
are of a probabilistic character and where cues refer
to distal objects with no more than relative certainty, that approach holds great risks. To fall back on
sheer rational thought processes may then lead to
transformations that are not at all adaptive. Effective behavior in an uncertain proximal environment
is, according to Brunswik, better guaranteed through
the use of an uncertainty-geared strategy. Instead
of rational behavior, ratiomorphic behavior is required there. That behavior is characterized by pro-
babilism instead of determinism, by continuity instead
of discontinuity, by compromise instead of lawfulness. It is the individual's task to bring about
agreement between his actual environment and a symbolic representation: agreement, not amalgamation. To
acquire control over the environment agreement is necessary and usually sufficient: identity between symbol and environment is superfluous.

Autistic thought or primary-process thinking
will henceforth be indicated as $S_x$-*thinking*. The difference from $S_y$-thinking lies primarily in the starting-points. $S_x$-thinking is always connected directly
with the topical environment, in which the individual
finds himself. The main function of that type of
thinking is to symbolize the topical situation $S_x$.
Each $S_x$ is unique, it may well be interpreted as a
general $S_y$, but that interpretation is arbitrary in
principle. The process is conceived as characterized
by alternation of a number of symbolizations to be
considered. It may be represented as follows:

$$S_{y_1........n}$$
$$\downarrow \uparrow$$
$$S_x$$

Logically, $S_x$-thinking precedes $S_y$-thinking, if the
latter is attached to the topical situation.
The whole process, in which $S_x$-thinking as well as
$S_y$-thinking are comprised, may be represented as
follows:

$$S_{y_1} \rightarrow R_{y_a} \rightarrow S_{y_2} \ldots \rightarrow S_{y_n}$$

$$\downarrow \uparrow$$

$$S_x$$

$S_x$-thinking serves to obtain control over a topical environment, $S_y$-thinking serves to maintain or enlarge control. The first process has the function of matching the second process with the environment. Basically, $S_y$-thinking is under social control, because its elements ($S_y$) as well as its operations ($R_y$) have been sanctioned by the community. In this type of thinking legitimacy is the main criterion. However, $S_x$-thinking is different: more than with $S_y$-thinking, we have to do here with individual patterns of choice and preference.

In the process of $S_x$-thinking two aspects may be distinguished. The first aspect is *validity*. $S_x$-thinking is to some extent perceptual, so that from the beginning the process is to be characterized as probabilistic. William James already pointed out that perception deals with probabilities: 'perception is of probable things'. Thorndike called the perceptual system the intuitive statistician. Thurstone stated that perception is always based on insufficient evidence. And finally, Brunswik saw each perception as a compromise, seldom leading to absolute precision, but seldom leading to disastrous mistakes either. According to the latter author, perception is based on the integration of environmental cues. Mathematically, the validity aspect of $S_x$-thinking may thus be represented as the comparison of a weighted sum of 'cue-scores' (in the $S_x$) with a norm defined in the $S_y$. In matrix language a vector of cues is multiplied by a vector of regression weights, after which the result is compared with the $S_y$-norm.

To compare the $S_x$ with *several* $S_y$'s, the $S_x$ cue vector has to be multiplied by a *matrix* containing the regression weights of each of the $S_y$'s. The resulting vector contains the 'scores' of the $S_x$ on each. To be able to exactly determine the $S_y$ that fits best

all cues in the $S_x$ should be known. This condition,
however, will be met with only very rarely. Consequently, on the basis of the perceptual character of
$S_x$-thinking, we shall always to some extent remain
uncertain about the validity of the $S_x$ with respect
to the $S_y$ (in this context validity is to be conceived as construct validity, rather than ecological validity).

The second element presumably playing a major
part in $S_x$-thinking is *utility*. It is assumed here
that utility in $S_x$-thinking will develop gradually
during life as a consequence of acculturation. The
young child, as yet unaware of opportunities for
transforming its present situation, will tend to interpret the $S_x$ in terms of direct biological gratification. Frequently, that interpretation will show severe bias in the eyes of adults who consider the
child's view to be merely wishful thinking. But later
on, as $S_y$-thinking develops, the child's policy will
gradually change. As the number of $S_y$ alternatives
increases, the validity aspect of $S_x$-thinking may be
further emphasized. The utility-aspect will be maintained, albeit in a different form. Instead of immediate gratification, the $S_y$ choice will tend to be
dominated by the aspect of *transformability*, resulting in a preference for those $S_y$'s that warrant
transformation to as many other $S_y$'s as possible.

Thus, in accordance with the principles of psychological adaptation outlined earlier, it is assumed that
a major characteristic of adult $S_x$-thinking is its
aim to avoid dead ends, as well as to favor high-
chance starting positions.

This strategy may at times lead to 'wishful
thinking' and 'irrationality' in adults as well as in
the young child, but to the individual this is not
necessarily at variance with the adaptive function of
$S_x$-thinking. An $S_y$, offering only limited prospects
for control is not likely to be chosen, even if it
almost perfectly matches the conditions in $S_x$. Thus,
the utility of an $S_y$ to be selected is not so much
defined in terms of direct biological utility, but

rather in terms of *expected control*. A more formal definition of the amount of control should be based on the number of different transformations that are permitted by the $S_y$. For the time being, the assumption is made that $S_y$'s may in principle be ordered according to their transformability and furthermore that this aspect is a relevant criterion for $S_x$-thinking.

The choice of the $S_y$ in $S_x$-thinking may be seen as a decision problem similarly as in $S_y$-thinking. According to decision theory, in decision making the chance of obtaining a particular result as well as the utility of that result are relevant considerations. The purpose of $S_x$-thinking is to establish control over the $S_x$, therefore the utility of the result is a function of the transformability of the $S_y$ to be chosen. The chance of obtaining that result is determined by the degree to which the $S_x$ satisfies the requirements of the $S_y$: its validity. Thus, expected control of a particular $S_y$-choice is a function of the validity of the $S_x$ with regard to the $S_y$, as well as of the transformability of the $S_y$ itself. The representation of $S_x$-thinking can on this basis be amplified as follows:

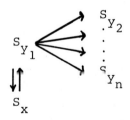

While covering the route from $S_x$ to $S_y$ we meet both ingredients of $S_x$-thinking. $S_{y_1}$ has a key function: it also is the only element that is at the option of the individual. The best $S_{y_1}$ to select is always the one with the highest value of both validity and transformability. In that case the individual

has the best guarantee of being able to cover the
route to $S_{y_n}$ .

   But, as a rule, in a particular situation the
optimum will not be attainable for both aspects simultaneously. Several interests will have to be weighed and a compromise will have to be attained. The
case in which a particular $S_y$ is chosen shall henceforth be designated as a *control compromise*. That compromise is characterized by the maximization of expected control. Expected control is defined here in
decision theoretical terms according to the formula:

$$C_E = f \; r_{x.y_1} , [ p \; ( \sum_{i=1}^{n} y_i ) / y_1 ]$$

in which
$C_E$ = expected control;
$r_{x.y_1}$ = the correlation between $S_x$ cues and $S_y$ seman-
      tic markers; and
$p [ ( \sum_{i=1}^{n} y_i ) / y_1 ]$ = the combined probability of trans-
                    forming $S_{y_1}$ to any other $S_y$.

The view that $S_x$-thinking does not only consist of
the combination of external cues, but that considerations of individual control are an essential factor,
has some far-reaching consequences for a multitude of
research areas. One of these is the study of judgment. For a long time, human judgment has been studied primarily with respect to its correctness, its
accuracy. An example is the process of judging other
people. Usually a criterion for the 'true state of
affairs' was developed first, and subsequently it was
tested whether or not judgement agreed with that true
state.
   During the fifties that line of attack was abandoned mainly because of methodological flaws (cf. Gage & Cronbach, 1955), but also because the function
of judgment was thoroughly revised. Instead of judgmental accuracy, the significance of judgment with
respect to general human functioning was emphasized.
Judgmental processes were studied instead of mere
judgmental achievement. The implicit theory of personality held by the subject became an object of study
in and of itself (Bruner & Tagiuri, 1954).
   The most recent developments tend toward a conception of judgment as an adaptive process. Rappoport

and Summers (1973) have formulated four basic assumptions to lay the foundations for this point of view.
They stated:
'1. Along with the major writers on cognitive develop-
    ment, we see thinking as an adaptive process, a
    "tool" gradually shaped out of experience with
    the physical and social environment.
 2. Judgment is a uniquely important functional as-
    pect of thinking that allows persons to cope
    with, or adapt to, uncertainty. It provides the
    psychological means of going beyond perceptual
    and cognitive "givens" while maintaining organi-
    zation and continuity in behavior.
 3. Because its central role of mediating between in-
    tentions or purposes of the person and uncertain-
    ties in his environment, judgment can only be un-
    derstood by scrutinizing person-environment in-
    teractions.
 4. Because judgment is here conceived of as cente-
    ring upon *relationships* between proximal "givens"
    and distal "unknowns", the person-environment in-
    teraction can best be understood as an interac-
    tion between cognitive and environmental systems'
    (p. 4).
The adaptive significance of judgment is premised in
this statement: its main function is to reduce environmental uncertainty for the sake of adaptation. Reference to judgmental accuracy is relegated to the
background: judgment has become a pragmatic instrument.

   A further elaboration of this statement can be
based on the control compromise. As was indicated before, a control compromise is attained by comparing
the validity of $S_x$ with respect to $S_y$, and the transformability of $S_y$. The first element (validity) is
basically intersubjective, because the $S_y$ definition
as such is assumed to be culturally determined and to
be precipitated in language. Yet, since environments
are considered to be uncertain, $S_x$-thinking is bound
to be to some degree *unreliable*, in that subjects
will not generally agree on the content of the control compromise when confronted with the same $S_x$.

   The second aspect, $S_y$ transformability, is primarily a function of individual experience, and will
be largely determined by the individual's learning
history. So, if the same environment ($S_x$) is judged

by different subjects, differences in $S_y$ choice will occur because the transformability of a particular $S_y$ is evaluated differently *(judgmental bias)*.

Judgmental unreliability as well as judgmental bias are phenomena that have repeatedly been pointed out in research publications in the area of judgment. Thus, for instance, Slovic and Lichtenstein (1973) concluded an extensive study of research on judgment by stating that 'judges are biased *and* unreliable in their weighting of information' (p. 94).

Hammond and Summers (1972) have attempted to further analyze the judgment process in terms of Brunswik's lens model. They succeeded in discriminating statistically between two important components of this process. These components - knowledge and control - show a clear relationship with the ingredients of the control compromise. Hammond and Summers succeeded in showing that both components can be identified empirically as well in divergent areas of investigation, such as multiple-cue probability learning, clinical judgment and interpersonal conflict.

In a study by Hammond and Brehmer (1973) on international conflict, both components of judgment were demonstrated again in a slightly different terminology, i.e. consistency versus policy. This study was connected with the means to be used to remove disagreement on strategies to be adopted in problem situations. The results showed that social interaction led to a reduction of policy differences, but, on the other hand, that consistency in the *application* of policies was reduced as well. All these findings lend support to the hypothesis that judgment may well be conceived as a process in which the judge typically establishes a compromise between appropriately applying culturally determined indices $(S_y)$ on the one hand and promoting his private interests on the other.

In this context, classical phenomena that have frequently been found in judgment research, as, for instance, stereotypy effects, relation effects, leniency effects, and the effects of implicit personality theory, may be looked at from a different point of view. Thus, person perception should not primarily be assigned claims of accuracy, but rather be viewed as an attempt to locate other individuals in one's own social ecology (cf. Hettema, 1972). Judgment categories to be utilized in that process have largely been adopted from culture. They are to

be considered crude outline categories that do not
easily lend themselves to representing subtle nuances in the ratee's behavior.

Application of these categories to real objects
is usually done in a very simple way. Contrary to
what judges themselves believe, the process of judgment can nearly always be described in terms of a
linear combination of judgmental cues. Experimental
research has indicated that in combining cues, judges do not even take account of redundancies, caused
by cue intercorrelations (Slovic and Lichtenstein,
1973). This finding indicates that judges utilize
every relevant cue, even if it provides no new information whatsoever. If this finding were to hold,
judgment could be described exhaustively as a classification in terms of a simple nominal scale, obtained
by an unweighted addition of relevant cues. A recent
study by the present author (Hettema, 1979) has provided evidence favoring this hypothesis. In a study
of judgment of teachers by their pupils, unweighted
addition of cues turned out to be a better predictor
of the judgmental result as compared to cue integration using multiple regression techniques.

These results taken together lend support to the
view that judgment can be characterized as a conven-
tional-pragmatic categorization of a nominal nature.
'Fathoming reality' can never be accomplished along
judgmental routes. The judgmental process is restricted to the location of other people in a system of
categories, aimed at obtaining an optimal behavioral fit to the social environment. Culture gives
support to that process in providing information in
the form of concepts. However, we do not take these
concepts to be 'depth'-concepts, but instead, to be
'surface'-concepts.

*Footnotes*

1. 'The following major difference exists between
   the actual process of adaptation and the process
   of acquisition: in biological adaptation the
   species' properties as well as the species' behavior are altered. In the process of acquisition,
   on the other hand, the individual reproduces the
   aptitudes and functions that have been accomplished historically. Through this process in human
   ontogeny is achieved what is acquired through
   heredity in animals: the results of species development are embodied in the properties of the

individual' (translation by the author).

2. 'What is comprised in psychoanalysis is not primarily the ways in which an acting individual be-
haves, but at the same time and above all structures of interaction to be understood within the
context of the communicating subject' (translation by the author).

3. 'Individual conscience as a specifically human way
to subjectively reflect objective reality, can
thus only be understood as a product of those relations and mediations that originate with society. Beyond the system of these relations (and beyond societal conscience) an individual psyche in
the form of conscience cannot exist' (translation
by the author).

CHAPTER IV

*CONTROL*

## 4.1  *The dimensionality of directed action*

Information processing is a necessary condition
for psychological adaptation, but it is not a sufficient condition. As has been pointed out before, between cognition and action there is a gap that has to
be bridged before real environmental changes can take
place. Personality theory comprises, among other
things, the study of overt individual behavior. So
personality cannot be restricted to cognitive processes, but has to include the investigation of directed
activities as they occur in the conditions of daily
living. Real actions co-determine environmental events
and may be seen as the overt manifestations of psychological adaptation as described before. At the sensomotor-operational level of functioning we look for the
*basis* of personality. This by no means implies that
study and theory construction should be restricted to
the description of overt activities, but it does imply that these activities are indispensable as a starting-point.

How should the actual process of transformation,
the overt activity, be conceived against the background
of the notions that have been developed before? Directed activities primarily emanate from the SRS-matrix.
Obviously the $R_y$ is relevant in connection with directed
action. The selection of an $R_y$ is closely connected
with the selection of an initial and a final $S_y$. But
an R-term coming from the matrix is no more than a
transformation rule, i.e. an activity defined at the
cognitive-symbolic level. That conceptual activity has
to be worked out in concrete operations that are mol-
ded to fit concrete external circumstances.

Directed action is conceived here as a complex
activity occurring simultaneously at different levels.
Thought processes as described in the previous chapter

are part of directed action. Directed $S_y$-thinking serves to transform a given $S_y$ in such a manner that directed action becomes possible. $S_x$-thinking is necessary to accomplish the connection of $S_y$-thinking to
the optical environment. In addition to internal activities, directed action comprises external activities: internal as well as external activities are assumed to be essential components of directed action.
Furthermore both activity types have to be connected
intimately to accomplish directed action. That connection may be established at any given moment, because
external and internal activities have corresponding
structures. We have made suggestions to this effect
in the preceding chapters, but the point has been
stated more explicitly by Leontiev (1977, p. 33).

However, structural correspondence as such is
not sufficient for connections to be established. For
that purpose, at any moment elements from either activity have to be linked up. To allow for these links
it will be necessary to distinguish a second dimension in addition to the *transformation* dimension.
That dimension is here called *equilibrium*. Introduction of this distinction as two separate dimensions
disengages the continuity aspect of behavior from the
testing aspect. Or, in other words, while behavior is
being executed, testing can go on *simultaneously* to
ascertain whether the execution proceeds adequately.
Behavioral models that have been developed thus far
have usually taken only one of the two aspects into
account: they are to be considered transformation models *or* equilibrium models.

The *transformation* dimension has especially been
emphasized by learning psychologists. The associatio-
nists assumed that by means of learning processes associative chains are established, that allow for effective behavior to occur in new situations. Those
chains are located within the organism and constitute
the foundations for thought processes that can develop on the basis of those structures (cf. Berlyne,
1965). However, learning processes have not merely
been described in terms of structural changes *within*
the organism. Notably, Skinner and his followers have
described transformational behavior in terms of external stimuli, functioning as reinforcers and controlling behavior via learning processes. To attribute an *operant* function to behavior, causing the environment to be actually transformed, is considered here an important step along the road to formulation of

a psychological adaptation concept. That development
is a necessary prerequisite to the conception of psychological adaptation as an extension of biological
adaptation.
   The second dimension of behavior, *equilibrium*,
has played a major part in psychological theorizing
as well, ever since Cannon's concept of homeostasis
was introduced. Authors like Dempsey (1951), Davis
(1958) and Stagner (1951) have attempted to develop
models of psychological homeostasis. Piaget (1967)
and Bresson (1967) consider equilibrium to be an essential component of adaptation and they have even
proposed to take an increase or decrease of equilibrium as *the* criterion for success or failure of a-
daptation. The most thorough elaboration of the notion of equilibrium can perhaps be found in the work
of Helson (1964) on the adaptation level. This author
has mainly based his endeavors on psychophysical investigations, in which he studied the effect of the
strength of stimuli from different sources (focal,
contextual, residual) upon the subjective zero-level,
established within the individual as a consequence of
stimulation. According to Helson, the perceiver may
be seen as a continuous integrator of stimuli im-
pinging upon him from all directions. These simuli
are perceived, weighed and integrated to constitute a
subjective zero-level, the adaptation level. In view
of the fact that the individual constantly enters new
surroundings, he is constantly confronted with new
stimuli as well, which then leads to constant changes
in his adaptation level. Therefore it can be stated
that adaptation level theory is concerned with adaptive processes, establishing internal (subjective)
constancy, while the external circumstances change.
Helson's theory is homeostatic in nature and may as
such be viewed as a theory of equilibrium.
   Another theory of similar stature which is based
primarily on perceptual research is the work of
Brunswik (1956). Originally Brunswik mainly occupied
himself with the study of constancy phenomena in perception, such as size constancy, brightness constancy, color constancy, and thing constancy. Later on,
his theory  evolved to become a more general theory
of cognition. Brunswik's lens model, like Helson's
model of adaptation level, is primarily concerned
with the integration of stimuli. One of the
major differences between the two is the fact that,
whereas Helson considers physical aspects of the environment to be the input, in Brunswik's conception

the input is primarily concerned with ecological aspects of the environment. Ecological aspects are transferred by means of cues, referring to the distal world
in which the organism lives. The lens  model provides
a meticulous description of the way in which the organism synthesizes perceptual data into a meaningful
whole. The latter is indicated as the organism's response. This response should be seen as a conceptual
one: the lens  model does not offer provisions for
real environmental transformations. It is merely concerned with combinations and re-combinations of data
that are available in the environment already. Thus,
Brunswik's model should primarily be viewed as a description of the way in which the organism manages to
establish a state of equilibrium between (external)
sensory data and (internal) symbolic structures.

Equilibrium is deemed to be of prime importance
for psychological adaptation by many authors. But it
is not the only criterion. Helson (1964), although
being one of the major representatives of equilibrium
theorists as a group, has stated: 'Although recogni-
zing such concepts as homeostasis, striving toward e-
quilibrium, desire for rest, and other more or less
steady states, we must not forget that individuals
and groups strive for variety, change and novelty as
well as for rest, quiet and the familiar' (p. 49).

Brunswik also came to realize the onesidedness
of his lens  model, and he notably made an attempt at
joint theory construction, together with an author
who had especially emphasized the transformation aspect: the learning psychologist Tolman. In 1935 they
published an article under the title 'The organism
and the causal texture of the environment'. In that
article Brunswik's contribution was directed at the
relationship between cues and objects, whereas Tolman's contribution was concerned with the relationship between behavioral means and ends. Their joint
model functions according to the so called lasso
principle, in which both aspects of behavior are represented separately, but mutually connected, to account for behavior. The lasso principle enables the
organism to create hypotheses concerning the state of
the environment, on the basis of previous experience.
Tolman and Brunswik concluded their joint effort by
stating the expectation that their model would become
of major interest for the development of psychology
as a whole. In fact, the impact of the model has been
rather limited.

Undoubtedly, this must partly be attributed to

the fact that at the time it was not yet possible to
fill up the model in great detail. Notably the question remained unanswered how precisely to conceive of
the interaction between the perception - equilibrium
dimension on the one hand, and the learning - transformation dimension on the other. At the time theory
lacked the possibility of transforming spatial structures into temporal structures: a spatio-temporal
translation mechanism was badly needed. It took 25
years before such a mechanism was introduced. The
form the mechanism finally received was that of a
*Plan* (Miller, Galanter & Pribram, 1960).

A plan consists of a complex hierarchy of so-called TOTE-units, a particular kind of control circuits,
postulated by Miller c.s. as the basic unit of behavior to replace the reflex arc. In the TOTE conception, feedback and control are included in the very
basic unit of behavior. Both T's in the model refer
to testing processes by which discrepancies, occurring between behavioral norm and reality, are registered. Discrepancies, if present, are eliminated by
means of internal operations (O), after which the
exit (E) occurs. An important aspect of TOTE functioning is the fact that it provides an opportunity for
further specifying the stimulus input of the organism.
The organism does not react to the stimulus *per se*
(defined physically, or in any other general way), but
to the stimulus in as far as it satisfies some standard or norm condition in the organism. It is precisely that aspect that makes the TOTE-unit particularly fit to accomplish the necessary coupling between
the two basic dimensions of directed action: equilibrium and transformation.

A plan can only be properly executed if the organism is able to specify in advance the conditions
in which it will be applied as well as the possible
results of action. The plan may be seen as the link
connecting the knowledge  that is at the individual's
disposal, and his actions, or, in the words of Miller,
Galanter and Pribram (1960): 'the individual's image
and his behavior'. With the authors just mentioned,
we conceive of the plan as a hierarchic process which
does not merely consist of a sequence of operations,
but which in addition includes several moments of
testing, allowing for control with respect to the a-
dequate execution of the plan. Correct execution of the
plan can be checked through the environmental cues successively manifesting themselves during the course of
behavior. In the assumption of those occasions of tes-

ting the very correlation  existing between the transformation rule as a conceptual structure and the real
environment as a sensomotor given  is indicated.
   The correlation mentioned may be viewed analogously to the correlation indicated formerly between
the $S_x$ and the $S_y$ in the control compromise. It is
therefore assumed that the level of functioning at
which the plan is executed is the same as the level of
functioning of the control compromise. That level was
indicated earlier as the *control level* and it was conceived as a third level located in between the sensomotor-operational level (cf. Chapter II) and the cognitive-symbolic level (cf. Chapter III). At the contro
level the encounter between organism and environment
takes place in the first instance. At that level the
very process of psychological adaptation is initiated.
In the next section this notion will be elaborated
further. For the time being, suffice it to point out
here that the execution of the plan as well as the establishment of the control compromise are conceived
at the control level: in both processes the confrontation of symbolic structures and environmental cues
is involved. In this context the plan may be seen as
a program of real environmental changes, tending towards an end state that has been specified in advance. Thus, the plan affects the nature of events as
well as the sequence in which events take place. Henceforth, theory construction will be based on the assumption that directed actions correspond to a plan
for the execution of those actions.
   Each of the two dimensions of directed action,
equilibrium and transformation, has its own function
with regard to psychological adaptation. Equilibrium
is concerned with keeping organism and environment
continuously connected, transformation is related to
environmental change as such. Considering the functional differences between the activities in the two
dimensions, it may be assumed that they will operate
according to different principles as well.
   To maintain equilibrium, continuous exchange of
information between organisms and environment is required to allow the necessary adjustments to be made.
We assume that this exchange is accomplished on the
principle of *efferent feedback*. This principle is defined here with Pribram (1971) as a process in which
environmental information is compared with and tested
against spontaneous or evoked neuronal activity in a
comparator. The result of this comparison sets some
operation going  which either affects other parts  of

the nervous system, or accomplishes alterations in
the environment. The results of either change are fed
back to the comparator, and the process is started all
over. It continues until a previously specified end
state is achieved. We assume that this end state may
be defined either in terms of the organism or in terms
of the environment.

The transformation dimension of directed action
concerns the specification of an end state based on a
particular initial state, as well as on the operations that are required to accomplish the end state.
Instead of feedback, transformation is achieved according to the principle of *feedforward*. In its usual
sense the term feedforward is conceived as information
on a task to be performed, while the information is
commonly supplied in the form of instruction (cf.
Björkman, 1972). But we prefer to use the term feedforward in a broader sense, so that it may be applied
to all kinds of purposive behavior. Not merely through
instruction but on the basis of private experience
as well, structures are established within the individual  that have a directive function with respect
to his behavior.

Recent neurophysiological research has led to the
insight that behavior is governed by feedback only in
relatively new situations. Thus, for instance, in conditioning experiments behavior in the initial trials
may be conceived as governed by a so-called feedback
organization. But at a later stage the organization
is gradually replaced by a feedforward organization
(Putnoky, 1973). Prolonged exposure to feedback is no
longer effective for learning achievement and may e-
ven lead to a reduction of control established at an
earlier stage (Hammond & Summers, 1972). These results demonstrate that confrontation with relatively
new environments requires strong activity in the e-
quilibrium dimension of behavior. However, after repeated confrontation with the same environment the
emphasis shifts to the transformation dimension, with
directed actions replacing the mere restoration of
equilibrium.

We assume that processes of feedback-feedforward
transformation (Putnoky, 1973) will manifest themselves in the structure of the *plan* as well. If the same
plan is utilized frequently, the plan structure will
gradually change. During the plan execution, feedback
will occur, enabling the individual to distinguish
between more and less effective subroutines and operations. On the basis of feedback, an elimination pro-

cess will be started that eventually simplifies the
original plan structure. Finally, a so-called skill
is established, that is a plan that can be executed
almost automatically and in which the number of tests
is reduced to a minimum. According to Osgood (1953)
a skill can be defined as a complex activity, governed mainly by proprioceptive cues. These cues have
gradually taken over the test function that had been
fulfilled by exteroceptive cues in the beginning of
the process of skill training. Research has indicated that prolonged training in psychomotor tasks
leads to simplification of the structure of behavior
(Fleishman & Hempel, 1954; Jones, 1962; Fruchter
& Fleishman, 1967). As stated earlier, we assume
that at the end of the training the plan has been
simplified as well. That simplification is assumed to
be expressed in a reduction of the number of alterna-
tions between operations and tests. The skilled individual requires less feedback and is more and more
able to have his behavior   determined by feedforward, thus gaining control.

Skills are important for the individual's psychological adaptation, because they allow for faster
and more effective transformations of the environment. On the other hand, they also hold risks, because in the long run they lead to inflexible, involun-
tary behavior that is effective only in environments
satisfying very precise conditions (Miller *c.s.*,
1960). Finally, they acquire the character of instinct
behavior with all its advantages and disadvantages.

## 4.2   *The control-paradigm*

The process of directed action as a further elaboration of psychological adaptation has been described thus far in terms of a number of subprocesses
and elements of processes. Thus, environmental transformation, the situation concept, the transformation
rule, $S_x$-thinking, $S_y$-thinking, the control compromise and the plan have successively been discussed. In
addition, interrelations between elements and processes have been pointed out occasionally. It will now
be attempted to integrate all subprocesses and process elements within the framework of a single system. To accomplish this task, use will be made of
system-theoretical notions that are employed in describing more complex processes.

In general systems theory, several types of system notation are utilized. One of the major types is

the so-called U.C.-structure, which is defined as a
structure in which all process elements and their relations are included. Formulated more accurately,
the U.C.-structure comprises the 'structure of universe of discourse' of the system, as well as all
couplings (cf. Orchard, 1971). The 'universe of discourse' is the collection of elements or subsystems
that determine the way in which the system operates.
The couplings are defined as the common external
quantities of the elements. The U.C.-structure then,
comprising the elements of the system as well as
their couplings, determines the permanent behavior of
the system as a whole.

The U.C.-structure of a system capable of accomplishing psychologically adaptive behavior should
satisfy a number of conditions that follow from earlier explications. For one thing, the U.C.-structure
should minimally comprise three phases as well as
three levels. In Chapter II the three phases were defined at the operational level and designated as the
initial environment, the transformation and the final
environment. In Chapter III they were discussed once
more, now at the cognitive-symbolic level, and they
were designated as the initial situation concept, the
transformation rule and the final situation concept.
At the control level the three phases were finally
designated as the control comprise, the plan and terminal control. Thus, the behavioral system comprises
nine elements and can provisionally be represented in
fig. 6.

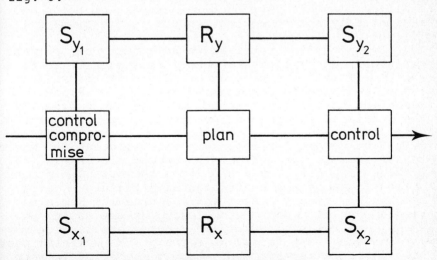

Fig. 6. Elements of the behavioral system.

This structure indicates that in a particular environment $S_{x_1}$ a control compromise is effected, so that a particular $S_{y_1}$ can be inserted in the appropriate element of the structure. This particular $S_y$ makes possible several directed transformations in the form of transformation rules $(R_y)$. Once a rule is chosen it can be worked out at the control level in the form of a plan, and subsequently executed at the operational level in the form of overt behavior $(R_x)$. The $S_{x_2}$, originating as a result, may be tested against the $S_{y_2}$, so that control with respect to an adequate execution is always guaranteed.

The system's continuity is conceived at the middle level (cf. Chapter II). Thus, it is indicated that at that level the *criterion* for psychological adaptation is located for the individual. The individual may develop a certain 'view' of the world at the symbolic level, but as such that view does not guarantee that psychological adaptation will be achieved. The testing of this view is possible only through actual execution of transformational behavior and through control of the results of that behavior. Thus, the criterion for psychological adaptation is conceived here as an *existential* criterion that is located at the very level where organism and environment meet. A negative result of the test mentioned earlier does create an existential problem for the individual. He realizes that his psychological adaptation fails, but is generally not sure with respect to the cause of failure.

Defining the system as we have just done permits two classical problems in theory construction to be avoided. First, the problem of *apriorism*, in which theory is based on a so-called *harmonie preétablie*. According to the aprioristic view the human organism has available an inner structure that virtually predestines him to solve his adaptation problems adequately. But no one has ever been able to point out where that structure comes from. The second problem is the problem of *empiricism*, which sees the organism as compelled to adopt the environmental structure 'as it *really is*'. In our conception the organism has a certain amount of reserve with regard to the world. However, that reserve is certainly not absolute, and may for instance take different forms on the basis of feedback. As a matter of fact, adaptive behavior is seen

here as the resultant of two subsystems, the symbolic
system on the one hand and the operational system on
the other. Adaptive behavior always results from a
unique confrontation of culture and nature. Thus, no
strict assumptions are required with regard to either
inner truth or outer coercion.

The U.C.-structure has thus far been described
in terms of the collection of elements constituting
the 'universe of discourse' of the system. With respect to the couplings connecting the elements, initially those processes are called upon that have been
taken earlier to be essential for the process of
psychological adaptation. We are referring to the
processes involved in $S_x$-thinking, $S_y$-thinking, the
control compromise and the plan. The couplings that
have been indicated there  might be conceived to be
sufficient for the execution of directed transformations of the environment  that, as we have seen,
characterize psychologically adaptive behavior.

However, two considerations necessitate a further
extension of the system of couplings. The first consideration concerns the relation between the control
compromise and the $S_x$. In establishing a control compromise, one of the main problems is to find an $S_y$
that fits the optical $S_x$. Thus far we have conceived
of the $S_x$ as a solid given, even though it is unde-
fined initially. However, at the sensomotor-operational level several relations may be assumed to exist
between organism and environment. Each of these relations can lead to a different selection of the $S_y$.
Thus, the organism may discover new environmental
cues through exploratory behavior. He may also restructure the environment by means of trial-and-er-
ror behavior in such a way that a different choice of
the $S_y$ becomes obvious. These arguments have led us
to assume the couplings between the control compromise and the $S_x$ to be bilateral.

The second ground for extending the system of
couplings is connected with the plan. With respect to
the plan some amplifying statements may be made. Our
exposition thus far might have led the reader to conclude  that the plan is to be conceived as an autonomous structure that is as such turned loose on the
environment. But, obviously, that is possible only
if the environment in the strictest sense satisfies

the conditions specified in the definition of the $S_y$, with which the plan in its conceptual form is connected. As we have seen before, this is not generally the case, so that behavior as planned has to be modified in order to maintain its fit to the environment. If the fit is retained, behavior will be linked up closely with the specific nature of the $S_x$. Therefore, between $S_x$ and $R_x$ couplings have to be postulated as well. If the fit is not retained, the organism may resort to a revision of the original plan by means of feedback to the $R_y$. Accordingly, bilateral couplings have to be assumed there. At the control level, finally, couplings have to be introduced as well, because the control compromise is indeed continually changed during the plan's execution, but we nevertheless assume that control is maintained until final control is obtained. The U.C.-structure in which the provisions mentioned are assimilated  finally takes the shape designated in fig. 7. This structure will henceforth be designated as the *complete U.C.-structure*. It encompasses nine elements connected with single horizontal couplings and double vertical couplings The complete U.C.-structure is based on the major assumptions that have been made and dealt with previously. The structure represents an *open system*, because the optical environment $S_x$ is included in it. Thus, the personality system is provided with a continuously changing element, and, as a function of that element overt behavior ($R_x$) will continuously change as well.

Within the structure *three phases* are distinguished  into which behavior may be divided, i.e. $S_1$, R and $S_2$. These three phases, it has been pointed out in Chapter II, are necessary for adaptive behavior. Behavior proceeds at *three levels* as well, i.e. the cognitive-symbolic level, the control level and the sensomotor-operational level. Each of these levels supposedly plays a major part in determining behavior. The *continuity* of behavior, considered to be finally decisive for the direction as well as the execution of behavior, is located at the control level. The other two levels are conceived as relatively discontinuous in the way they function.

The system as a whole may be described in terms of *two* distinct *dimensions* representing behavioral aspects that are both indispensable for directed action, notably equilibrium (the vertical dimension of the U.C.-structure) and transformation (the horizontal

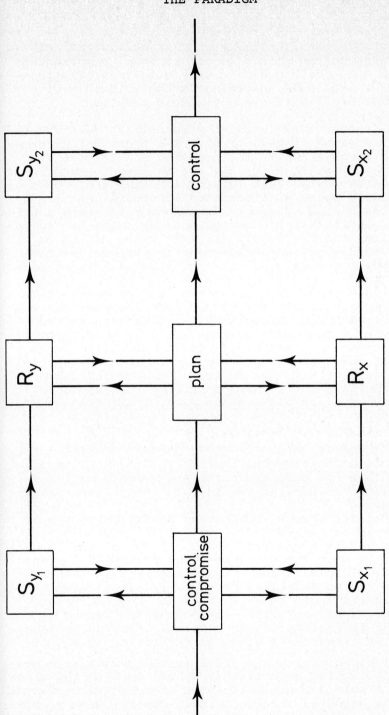

Fig. 7. Complete U.C.-structure.

dimension). Equilibrium is established and maintained according to the principle of *feedback*, represented in the U.C.-structure by double couplings. Transformation is achieved according to the principle of *feedforward*, represented by single couplings.

The U.C.-structure is meant primarily to describe behavior at a high level of adaptive functioning, namely the level at which the organism is directedly altering the environment in which he lives. Psychologists have always been looking for the 'basic unit of behavior', being an elementary structure that may be found as a kind of common denominator in every single behavior. In this connection one may think of the reflex arc, the S-R model, the TOTE-unit, and so on. Our strategy has been different on purpose: we have attempted to develop a structure that is the minimally necessary condition for a very complex activity: directed action. That structure is thus meant to be the common multiple of every single behavior. This implies that more elementary functions can be made feasible by parts of the complete U.C.-structure. It also impliesthat approaches 'from below', in which complex behavior is described in terms of repetition (for instance S-R), or in terms of hierarchization (for instance TOTE), are considered inadequate to describe such complex behavior as, for instance, direc ted action. The simple S-R model is usually defined on the operational level, it only comprises two elements ($S_x$ and $R_x$) of the structure. The more complex S-O-R model is hard to define in terms of the U.C.-structure, unless one were to substitute symbolic and control elements for the O-term, but this is not usually done.

Skinner's model of operant conditioning may be conceived as representing part of the complete U.C.-structure. In elementary terms, the model may be described as $S^d \rightarrow R \rightarrow S^r$, in which the first S represents a discriminative stimulus, and the second S represents a reinforcing stimulus. At the operational level this formulation seems to agree with the U.C.-structure. But discrepancies arise  as soon as the nature of the stimuli is further defined. Notably, the definition of $S^r$ is at variance with the definition of $S_{x_2}$ as conceived here. Skinner views reinforcement as a stimulus following a particular behavior, with the capacity to maintain or to re-evoke that behavior. That view is based on a conception of control that is al-

together different, fundamentally, from the conception developed here. In Skinner's view the basis of
control is located *outside* the organism. In the control of behavior the organism itself remains outside
it: control is accomplished solely by external stimuli, or, more accurately, by the contingency between a
response and its consequences (cf. Skinner, 1963).
Manipulation of contingencies enables the experimen-
ter to control the behavior of animals in experiments.
In non-experimental settings the natural contingencies emanating from the'causal texture of the environment' are supposed to determine learning behavior
(Skinner, 1969, p. 7).

A resemblance may be noted here between the conceptions of Skinner and Brunswik, who both appear to
assume a natural order in the organism's environment.
That order is 'discovered' by the organism by means
of its behavior, and subsequently behavior is adjus-
ted to fit that order. We have pointed out before (in
Chapter III) that we are not prepared to make such
strong assumptions with respect to the environment.
We have indicated, also, that in man a major part of
the order mentioned is not established by means of individual behavior but through processes of information
exchange and communication. We agree that, initially,
relative certainty with respect to the environment is
attained through individual behavior. New or strange
environments can be explored by way of small interventions in the environment. Alterations that occur
in the environment as a consequence of these interventions, are registered. If these alterations occur
repeatedly after the same interventions, environmental uncertainty is gradually reduced: the organism
acquires control over the environment. With Skinner,
we consider overt operant behavior to be a necessary
condition for control. But unlike Skinner, maintaining
equilibrium is here seen as an additional necessary
condition for control. In Skinner's model, that condition is not stipulated, so we conceive of it as a
model of pure transformation.

On the other hand, there are behavioral theorists
who completely leave the transformation aspect out of
consideration in their conception of control. One of
them is Kelly, who sees control merely as a *point of
view* used to explain external events: 'To say that
something is out of control is merely to say that we
have given up trying to explain it. To abandon the notion of control, with respect to any behavior whatsoever, is to abandon the notion of lawfulness' (Kelly,

1955, p. 127).

In Kelly's theory, situations are constructed according to typical patterns. One of these patterns is the C-P-C cycle, in which a fixed succession of the elements circumspection, pre-emption and control finally leads to a choice made by the individual. That choice determines his conception of the situation. In Kelly's view the concepts of choice and control are situated closely together. Control is achieved as soon as the individual has created such clarity with respect to the situation  that only one line of action remains possible. Clarity is seen as an end product of complex processes in which several alternatives are considered, after which reductions are made until the final choice is made. From the perspective of his personal construct theory Kelly prefers to assume a subjective definition of the concept of control: control is achieved as soon as the subject has made his choice. The criterion for that choice is the subject's expectation to maximally define and elaborate his contruct system. Whether or not that expectation is based on solid grounds is not debated any further.

In Kelly's view the function of control has to be located within the person and his construct system, and certainly not within the situation or the person's behavior. What is called control in  his theory is similar to what we have called equilibrium. In terms of the U.C.-structure, Kelly would speak of control as soon as the control compromise is established. We define control on the basis of the final comparison of $S_x$ and $S_y$. According to our conception of control, planned behavior has to be counted in, and furthermore the world has to be given the opportunity to answer.

The discrepancy between the two views is indicated nicely by Berlyne (1965), who makes an important distinction between prediction and control: 'To predict means to anticipate the outcome of a projected series of transformations, while to control means to select transformations  that will bring about the desired state of affairs in the future' (p. 82). Thus, Berlyne endorses the meaning of the concept of control as used in informatica and cybernetics (Ashby, 1952, 1956; Miller c.s., 1960; Powers, 1973). The latter author (Powers, 1973) defines control as 'achievement and maintainance of a preselected perceptual state in the controlling system, through actions on the environment that also cancel the effects of disturbances'.

This preselected perceptual state may be conceived as a criterion  against which the external environment is tested. In the context of the U.C.-structure that criterion function is accounted for by the $S_{Y2}$. Control is achieved only if the test leads to a positive result. Therefore, control is located on the borderline of organism and environment, where it becomes manifest as a state of equilibrium. Control is always available  when the organism succeeds in transforming the environment, simultaneously retaining equilibrium: *control is equilibrious transformation*.

The control model has been developed here as a background for directed action. But we assume that other activities and functions of the organism may be located in the model as well. Some activities merely call on parts of the provisions allowed for by the model; yet, also in those cases one may very well speak of environmental control. For instance, the radar observer watching for enemy attacks cannot interfere actively with the events occurring, but he is very well aware of the signals he has to pay attention to. In the context of the system developed here, vigilance should be seen as a situation in which the $R_x$ is basically absent, but control may nevertheless be achieved by means of the other system elements.

The carrying out of purely executive tasks, led by others, may be controlled *by the executor*, even though he cannot call on processes of directed thought to define the goals of his actions.

Attendance to courses or instruction  frequently causes problems, because the pupil is not enabled to use all mechanisms of control that are at his disposal. Yet, participation in the process of education cannot be characterized as an activity in which the pupil is entirely deprived of control. In the past, however, symbolic activities have been too exclusively emphasized, thereby insufficiently  providing for activities at the operational level. In modern education some gradual changes may be noted in the emphasis on those activities.

In the previous chapter it has been indicated how control aspects affect thought processes in the form of $S_x$-thinking as well as $S_y$-thinking. Decision processes, judgment and appraisal of the environment are all subject to control bias even if they thus come into conflict with logic or rationality. In addition,

we assume that perception, exploration and searching
behavior should be seen primarily against the background of the control principle. This is not meant to
imply that each elementary activity is as such determined by the control principle, but is does imply that
the *cooperation* of several functions can only be explained in the context of control. Thus, the control
paradigm should be seen as an integrative system, the
partial activities of which together determine the
molar actions of the individual. Personality theory
is primarily concerned with the idiosyncratic *relationships between* subsystems, affecting individual
behavior. These relationships always show the restrictions imposed by behavioral capacities (competencies)
of the individual as well as behavioral opportunities
allowed for by the actual environment ($S_x$). It should
be kept in mind, however, that regarding those behavioral opportunities  environmental transformation is
not the only way to acquire psychological adaptation.
In addition, the control model provides a framework
to account for adaptive escape and avoidance behavior.
Thus, completely unknown environments will be avoided
because a control compromise cannot be acquired on
the basis of lacking validity. Dangerous environments
will not lead to a control compromise in default of
transformability of the $S_x$. In both instances
lack of equilibrium between organism and environment
may cause adaptive escape and avoidance behavior.

### 4.3  *Disequilibrium and short-term adaptation*

The control model as developed thus far represents an ideal structure: the system functions without any friction as long as the external world abi-
des by the rules (situation definitions and transformation rules), as formulated at the cognitive-symbolic level of the system. It will be obvious from the
preceding pages, however, that we are not prepared
to base our model on such an assumption.In fact, we
do expect frictions to occur and furthermore we expect them to be the rule rather than the exception.
Therefore we cannot restrict ourselves to designating
an ideal structure, functioning according to rules
derived from logic.
In that respect there is a major difference from
customary practice in theory construction in psychology. For quite some time now psychology has shown a clea
preference for strictly rationalistic models, but ti-

me and again it has been demonstrated that human behavior does not conform to these models. The literature on cognitive functioning provides many examples to illustrate this statement. One merely has to think of models in the areas of decision making, problem solving, directed thinking, and the like. The rational decision maker accurately weighs probability and utility factors, but decision making behavior of persons in realistic situations seldom takes a course in compliance with the model (cf. Edwards, 1954). Problem solvers have provided us with sophisticated descriptions of the way they think, but it is improbable that these descriptions have any connection with the actual process (cf. section 3.1).

Analogous problems are bound to occur with respect to the conception of intelligence as a personality variable. For a long time it has been assumed that intelligence constitutes some kind of super trait within personality, basically to be seen as tantamount to adaptive capacity (for instance Stern, 1935). But countless empirical studies have demonstrated that intelligence only permits modest predictions, even in contexts where on *a priori* grounds high expectancies seemed to be justified, as, for instance, in educational research.

Within the framework of the control paradigm these results are only to be expected. A well-built intelligence test typically consists of items with unequivocal answers, that is to say that consensus exists with regard to the question as to which answer is right. Thus, the test has obtained the character of a well-shaped instrument to measure the presence or absence in the individual of culturally accepted and widely sanctioned definitions and rules. There may even be a case for the intelligence test to be the best conceivable measure of cultural achievements. The type of thinking the intelligence test elicits is $S_y$-thinking in an almost pure form.

It cannot be denied, indeed, that $S_y$-thinking plays an important role in accomplishing adaptive behavior. but it is certainly *not* adaptive behavior itself. It is basically restricted to the aspect of symbolic transformation and thus leaves an important part of the U.C.-structure out of consideration. We conceive of intelligence as an important marginal condition of psychological adaptation. For the behaving individual, intelligence becomes increasingly significant to the extent that concrete environmental circumstances are more in agreement with existing situation concepts. But in the case of discrepancies between the two, adaptation problems can no longer be solved solely on the basis of an adequate knowledge of rules and concepts.

Adaptation problems will become manifest for the behaving individual in the form of discrepancies between the intended and the actual result of his actions. In the context of the control paradigm they will become manifest as disturbances of the *equilibrium* between organism and environment. Here we come upon the very core of the idea of psychological adaptation. If the relationship between organism and environment is metaphorically represented as a bridge, then disequilibrium is equivalent to the threatening collapse of that bridge. In view of the priorities stated before, the utmost will be done to secure the connection between the two banks. To this end, all means are basically permissible, with respect to the nature of the connection itself, as well as with respect to its points of support on either bank. The nature of the connection depends on the opportunities afforded by the banks. Therefore, in case of a threatening collapse, the first thing to do is to look for *new* points of support.

In the model this amounts to an alteration in one of the system elements to restore equilibrium. In view of the couplings that exist in the system, such an alteration will always cause an alteration to occur at the control level as well, where it will become manifest in the control compromise, the plan or the nature of control as such.

States of disequilibrium can be described in several ways, depending on the level of functioning that is emphasized in the description. If disequilibrium is regarded primarily against the background of the cognitive-symbolic level of functioning, one might speak of a discrepancy between an expectation or hypothesis stated earlier and the actual result of behavior. Against the background of the sensomotor-operational level, one could speak of an interruption of the ongoing stream of behavior, an interruption of an organized sequence of behavior. At the control level one could speak of a disturbance of the relationship between organism and environment, issuing in loss of control. All formulations mentioned thus far have received ample attention in the literature. Almost unanimously the point is made that the disturbance leads to a state of arousal of the autonomous nervous system.

As early as 1930 Cannon had stated in general
terms that every important alteration in the environment is answered by the organism with a process of recovery. In this context the main weapon of the organism is the sympathetic part of the autonomous nervous system. Subsequent authors have connected the recovery reaction with a vast number of divergent phenomena, all supposed to be *the* cause of that reaction.
Thus, for instance, the reaction has been connected
with the disturbance of expectancies (Pribram, 1967;
Epstein, 1972), with conflict and disequilibirum
(Berlyne, 1965), interference with the organization
of behavior (Hebb, 1962), states of helplessness and
disorganization (Mandler, 1964, 1975), states of dis-
congruity (Miller, *c.s.*1960; Pribram, 1967) and the
interruption of organized behavior (Mandler, 1964).

The causes of the arousal reaction mentioned
thus far can all be fitted to the control conception
developed here, because they are all in some way connected with disequilibrium between the organism and
the environment. Differences between single causes
may well be attributed to the level of functioning at
which the disturbance is primarily located. Later we
will come back to the issue of causality in greater
detail, let us now turn to the issue of functionality.

The function of the arousal state of the autonomous nervous system has been subject to divergent conceptions. Cannon (1939) for instance, has put special
emphasis on the maintenance, and the restoration, of
*internal* equilibrium, occurring as a consequence of
external disturbances (homeostasis). However, psychologists have connected the function of  arousal primarily with behavior, overt as well as covert. Thus,
Berlyne (1960, 1965) conceived of arousal as a drive
state accomplishing orienting and exploratory behavi-
or. Arnold (1970) and Lazarus (1966) in particular
emphasized the effects of arousal with respect to cognitive functioning. According to these authors, arousal leads to an emotional state, bringing about a new
meaning to the actual environment. This meaning takes
the form of an evaluation or appraisal, that has consequences for the position the individual takes with
respect to the environment. Mandler, who would certainly not reject such a cognitive interpretation, has
particularly emphasized behavioral change, covert as
well as overt, as a consequence of arousal. In his
view, interruption of behavior is usually followed by
repetition of the interrupted behavior, the occurrence

of substitute behavior, and, if unsuccessful, an increase of the vigor with which behavior is executed
(Mandler, 1964,1975).

At first sight these divergent conceptions with
respect to the function of arousal are hard to recon-
cile. However, in the context of the U.C.-structure
they may well be harmonized if they are conceived as
different mechanisms to restore equilibrium, functioning at different points in that structure. In this
connection, for better understanding it should be realized that equilibrium, as well as disequilibrium,
is ultimately determined by the *state* of the system as
a whole. This state is in its turn determined by the
values that each of the system quantities acquires at
any given moment in time (cf. Orchard, 1972). Within
the control paradigm the system quantities are the
values of each of the subsystems $S_{y_1}$, $S_{y_2}$, $R_x$, $R_y$,
$S_{x_1}$ and $S_{x_2}$. Together these values are crucial for
the question as to whether control is present in the
system as a whole. In the case of non-control the
system will tend to restore control by means of
alterations in one or more of the subsystems.

An important question in this connection is, how
we should conceive of state change in the system.
First and foremost then, the vertical couplings in
the U.C.-structure offer an opportunity to restore
control. The *afferent* arrows represent activities of
testing information against criteria derived from
information emanating from other elements of the system. These testing activities are assumed to take
place at the control level. Well then, the *efferent*
arrows, pointing away from the control level, represent the activation of internal or external operations, intended to accomplish alteration of the values
in various elements of the system, with the object of
acquiring *new* information.

Thus, for instance, the arrow pointing upwards
from the control compromise, represents a process indicated as *reflection*. This term is not meant here to
indicate introspection, but rather a process of 'going over the significance of experiences, facts or
events' (cf. Wolman , 1973). The main function of
this process is to scan the existing $S_y$-structure in
order to generate an $S_y$ that fits the actual $S_x$. By
means of this process a disturbed equilibrium can be
restored through the establishment of a new control
compromise. Reflection may thus result in a new $S_{y_1}$,

a new 'appraisal' of the environment as conceived by
Arnold (1970) and Lazarus (1966).

The arrow pointing downwards from the control
compromise indicates operations upon the $S_x$. It represents *exploration* and searching activities in the
actual environment, with a view to achieving a new
orientation for the organism. In emphasizing other
environmental aspects than before, this activity may
contribute, in much the same way as reflection, to
the establishment of a new control compromise aimed
at eliminating an existing state of disequilibrium.
Exploration changes the $S_x$ offering insufficient cues
for directed action to be based upon. The process of
exploration contains elements of orienting behavior
as described by Russian investigators like Sokolow
(1960) and subsequently by Berlyne (1965).

The efferent connection upwards from the plan
represents an acitivity directed at generating a new
transformation rule. This rule might replace a rule
that was chosen earlier, and as such it might again
serve to restore equilibrium. This activity will be
indicated here as *uncoupling:* it loosens an $R_y$ chosen
before, and may thus contribute to the restoration of
control. Processes of uncoupling have been described
in more detail by Pribram *c.s.* (1975).

From the plan downwards another connection exists
that relates to changes in the execution of the plan.
These activities have been described by Mandler (1964)
and have been indicated by that author as *substitution*. The term refers to the insertion of alternative
operations within the context of an existing plan
structure, thus maintaining the transformation rule:
$R_x$ is altered whereas $R_y$ remains constant.

The main function of the vertical couplings as a
group is to maintain or restore equilibrium. It is assumed that the processes represented by the vertical
arrows operate according to the principle of *efferent
feedback control* (Miller *c.s.* 1960; Pribram, 1971).
As has become clear from the preceding descriptions
of the processes involved, it is assumed that mechanisms for restoring equilibrium can be effective with
regard to internal as well as to external elements of
the structure.

Control has been defined before as equilibrious
transformation. Therefore, loss of control may be
corrected directly through restoration of equilibrium,
as well as indirectly by means of new transformations. The latter's objective is to alter the state of

the elements $S_{y_2}$ or $S_{x_2}$. Two mechanisms may serve
that function. The first is located at the cognitive-
symbolic level: the processes belonging to this mechanism are indicated here as *redirection* of previously intended goals. This mechanism makes it possible to proceed from the same $S_{y_1}$ to different $S_{y_2}$'s,
of course within the competence of the individual.
In a situation where an $S_{y_2}$, originally intended,
fails to be matched by $S_{x_2}$, the redirection mechanism
provides the opportunity to replace the original $S_{y_2}$
by a new one, to regain control.

The second transformation mechanism reactivates
the overt instrumental behavior $R_x$. In case $R_x$ initially does not succeed in providing control, the organism may resort to repetition to change the state of
$S_{x_2}$ as yet. Repetition may be accompanied by trial-
and-error behavior and by an increase in executionary
vigor in order to re-establish control. These aspects
of behavior have been described by Mandler (1964) in
the framework of the study of the interruption of
fixed, overlearned behavioral sequences. Mandler has
indicated these aspects as *persistence*.

To summarize briefly, six restoration mechanisms
have been distinguished here on the basis of structural properties of the U.C.-structure. Each of these
mechanisms - reflection, exploration, uncoupling,
substitution, redirection and persistence - may serve
to restore control through state transition. But in
each separate mechanism the point of contact in the
U.C.-structure is different (cf. fig. 8).

In view of the fact that couplings exist between
different elements of the U.C.-structure, we must assume that state transition in one element has consequences with respect to the state of the elements that
are located *later* in the U.C.-structure. Thus, an
early restoration mechanism like reflection will trig-
ger a new $S_y$ and this in turn may lead to the choice
of a new $R_y$. Taking this kind of consideration into
account, a structure may be derived in which transitions of several states are represented, as well as
the consequences which these state transitions have
with respect to the states of the other elements. In
general systems theory such a structure is called the
S.T. (State-Transition)-structure (cf. Orchard, 1972).
The state transition structure of the control system

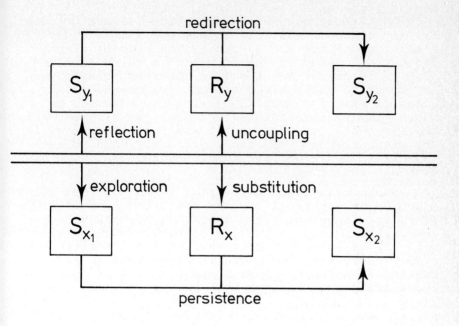

Fig. 8. S.T.-mechanisms and their effects upon the states of several system elements.

| S.T.-mechanisms | Elements | | | | | |
|---|---|---|---|---|---|---|
| | $S_{y_1}$ | $S_{x_1}$ | $R_y$ | $R_x$ | $S_{y_2}$ | $S_{x_2}$ |
| Reflection | x | – | 0 | 0 | 0 | 0 |
| Exploration | – | x | 0 | 0 | 0 | 0 |
| Uncoupling | – | – | x | – | 0 | 0 |
| Substitution | – | – | – | x | 0 | 0 |
| Redirection | – | – | – | – | x | – |
| Persistence | – | – | – | – | – | x |

Table 3. *Elementary state alterations as a consequence of several S.T.-mechanisms*

x = primary alteration
0 = derived alteration
– = no alteration

may be represented according to table 3.

In this structure a distinction is made between primary state transitions on the one hand and derived state transitions on the other. The primary transitions are located in the elements in which each mechanism is primarily effective. Derived transitions may occur in those elements that are connected, by means of existing couplings, with the elements in which primary transitions have been established. This implies that transitions will manifest themselves in the element where they occur primarily, and subsequently to the right of the U.C.-structure, to end up with $S_{x_2}$ and/or $S_{y_2}$.

State transition mechanisms taken together offer a number of opportunities for restoring control. However, that does not imply that each mechanism is *necessary* to obtain control. Frequently, the individual will not be able to perform particular transitions, simply because of the specific properties of the situation in which he finds himself. But that does not necessarily mean that he will lose control.

The six state transition mechanisms distinguished here have been derived from he U.C.-structure, i.e. a structure designated to represent a particular theoretical position with respect to behavior, and the assumptions underlying that position. It is of some interest with regard to the firmness of the theoretical position taken here, to investigate whether the S.T.-mechanisms mentioned do have a basis in *physiological* states that, presumably, determine their activities. Miller *c.s.* (1960) have proposed to search for the anatomical substratum of regulatory mechanisms of this type in the brainstem, notably the hypothalamus and the mesencephalous reticular structures. Recent years have brought more clarity with respect to the precise nature of these mechanisms and structures, as well as to the physiological and biochemical states involved, especially through the work of Karl Pribram.

A major renovation has been his view that the arousal state, originating as a consequence of disturbances, is no longer to be conceived as a general facilitative process accelerating neural transmission. In contrast to this conception Pribram (1971) suggested that arousal be conceived of as an impetus to specific configural changes. This suggestion basically agrees with the present position and has some interesting consequences with regard to that position. In

Pribram's conception the distinction between the physiological states of arousal and activation has regained importance.
'    Parallel to that distinction he has made the
psychological distinction between emotion and motivation: 'To *e-mote* implies to be *out of* or *away from*
action. In terms of the TOTE-unit the emotions are
concerned with the regulation of input, which is to
say with the feedbacks, the preparatory and anticipatory processes effecting efferent control over input
.....Motive, on the other hand, involves the organism
in action, in the execution of its plan. Emotion and
motivation, passion and action: these are the two
poles of the Plan' (Pribram, 1971, p. 38). Translated
in terms of the control paradigm, motivation is obviously connected with the dimension of transformation,
whereas emotion is connected with equilibrium. In the
U.C.-structure motivation is represented by the horizontal couplings and emotion is represented by the
vertical couplings.
      In Pribram's terminology motivational mechanisms
must be conceived as *'go'-mechanisms*, emotional mechanisms on the other hand as *'stop'-mechanisms*. If, in
terms of a hackneyed metaphor, motivation is characterized as the engine of the organism, emotions might
be characterized in the same vein as the organism's
pneumatic tyres and springs.
      This dichotomy has recently been superseded by
a trichotomy in the work of Pribram and McGuiness
(1975). In addition to arousal and activation they
have distinguished a third process, called *effort*. In
this process the go-mechanisms as well as the stop-
mechanisms are involved, in the sense that effort affects the uncoupling of stimulus and response. Effort
serves to bring about change in intended action. That
change then pertains to an existing set, or reaction
tendency, that is concretized in the plan. According
to Pribram and McGuiness the stop-mechanisms are regulated by the amygdala, the go-mechanisms by the basel
ganglia while the effort-process is regulated by the
hippocampus (in the latter process use is made of the
so-called Papez-circuit). The authors have also suggested that neurotransmission is regulated in the
stop-mechanisms by means of indole-amines, notably
serotonine, and in the go-mechanisms by means of catecholamines, as, for instance dopamine.
      The classification as proposed by Pribram and
McGuiness, into arousal, activation and effort, shows
a clear parallel with our own classification of state

transition mechanisms. Reflection and exploration in that terminology both represent stop-mechanisms: they are put to work by arousal. Redirection and persistence are go-mechanisms: they require activation. Uncoupling and substitution are mechanisms that become effective on the basis of effort.

An important example of *arousal* functioning is the orienting reaction, which occurs if the organism is confronted with unexpected stimuli (Sokolov, 1960). The orienting reaction is the result of a complex composition of subprocesses, part of which can be explained from processes of input registration as described by Pribram and McGuiness (1975). In these processes the unexpected stimulus is compared with previous experiences. In this comparison the amygdala function by means of a serial registration of relevant events in memory (Pribram, 1971).

In animals from which the amygdala have been removed, a number of typical phenomena disappear from the orientation reaction, as, for instance, changes in skin conductance, heart rate and respiration. On the other hand the typical behavioral orientation is maintained in these animals, and this orientation even shows an increased resistance to habituation. These observations have led Pribram (1971) to distinguish at least two components in the orienting reaction. One component refers to registration and the other to searching behavior, directed at environmental sampling and the scanning of novelty.

In these descriptions some elements can be recognized that were used earlier to describe reflection and exploration in the framework of the control paradigm. We assume that reflection and exploration both have the function of establishing or restoring a control compromise. It may be recalled here that the control compromise essentially consists of an agreement or compromise between situation concepts on the one hand and environmental cues on the other. If the compromise fails to become established or if an existing compromise is disturbed, two strategies are possible to restore equilibrium. By means of reflection a new situation concept may be generated to fit environmental cues: this process runs parallel to the process of registration as discussed by Pribram. And, secondly, by means of exploration new environmental cues may be generated to fit the existing situation concept: this second process is much the same as Pribram's process of environmental sampling.

Thus far the processes concerned orienting behavior as an example of arousal. In contrast to the pha-
sic arousal reaction, *activation* refers to a tonic
reaction that lasts longer and enables the organism
to maintain a particular intentional state for a longer period. The activation mechanism has been related by Pribram and McGuiness (1975) to the occurrence of contingent negative variation (CNV), slow changes in the electric activity of the brain as a function of expectancy and motor preparation for action.
In Pribram's (1971) view CNV's are induced by a variety of expectancy states, and the locus of the change in electric potential depends on the type of task
for which preparation is wanted. If no overt action
is required, the CNV becomes manifest mainly in the
frontal cortex. If overt action is required, it becomes manifest in the motor area of the cortex and precedes execution of the action.

Pribram and McGuiness (1975) have made the assumption that the CNV occurs as soon as a piece of
brain tissue gets ready or remains ready for action.
We see a mechanism here that seems particularly suited
to perform activities going together with the direction and redirection of action, as well as with firmly maintaining that direction in a state of persistence against disturbances.

As the emergency character of the situation increases, sympathetic activity of the autonomous nervous system will increase as well. As Mandler (1964)
has shown, this will also happen if planned behavior
is interrupted, especially if the behavior is highly
organized by overlearning. A state of increased activation as a consequence of behavior interruption
may become visible in emotional expressions of several kinds. But it may also lead to directed attempts
to complete behavior as yet. Mandler has stated in
this connection: 'Once an organized response has been
interrupted it is assumed that a tendency to comple-
tion persists as long as the situation remains essentially unchanged' (p. 169).

Typical examples of *effort* are demonstrated during problem solving behavior in concrete situations,
if a solution strategy once chosen appears not to be
successful. In a situation like this, the individual
may proceed to adopt a completely new strategy by replacing the initial transformation rule by a new one.
But he may equally proceed less drastically and restrict himself to replacing elements of the original
strategy that merely concern the execution or the

order in which activities are carried out. In both
instances effort is assumed to be at the basis of recovery  behavior to restore equilibrium.
    Thus far, six state transition mechanisms have
been described, together supposedly regulating individual short-term adaptation. The specific stimulus
of all S.T.-mechanisms is a state of disequilibrium,
originating at the control level of the control system. The typical reaction to that state is conceived
here as an attempt to alter the state of one or more
system elements by means of configural change. New
developments in neurophysiological research have recently been put forward to lend support to this conception. It may be concluded that specific anatomical
structures and physiological processes have been identified and described  that offer a basis for the S.T.-
mechanisms as  postulated here.

A final question deserving attention in this section
concerns  the *choice* of a particular S.T.-mechanism
in a concrete situation. Several hypotheses may be
considered to account for the choice that is actually made. Thus, for example, one hypothesis may state
that individuals have a preference for S.T.-mechanisms
that affect a particular *level* in the U.C.-structu-
re. Another hypothesis may state that individuals have a preference for a special *phase* in the process
chain. Both types of hypothesis deserve a somewhat
closer examination.
    In elaborating the first option, the 'level hypo-
thesis', for convenience we shall restrict ourselves
to one particular process phase, notably the first
phase in which the control compromise is established.
In situations characterized by ambiguous or contra-
dictory stimulation a control compromise will be hard
to attain. According to the control model an individual in such a situation will resort to either reflection or exploration to acquire control. In those
circumstances we can expect the preference for reflection as opposed to exploration to be a function
of the individual's *competence* with respect to the
situation in question: highly competent individuals
will show a preference for reflection.
    This statement may seem obvious at first sight,
since without any competence reflection would not
make sense. However, there is also some empirical e-
vidence to support it. This evidence has been obtained in animal research, directed at questions concerning the biochemical substrate of behavior. In a
series of classical investigations Krech, Rosenzweig

and Bennett (1956, 1962) were able to show that competence in rats is correlated with the amount of acetylcholine in particular brain tissues. Other studies have subsequently indicated a relationship between the amount of acetylcholine in those areas and the tendency to explore. Thus, Grossman c.s.(1965) and Vossen (1966) classified rats according to preference for exploration and they found that higly explorative rats do have smaller amounts of ACh as compared with their less explorative congeners. In the present context this evidence is suggestive rather than decisive. However, if it could be generalized, it would imply that competence is an important factor regarding the preference for cognitive-symbolic as opposed to sensomotor-operational S.T.-mechanisms.

The second option, the 'phase-hypothesis', would state that the choice of S.T.-mechanisms is connected with the phase in which the disturbance occurs. Early disturbances would lead to a preference for reflection and exploration, disturbances in the middle of the process to uncoupling and substitution, and late disturbances to redirection and persistence. But in this hypothesis the assumption is made that the organism knows when the disturbance took place and that will generally not be the case. For instance, a disturbance might become manifest during the *execution* of behavior, whereas the real cause of the disturbance was an inadequate control compromise. The basic position we have adopted before (in Chapter II) does not include any strong assumptions with respect to the certainty of the world or the adequacy of our knowledge concerning that world. Therefore, this solution with respect to the choice of S.T.-mechanisms must be rejected. The feedback that is obtained by the acting individual is restricted and does not provide him with certainty with respect to the cause of disequilibrium. The organism basically has a problem of attribution regarding the cause of the disturbance.

Now, it could be hypothesized that *competence* plays a part with respect to the phase of disturbance as well as to level. The competent individual knows better what aspects have to be attended to, he obtains more feedback and will be able to detect the disturbance earlier. One of the implications would be for competent individuals to 'work back' directly from the phase of disturbance. Mandler's (1964) study has provided evidence with respect to this hypothesis. His data have shown that competent individuals, when interrupted, have stronger galvanic skin reactions

and a more increased heart rate as compared with less
competent individuals. This result might be interpreted as a connection between competence and persistence when a task is interrupted. But the same study
has demonstrated that competent individuals also
show a higher amount of *other* reactions (exploration,
substitution) as compared with less competent individuals. The general conclusion to be drawn seems to
be that competence favors the use of S.T.-mechanisms
*in general:* incompetent individuals give up earlier.

The question of whether an individual will react
with arousal, with effort or activation, after disturbance in a particular situation, is presumably not
to be answered in any more general way: the individual usually  does not know where the disturbance originated, and to which cause it should be attributed.
The individual learning history will probably play a
major part on this score. Wagner (1963) has shown that
emotional and motivational consequences of interruption are connected with the situation in which the
interruption occurred, according to the principles
of classical conditioning. Analogous results have
been obtained by Campbell, *c.s.* (1964). We therefore
assume that S.T.-mechanisms will be coupled with the
situation in which they had appeared originally. In
a renewed confrontation which such a situation the
S.T.-mechanism may be assumed to be ready, even before disturbances occur.

## 4.4  *Long-term adaptation*

Maintenance and restoration of equilibrium are
possible only as long as the organism's competence is
capable of satisfying environmental conditions. But
in many cases that is impossible. If the individual
is confronted with the definitive  failure of his a-
daptive equipment, states of extreme arousal or panic
may occur. Conditions like natural calamities, war,
suddenly arising danger, injuries, death of relatives and the like, in which man is completely power-
less, are well-known causes of panic. However, it is
not only this sort of major threats, but also minor
occurrences indicating the failure of adaptation
which may cause panic. Mandler (1975) who has dealt
with this state, noted in this connection: 'Panic-
like behavior may be found in rather innocuous situations. We may find that it is suddenly not possible
to open the door leading from a room - for some reason it is stuck. Again and again we may try to go

through the same motions, pushing, pulling, exerting
more force, or even more intelligence. We run through
the gamut of possible reactions to interruption but,
with each interruption, we potentiate further the
autonomic arousal that follows interruption. The more
intensive and demanding the signals that initiate the
actions, the more likely the repetition, the greater
the subjective perception of interruption, and the
more intense the degree of arousal. At the extremes
we find the kind of behavior usually described as
panic' (p. 238).

The major condition for panic to occur is a per-
manently disturbed equilibrium. A possible cause of
a disturbed equilibrium might be the introduction of
radical changes in someone's familiar direct life environment. Pavlov (1924) has demonstrated what happens in the case of such radical changes, by means of
animal research. He started from the notion of *dynamic stereotype*, to indicate a conditioned, well-balanced system of internal processes, originating in
the animal as a consequence of constant external influences. In the present context the dynamic stereotype is clearly related functionally with what has
been called competence here. To organize such a system requires an enormous amount of neural energy.
This may be demonstrated by studying the processes
occurring when an existing system is demolished and
replaced by a new system. Pavlov (1924) has shown
what happens in such a case, by means of experiments
with dogs that had been conditioned according to a
particular schedule long enough to cause a differentiated dynamic stereotype to be developed. If a *new*
stimulus was introduced after several conditioned
stimuli, and this new stimulus was accompanied by the
unconditioned stimulus only in some instances, a new
reflex began to develop soon. However, that development was attended by extreme arousal on the part of
the animal. This state continued for several months
until a new dynamic stereotype was established.

According to Pavlov a large amount of neural e-
nergy is required to achieve the new stereotype, so
that only animals with a strong and well-balanced
nervous system are capable of mustering that energy,
and to replace the existing organization by a new one.
Animals that do not satisfy these conditions show
chaotic behavior, thus interrupting the process of
conditioning for a long period of time. On the basis
of these experiments Pavlov has related the neurological system of emotions to a process of disruption
of the existing stereotype and its replacement by a

new adaptive system.

In the forties, the fundamentals of Pavlov's stance were taken over by Hebb to develop a theory, as bold as it was speculative, concerning the processes occurring in strongly emotional behavior. Hebb (1949,1962) also started from disturbances in the familiar life environment. He observed fear reactions occurring in chimpanzees when confronted with incomplete, mutilated or inanimate pictures of well-known objects, men and animals. The results showed that fear reactions are caused by a lack of reactivity in complete animals, as well as by evidently missing important parts.

Hebb (1949) explained these results as a consequence of 'the disruption of temporally and spatially organized cerebral activities'. This disruption causes spontaneous fear to arise, in turn causing the animal to *avoid* the fear-provoking object. Fear behavior thus has an important function with respect to long-term adaptation, because it induces the organism to avoid non-coordinated elements in future, and thus to restore its cerebral equilibrium. Once the disruption process has occurred, the typical fear reaction disappears even if the fear-provoking object is met anew, because the object will be shunned on sight.

Hebb's conception may be summarized as follows: negative emotions always contain an element of disturbance, whose function it is to prevent every occasion leading up to it in the future. In this process the following stages can be distinguished:
1. At the basis of the disturbance is some form of disorganization of cerebral structures, as a result of either conflict, sensory deprivation or constitutional change.
2. As a reaction a strong spontaneous emotional state appears.
3. This state leads to disorganization of an existing behavioral structure in the cerebrum ånd to organization of escape behavior.
4. Repeated confrontations with the same environment cause the organized escape behavior to become better organized each time.
5. In subsequent confrontations the disorganized part of emotional behavior decreases each time.
6. In the final stage a perfect avoidance response is learned, whereas the emotional component is completely extinguished (avoidance without fear).
   The core of this conception is represented in

the third point, referring to moments of uncoordina-
tion as well as moments of coordination in emotional
behavior. According to Hebb, the first moment is the
consequence of a disruption in the timing of cerebral
activities and causes elimination of the original behavior. The second moment serves to prevent the un-
pleasant stimulation in the future. Since Hebb's publications several studies have been devoted to coordinated as well as to uncoordinated elements of emotional behavior and these studies have led to some
important new points of view. A number of these studies will be dealt with here and, for convenience,
they will be categorized according to the dominant
behavioral aspect in studies concerned with states of
*fear, helplessness or frustration.*

A state of *fear* is characterized by a number of
typical aspects in the behavior of organisms that are
subject to this state. Thus, for instance, fear has
an inhibitory effect upon  the amount of exploratory
behavior of rats (Montgomery &  Monkman, 1955; Aulich, 1978). Furthermore, fearful individuals show a
typical reduction of the degree to which they utilize
environmental cues (Bacon, 1974; Baddeley, 1972;
Easterbrook, 1959). Notably the sensitivity to peripheral cues decreases, whereas in the view of some
authors the sensitivity to central cues increases.

Baddeley (1972) has suggested that the adaptive
character of this reaction is concentration on aspects
that are considered important by the individual. Thus,
in dangerous situations opportunities for escape would
be enhanced. However, in contrast to this view, many
studies have revealed that fear has a negative influence on the effectiveness of mental functioning as a
whole (for example Beier, 1951; Osler, 1954; Berkun
*et al*, 1962).   Therefore it does not seem to be useful to look for the adaptive significance of fear in
the very situation where it originated. Rather, with
Hebb (1949), we should look for the significance of
fear in future situations of the same character as the
original situation, and notably concentrate on the
avoidance of these situations. In the threatening situation the organism develops a high degree of sensitivity to cues that are typical of this situation,
and that may be used to discriminate it from other
situations. As a result there is an increase in the
sensitivity to threat cues (Janis, *c.s.* 1969). On the
basis of these threat cues the organism is able to
subsequently avoid situations of that type or to enter them only after it has taken special precautions.

*Helplessness* occurs whenever the organism is not successful in mobilizing effective behavior. Recent research (Seligman *et al*, 1969) has shown that in states of complete helplessness, learning processes may take place in the organism, serving to maintain the original state of affairs, although the situation might be escaped from along another route (learned helplessness). In the investigation mentioned, dogs were subjected to electrical shocks which, initially, were unescapable. Subsequently, however, when the experimental conditions were changed to provide opportunities of escape, the animals were no longer capable of learning the escape behavior, however simple that might be as such.

To persist in non-effective behavior, once it has been demonstrated for the first time, is a well-known phenomenon in the literature on problem solving, where it is usually conceived as rigidity. Many studies have shown that in problem solving, rigidity particularly manifests itself in states of increased emotionality (Beier, 1951; Cowen, 1952; Pally, 1954; Davis, c.s. 1958; Maier, 1956; Van de Geer, 1957).

The adaptive significance of sticking to non-effective behavior is sought here, once again, in the direction of long-term adaptation, notably adaptation by means of directed extinction of non-effective behavior. An argument for this conception may be adopted from the work of Mandler (1964), who demonstrated clearly that the extinction of overlearned behavior is achieved more efficiently as opposed to the extinction of newly acquired behavior.

*Frustration* occurs especially when in a familiar situation a line of action is established and also executed but does not lead to the result that was intended. For a long time, in the wake of Freud, it was assumed that frustration is bound to cause aggressive behavior, but eventually experimental research has shown that frustration may be followed by different kinds of behavior (cf. Barker, *et al*, 1941). A core element in all these behaviors is a decrease of the constructivity of behavior: frustration presumably interferes with constructive aspects like attention, thinking, planning and other cognitive processes. A second important phenomenon usually occurring under frustration is the organism's tendency to continue the activity in which he is currently involved, no matter what its contribution with respect to the original purpose (Child & Waterhouse, 1952). This may be seen as a phenomenon of distraction from the goal

that was intended originally, which is frequently accompanied by an increase in the vigor of behavioral
execution.

Just like the states of fear and helplessness
mentioned earlier, frustration is characterized by a
process of disruption, in this case being exacerbated
to include elements of the behavioral chain that was
intended initially. Its significance with respect to
long-term adaptation might be that frustration has
the effect of demonstrating that particular elements
of the behavioral chain are effective, even though
behavior as a whole fails to be effective. In a social context, behavior following frustration will frequently be interpreted as aggressive, as a consequence of its lack of constructivity and the great vigor
of its execution. Naturally, under extreme frustration great damage may be done to the health and the
life of others. But is is assumed here that the damage
is not to be explained on the basis of primarily aggressive instincts, but rather as an expression of
the vital interest of adaptation for the individual.

In the descriptions given thus far  of the states of panic, occurring typically from fear, helplessness, and frustration, there are, as well as all
the differences, some general characteristics to be
observed. In all three states, there is initially a
question of definite *failure of the S.T.mechanisms*
for short-term adaptation to be effective. As a consequence, a strong *increase* occurs in the *emotional
state* of the individual. And, finally, a remarkable
*reduction* takes place with respect to vital elements
in the *organization of behavior*. This reduction is
manifested in fear as a restriction of the perceptual
field. In helplessness, the reduction is demonstrated
in the response repertoire that the individual has at
his disposal. And finally, in frustration there is a
marked reduction with respect to the goal structure
of behavior, as compared with the goals originally set.

To provide an interpretation of these findings,
our line of reasoning will be based on the general
assumption that, ultimately, environmental control
has top priority for the organism. This statement has
been worked out in Chapter II and needs no further
comment. In short-term adaptation this general assumption is translated into the precept, to *maximize
environmental* control by means of S.T.-mechanisms.
If successful, short-term adaptation enables the organism to gradually master his environment, while
control is being maintained or restored at any given
moment.

However, an important new development takes place as soon as short-term adaptation definitely fails.
Instead of maximizing control the organism changes
his strategy and proceeds to *minimize noncontrol*. The
major effect of this new strategy is to precisely
establish the boundaries of psychological adaptation
at that particular moment as well as in that particular environment. The processes occurring to minimize
noncontrol might be interpreted as a withdrawal of
the organism, that is to say, a withdrawal as far as
necessary.

In a very global sense the same function is being fulfilled here that has been attributed to
strong emotional behavior by Hebb (1949). However,
with respect to the processes and mechanisms involved,
our position is at variance with the conception of
the author mentioned. In Hebb's view an *internal* conflict is at the basis of disruption, while in the
present conception there is a conflict between organism and environment in the form of an irreparable
disturbance of equilibrium. In Hebb's view the coordinated part of emotional behavior basically originates
*within the organism*. The organism has available internal tendencies to flight, avoidance, anger, aggressive behavior, and so on. In our conception the
coordinated part as well as the uncoordinated part
of emotional behavior is born out of the very connection between organism and environment. We assume a
new coordination to be established as a direct consequence of a *temporary intensification of the connection* between organism and environment.

To explain this statement we must go back to the
control paradigm and the assumptions made there, to
show that it is only a logical consequence of those
assumptions. The point was made then  that panic occurs whenever the competence of the organism appears
to be insufficient to obtain control over the environment. The origin of panic is characterized by can-
cellation of all S.T.-mechanisms, so that efferent
feedback control as well as feedforward control are
stopped. Thus, the organism is no longer capable of
testing environmental information, so that, tempora-
rily, there is no criterion at all to serve as a
background against which information may be rejected.
As a consequence, an *open connection* between organism
and environment will be established.

This open connection will allow untested concrete environmental information to enter the system
and to be taken up in the cerebral structures of the

organism. We assume that this concrete information will form part of the organism's competence, and subsequently codetermine behavior in environments similar to the one in which the disturbance had occurred in the first place. Only if that assumption is granted can the process lead to long-term adaptation by means of minimizing noncontrol.

In this respect there is a significant place for the finding that in fear, helplessness as well as frustration, behavior is definitely reduced at the sensomotor-operational level. For, unrestrained assimilation of information can occur only if the source of information is restricted in the way it operates. On the basis of the concrete nature of the assimilated information, we must assume that any change in the organism's informational structures, established by emotional disruption, will be of an idiosyncratic character. The net result of the whole process is conceived as consisting of concrete environmental data being superimposed upon existing symbolic structures. For that purpose a disruption of the existing state of affairs seems to be required.

It is important to point out here that disruption will have no effects upon strictly defined parts of the symbolic structure. Rather, we assume that the effects will be scattered over larger areas of that structure, on the understanding that the amount of spreading will be a function of the strength of panic. This may be explained as follows. According to our position as described earlier, no one to one relationship is assumed to exist between symbolic elements and sensomotor elements. In directed action this principle has led us to assume that one $S_y$ may be coupled with many $S_x$'s through probabilistic relations. In states of panic the picture is reversed in the sense that the $S_x$ or $R_x$ is the starting point, whereas the effects are being considered with respect to $S_y$ or $R_y$. So, in those states it is only logical to assume that confrontation with one sensomotor element spreads its effects over several symbolic elements.

As stated before, it is also assumed that the amount of spreading is a function of panic strength. To elucidate this statement, we must go back to the relationship between panic and the reduction of behavior. If one assumes that relation to be positive, or at least monotonic, it follows that reduction be-

comes stronger as panic increases. In strong panic
*less* cues will be admitted as compared to weaker
forms of panic. This implies that in strong panic it
is harder to discriminate these cues in terms of $S_y$
or $R_y$, and consequently they are pertinent to more
symbolic elements.

In summary, it is assumed here that panic always
has generalized effects upon the symbolic structure
on the very basis of the reduction occurring in panic
behavior, and in addition it is assumed that the a-
mount of generalization will be a function of panic
strength. The adaptive nature of this development is
that it enables the organism in the future to establish his position with respect to specific environments  that appear to share essential features with
the environment in which panic took place.

Disruption may arise in different phases of the U.C.-
structure. Thus, panic may arise if a control compromise fails to be established: in that case it is called *fear*. Panic may also arise because a plan cannot
be accomplished: in that case it is called *helplessness*. And, finally, panic may arise because control
at the end of the process fails to be achieved: that
state is called *frustration*.

In the following pages an attempt will be made
to explain in more detail what happens in terms of
the system in each of the panic states distinguished
here. Let us turn once more to the state of *fear*. It
has already been explained that the establishment of
a control compromise is a major condition for directed activity. The nature of a particular control compromise is determined by considerations of validity
and transformability (cf. Chapter III) together determining the amount of expected control. The individual will sometimes find himself in an environment in
which the amount of expected control for any control
compromise is so small that establishment of a control compromise is virtually impossible.

On the basis of the definition of expected control it follows that those circumstances will occur
if either validity or transformability (or both) are
too small. In the first case we may speak of an $S_x$
that is basically undefinable, i.e. there is no way
to locate the $S_x$ within the symbolic $S_y$-structure.
The environment causes fear because of its unfamiliarity: fear is conceived here in the sense of Freud's
concept of anxiety (*Angst*).

In addition, there is a second type of fear, occurring on the basis of transformability. This type
of fear will arise if the environment may indeed be
located within the $S_y$-structure, but if, in addition,
the $S_y$-structure indicates that there is no possibility whatsoever of transforming the pertinent $S_y$ into
a direction that is acceptable to the individual.
Dangerous or threatening situations, where the individual does not know how to remove the threat, belong to this category. In Freud's terminology the
term fear (*Furcht*) would be appropriate in this case
as well.

The occurrence of fear as a consequence of either unfamiliarity or threat will eventually lead to
an extension of the individual's $S_y$-structure by way
of the introduction of a new 'idiosyncratic $S_y$'. With
the aid of that new $S_y$ the threatening situation, as
well as other situations with common features, can be
avoided in the future.

An interesting question in this connection is,
what would happen to the fear reaction if the individual did not avoid a threatening situation but on
the contrary re-entered it. A study, pertinent to
this question, has been undertaken by Epstein and
Fenz (1965), who observed the behavior of parachutists, before, during and after the jump. In that
study a remarkable difference was found between
novices and experienced jumpers. Novices appeared
to show signs of panic, accompanied by ten-
sion and behavioral disorganization just before the
moment of the jump. Experienced parachutists on the
other hand, showed panic signs as well, but the moment at which panic became manifest, was removed
from the moment right before the jump to a much earlier moment, i.e. the morning preceding the jump.

This extraordinary finding may be reconciled
with our conception of long-term adaptation, in that
even very experienced jumpers will enter a dangerous
situation each time they prepare themselves for a
jump. Thus, according to the present point of view,
fear should become manifest on the basis of the second component of the control compromise: low transformability of the situation. The advantage an experienced parachutist has as compared with a novice is,
that the former has managed to untie the moment
at which fear becomes manifest from the actual
moment of jumping, thus avoiding the disorganizing

effects of panic to interfere with jumping behavior
itself. The processes required to accomplish untying
cannot be pointed out precisely as yet, but one might
hypothesize that the process of symbolic $S_y$-chaining
referred to in the previous chapter has something to
do with it.

A state of *helplessness* occurs whenever the individual, after having established a control compromise, appears not to be able to find an adequate
transformation rule. Either by means of thinking, or
by means of overt action he comes to realize that his
preferent transformation cannot be applied in this
case. He may try subsequently to find an appropriate
transformation rule yet by means of uncoupling or
substitution, but if these processes fail, a state of
helplessness will arise that cannot be resolved within the context of the actual situation. In such a
case a state of panic may become manifest, causing
behavior to become entirely rigid. The effort mechanisms will cease to function, and the individual will
repeat the same behavior over and over again, even
though it never leads to any result whatsoever.

These continuous panicky repetitions of the same
behavior will finally yield irrefutable proof to the
individual  that this behavior in this situation is
totally ineffective. Extinction will occur at an ac-
celerated rate, so that eventually the transformation
rule, governing the panic behavior, will disappear
from the pertinent place in the symbolic behavioral
structure.

*Frustration* takes place if the control compromise as well as the plan are established  but in the
final stage of the process there is still no agreement between $S_x$ and $S_y$, so that control is prevented
from being established. In such circumstances the individual may mobilize his S.T.-mechanisms,  but if
these mechanisms fail to accomplish control, frustration occurs and may become manifest in panic and vio-
lent emotional behavior. The effect of frustration
will be that, eventually, the original goal of behavior is abandoned.

But there will be other effects as well. Behavior in a frustrating situation will often cause some
change to occur in the environment, even though the
alterations achieved are not usually the transformations that were intended in the first place. Thus,
particular subgoals may indeed be accomplished, or
behavior may cause alterations that were not at all

to be expected. It is our hypothesis that this type
of products resulting from panic behavior under frustrating conditions, will be registered in the symbolic structures, take their place among the existing
$S_y$'s, and will be considered in the future to act as
intended products of transformation as well.

In the description of the states of fear, helplessness and frustration, each time the cessation of
particular S.T.-mechanisms was observed to initiate
a state of panic. In more peaceful circumstances S.T.-
mechanisms provide for a flexible relationship to
occur between individual and environment. So, clearly, cessation of these mechanisms will cause a loss
of efficiency to occur in the actual behavior. A negative relationship between strong emotionality and
behavioral efficiency as outlined here, is in agreement with the so-called law of Yerkes and Dodson
(1908), in which a curvilinear relationship is postulated between drive level and performance. However,
if our conception is correct, that relationship can
only be established if performance is solely conceived as short-term adaptation. If long-term adaptation was to be considered instead, the curve connecting drive and performance would take quite a different
shape: our expectation would be that the relationship
would be curvilineair as well, but with a deflection
in the opposite direction.
      Unfortunately, long-term effects of panic are
hard to investigate directly. Ethical considerations
prevent experimental research in which these effects
are studied in human subjects.
Therefore, we have to fall back on research in natural settings, where panic is supposed to occur either voluntarily or inevitably. Examples of settings of
this type are parachute jumping (Epstein & Fenz,
1965), deep-sea diving (Baddeley, 1972), army excercises (Berkun, *et al*, 1962) and hospitalization for
surgical operations (Janis, 1958). Customarily, this
research is of a correlational nature, and physiological measures are frequently used as predictors to
represent the intensity of emotional reactions. Thus,
it seems relevant to focus primarily on physiological variables presumably connected with panic reactions as distinguished here.
      The pertinent literature may be found under the
heading of 'stress behavior' and within that area
special attention should be paid to physiological
stress reactions. Three measures of endocrine secre-

tion are applied with some regularity in that type of
research, i.e. the adrenal medullary hormones, the
catecholamines epinephrine and norepinephrine, and
the adrenal cortical hormones, especially 17-OHCS (cf.
Reynolds, 1976; Kety, 1967; Levi, 1972; Brady, 1967).

Regarding the definition of the precise function
of these hormones in the process of adaptation no
complete consensus exists as yet. Obviously this is
caused at least in part by ambiguities with respect
to the divergent models of behavior that are used.
Levi (1972) has reviewed research outcomes regarding
the three hormones, and specifically mentioned increasing 17-OHCS secretion   in subjects *previous to*
hospitalization, laboratory tests, surgical operations, exams, psychological interviews and tests, riding motor cycles, flying airplanes, and combat situations. An increased secretion of the catecholamines
appears to occur during exams, dentist treatment,
hospitalization, acrobatic excercises, supersonic
flights and motor riding, in centrifuges, sensory
deprivation and during submergence.

Brady (1967) investigated emotional conditioning
in monkeys in stress situations and found specific
results for each of the three measures. Thus, for instance, during the process of aversive conditioning
a strong increase was noted in the 17-OHCS level. In
a later stage of the study a clear difference was
found between reactions in both catecholamines, epinephrine and norepinephrine. For instance, during the
warning signal preceding the administration of an e-
lectrical shock, Brady found a strong increase in norepinephrine secretion whereas the epinephrine level
remained essentially constant. If 'free shocks' were
administered, secretion of both catecholamines was
increased. But if, in an avoidance experiment the
response-lever had been removed, the warning signal
was accompanied by an increase of epinephrine secretion.

Kety (1967), after summarizing the results of
Brady's research, advanced the hypothesis that epinephrine is secreted particularly if there is uncertainty regarding the response, whereas norepinephrine
secretion is raised when the outcome is inevitable.
For Kety, the adaptive function of the corticoste-
roids is considerably less obvious. Reynolds (1976)
has connected an increase in 17-OHCS secretion  with
fear and with uncertainty regarding the manageabili-
ty of the situation. An increase of catecholamine secretion, according to Reynolds, primarily concerns

motor activity: he states that a connection of catecholamines with psychological activity requires further confirmation to be conclusive.

In a provisional summary it may be stated that
there seems to be an obvious effect of stress conditions upon the secretion of 17-OHCS as well as epinephrine and norepinephrine. In addition there are some
indications that the effects are specific in that they
are caused by specific experimental conditions. However, the precise function of each of these products
in the context of adaptation is as yet far from clear.
On the basis of the results mentioned, within the
context of our own conception of long-term adaptation,
we shall as a tentative working hypothesis start
from the idea that 17-OHCS secretion  is increased
particularly in states of fear, norepinephrine in
states of helplessness and epinephrine in states of
frustration.

A strong increase of autonomous reactivity in stress
conditions has for a long time been conceived as an
indication of inadequate adaptation to external conditions. However, a number of studies in the area of
stress behavior have largely led to the conclusion
that autonomous reactions should rather be seen as
indications of organized attempts to cope with threatening environments, whereas precisely the absence of
such reactions points in the direction of disorganization and defensiveness (cf. Shapiro &  Crider,
1969). Therefore, with respect to *long-term effects*
of panic behavior the best assumption seems to be that
strong autonomous reactivity generally furthers a more active position with regard to stress conditions
and thus makes an important contribution to their
mastering. Frankenhaeuser (1975), for instance, has
demonstrated that an increased catecholamine secretion is associated with a more adequate long-term
adaptation. In addition she has observed that it is
not just the *increase per se*, but also a fast *decrease*
that is beneficial for adaptation.

Frankenhaeuser and her co-workers have specially emphasized the effects of adrenal medullary secretion upon behavior in special tasks, so that in their
work adaptation is primarily viewed as the capacity
for solving problems. But there are other aspects of
life in which similar results have been found. For
instance in research directed at adaptation problems
connected with threats to health, material well-be-
ing and social relations, results have indicated that

strong autonomous activity has beneficial effects and
is of prime importance for long-term adaptation.
Thus, for instance, patients being admitted to hospital for a surgical operation, usually demonstrate reactions in the form of increased catecholamine secretion, in which epinephrine as well as norepinephrine
are involved. Noteworthy, just before the operation
only norepinephrine reactions may be established
(Tolson *et al*, 1965) which might point in the direction of a state of sheer helplessness.

After the operation has been completed, the pa-
tient typically finds himself for a rather long time
in a state of uncertainty and fear with respect to
the final result. It appears to be possible to partly reduce this so-called post-operative fear, notably
by having it *precede* the operation. In this connection Janis (1969) speaks of 'the work of worrying' and
of 'the work of mourning' depending on the moment at
which the reaction actually occurs. Through special
treatment it is possible to raise anticipatory fear,
much by way of an emotional inoculation. Anticipatory
fear may have the effect of stimulating special mechanisms, enabling the individual to be ready and cope with the intervention more adequately. Research has
in fact demonstrated that anticipatory fear has positive effects on the psychic recovery of patients *after* the operation has taken place (Egbert, *et al*,
1964).

If, on the contrary, the individual is not able
to emotionally prepare himself for the impending sur-
gery, coping will have to be effected afterwards. In
general, the suddenness of the confrontation appears
to be an important factor with respect to the effects
of disruptive states. Thus, the sudden loss of belo-
ved persons or the disclosure that one is suffering
from an incurable disease may initially lead to
vigorous emotional outbursts, followed by longer
periods of grief. These reactions have as their
primary function the establishment of a radical
change in the individual's cognitive system so that
a new equilibrium may be attained: 'Grieving is a
response to the loss of a whole system of assumptions
and expectations upon which human beings build a view
of the world. In some manner the weeping reaction....
serves to 'dissolve' the old system in such a way that
it can be replaced by a new' (Shands, 1955).

# CHAPTER V

## PERSONALITY

### 5.1 The open-system theory of personality

In the previous chapters a number of general
views have been developed and elaborated that are considered to be of the utmost importance for man's functioning in his natural habitat. In this context special emphasis has been placed on adaptational aspects.
As yet, no presuppositions have been made regarding
individual parameters to be held responsible for individual differences in behavior. This is the consequence of a well-considered choice which conceives of
the personality problem as a particularization of more
general principles of behavior, presumably operating
within each individual.

In the pages that follow an attempt will be made
to achieve a more definite formulation of a theory comprising the various aspects that have been dealt with
hitherto. Thus, a first impetus will be given to the
development of a theory of personality that, as yet,
needs further elaboration in many respects. Like other personality theories, this theory shows restrictions regarding its reach, or - to use a term coined
by Kelly - its range of convenience. The interactionistic nature of the theory puts special emphasis upon
the situation in which the behaving individual finds
himself. The theory is of a molar character and is
primarily directed at the description of individual
behavior within the context of real environments. For
that purpose symbolic structures were introduced into
the theory in the form of situation concepts and transformation rules, derived from everyday language, to
represent the environment as well as behavior executed in the environment. Thus, the theory's focus of
convenience is defined as human behavior in the real
conditions of daily life.

The individual is viewed as one who is confron-

ted with divergent situations day by day, who strives
for goals and takes action to achieve them, who makes
decisions regarding goals as well as actions, is frequently unsuccessful in accomplishing his aims, is
subject to frustrations as well as to states of helplessness and fear, is usually able to recover from
those states; who knows what it is to be in trouble
but also to be satisfied and happy to accomplish his
goals, maintains a number of relationships with other people, some of which are gratifying while others
are just obligations emanating from the constraints of
life.

The indidivual is neither seen as free, nor as
captive: first and foremost he interacts with his environment. The latter makes its demands, which are at
least in part to be considered as extensions of culturally determined contingencies. The individual will
accomplish his aims and desires only in sofar as the
environment enables him to. Of particular interest is
the fact that the individual is basically free to
choose the environment to live in, although it should
be added immediately that his actual movements are
restricted by limits, in and of themselves to be viewed
as constraints. Individual existence is considered
here to be an ongoing stream of transactions in daily
life between individual and environment, characterized by changing outcomes and perspectives.

Traditional global-dispositional theories of
personality have not intensively occupied themselves
with daily events. They have typically studied personality in its own right, thus implying that individual actions are the direct consequences of the 'nature' of personality. A discipline like social psychology might be expected to be more inclined to study
daily-life conditions but with a few exceptions that
does not appear to be the case either.

Very recently, Secord (1977) has ardently advocated a new paradigmatic approach within that area. To
become a full-fledged scientific endeavor, according
to Secord, social psychology would especially have to
study behavior in the context of real life
situations. Study of environments requires that they
should be analyzed in smaller units on the basis of
a taxonomy of situations, allowing for investigations
of person-situation interactions to be made. Notably,
Secord has pleaded for an approach in which interactions with 'true life' conditions are put in the fo-
refront: 'Sometimes, in life situations people *are*
severely constrained....But in many other situations
people have a variety of choices, paths they can go

down. The very essence of social behavior is that individuals avoid some situations and enter others. Moreover they modify situations to suit themselves. They also create situations that facilitate certain kinds of behaviors. Depending on their own natures, they also evoke certain kinds of behaviors from people with whom they interact. Most of the time they are either modifying or creating situations that facilitate things that they want to do. If this is the true character of social behavior, then the kinds of experiments we have mostly been doing, even if we do a million or a billion of them, will give us a piecemeal, fragmented, terribly incomplete view of social behavior. We need to develop a theory of how individuals move into and out of situations, how they modify situations, and how they create new situations, and how these actions relate to the behaviors that they enact' (Secord, 1977, p. 46).

The program of study that is announced in this statement is by no means a simple one. To theorize about daily life implies the development of concepts and rules to define the events that may be distinguished there. For one thing, it is not hard to refer to situations as a common sense notion, but to define situations in such manner that they may be dealt with scientifically, is quite something else. In a very global sense the type of theorizing advocated in this book does answer the description made by Secord. But a number of additional requirements had to be fulfilled to permit a more accurate treatment of daily life events.

The present theory especially emphasizes the nature of the specific relations an  individual may enter into, with regard to the situation. First of all the question of control versus non-control has to be settled, and only subsequently can attention be directed towards the activities utilized to extend, maintain or restore control. To be able to do justice to this emphasis, it was necessary to further specify the concept of control. That emphasis is of utmost importance, since *personality development* is considered here to be determined mainly by control activities demonstrated by the individual in different situations. In the first chapter personality was provisionally defined as 'a system of interacting biological and culturally determined elements, which maintains an open relation with the environment actually obtaining'. This definition may now be extended into a formal theory on the basis of the conclusions obtained in the

previous chapters after the analysis of a number of
relevant topics.

The assumptions constituting the theory will
conveniently be divided into three groups. The first
group is connected with the personality *system* and
the general permanent elements of that system. What
we call system here, is usually referred to as personality structure in the handbooks. The second group
of assumptions concerns the dynamic or *process* aspects that determine the way the personality system
functions. Personality processes accomplish particular results in the environment as well as in the personality system itself. The latter results or *products* are included as permanent aspects in the individual, to participate in the structure of personality. They will be dealt with here as a separate third
group of assumptions to indicate clearly, that they
are being conceived as structural aspects originating
as a direct consequence of individual activities.

The assumptions of the theory will be formulated
henceforth in terms of single statements. Each of the
assumptions has received attention in the course of
this book. Only in those cases where for the sake of
clarity further explanation is considered necessary,
will additional information be briefly supplied.

## 5.1.1 SYSTEM ASSUMPTIONS

*5.1.1.1 The open-system assumption*
      *Personality is an open system: the system
comprises a number of relatively permanent subsystems
and, in addition, an environment that is altered continually.*

*5.1.1.2 The level assumption*
      *The personality system functions at three
different levels: the cognitive-symbolic level, the
sensomotor-operational level and, in between, the
control level.*

*5.1.1.3 The transaction assumption*
      *Among the three levels of the personality
system transactions occur continuously.*

*5.1.1.4 The input assumption*
      *The input of the personality system may be
defined either at the cognitive-symbolic level or at
the sensomotor-operational level of functioning.*
      The cognitive-symbolic input of the system compri-
ses information which is part of the culture of the

society in which the individual lives. The senso-mo-
tor-operational input consists of segments of the environment.

*5.1.1.5 The output assumption*
     *The system's output may be defined as well as*
*the input at the cognitive-symbolic level or at the*
*sensomotor-operational level.*
     The output will generally show the characte-
ristics of transformations as accomplished by the individual.

## 5.1.2 PROCESS ASSUMPTIONS

*5.1.2.1 The control assumption*
     *Internal as well as external activities of*
*the individual are governed by the leading principle*
*of psychological adaptation: acquiring and maintaining*
*control over the environment.*
     This is a fundamental assumption in the sense
that the other process assumptions may be conceived
as particularizations of the control assumption. In
case of conflict between the control assumption and
the other process assumptions the former will always
obtain priority. The control assumption constitutes
the basis for the competence aspect as well as for
the motivation aspect of personality.
     Control is located at the control level of
the personality system, where three different elements
are distinguished, i.e. the control compromise, the
plan and terminal control. Control is defined as e-
quilibrious transformation, and, as such, it constitutes an integration of two separate process types:
equilibrium and transformation. For the individual,
equilibrium is the criterion for *maintenance* of control, whereas transformation determines *extension* of
control.

*5.1.2.2 The information assumption*
     *The individual utilizes information that is*
*available in his culture for the purpose of furthering*
*control over the environment.*
     Control always assumes information to exist
in the system, because information is a necessary
condition as a criterion to test environmental change. Cultures offer information in the form of situation concepts and transformation rules for efficient
transformation of the environment. Without that information control could basically be obtained as well;

however, the individual would be obliged to acquire
control entirely on the basis of his own strength and
by means of his own activities.

Cultural information is of a superindividual
nature and may serve the function of a norm for individual actions. These characteristics make cultural
information particularly fit to enhance cooperation
and coexistence with other individuals. The individual can utilize this information in directed thinking, enabling him to determine the goals of his actions and the means to be used to attain those goals.

*5.1.2.3 The transformation assumption*

*Transformation activities may cause real mo-
difications to occur in the environment that are fed
back to the personality system.*

This assumption constitutes a necessary element of the theory as the counterpart of the information assumption. Confrontation of individual and
environment is essential for control to originate,
because only by means of that confrontation can it be
tested whether or not an existing informational structure is effective. By this assumption the theory is
raised above the level of downright cognitivism which
is logically bound to issue in sociologism.

In this connection we agree with Leontiev
(1977) when he states that: 'die reale Basis der Per-
sönlichkeit des Menschen die Gesamtheit der seiner
Natur nach gesellschaftlichen Beziehungen zur Welt
ist, aber der Beziehungen, die *realisiert* werden: sie
werden realisiert durch seine Tätigkeit, genauer ge-
sagt, durch die Gesamtheit seiner mannigfaltigen Tä-
tigkeiten' (1) (p. 77).

*5.1.2.4 The maximizing assumption*

*If the equilibrium between organism and envi-
ronment is disturbed, S.T.-mechanisms are started to
maximize control within the conditions in which the
disturbance occurred.*

The assumption is connected with short-term
restoration of control. Without this assumption the
individual would have to be continuously ready with
his optimal adaptive equipment in order to give the
right reaction to avoid a permanent loss of control.
In a closed system that is what would indeed happen.
However, as soon as we conceive of personality as an
open system (assumption 5.1.1.1) the organism is always in a state of *dynamic equilibrium* with the environment.

Since furthermore the principle of *equifinali-*

*ty* is applicable (cf. Chapter II), in an open system
it is possible to attain a previously projected end
state, starting from different initial states. By
this very property restoration of a state of disturbed equilibrium is always possible on principle. Restoration of equilibrium is accomplished by the principle of *state transition*, by which the state of one
or more elements or subsystems is altered to restore
equilibrium. In that context six S.T.-mechanisms have
been distinguished, viz. exploration, reflection, redirection, uncoupling, substitution, and persistence.

*5.1.2.5 The minimizing assumption*
        *If the application of S.T.-mechanisms fails to
restore equilibrium, disruption mechanisms are started to minimize loss of control.*
        To the individual, a final loss of control
constitutes an existential problem with respect to
adaptation as a whole. Establishment of incompetence
necessitates revision of the symbolic structure, but
that revision should not extend any farther than is
strictly required. Disruption mechanisms serve to
establish the boundaries of the alterations needed
within the cognitive system. Without these mechanisms
a generalized incompetence would arise, requiring the
individual to revise his competence structure entirely. The three disruption mechanisms distinguished here - fear, helplessness and frustration - are considered to be effective in different parts of the
structure.

5.1.3 PRODUCT ASSUMPTIONS

*5.1.3.1 The differentiation assumption*
        *Admitting cultural information into the sys-
tem causes progressive differentiation to occur in
the symbolic behavioral structure of the individual.*
        The learning of situation concepts and trans-
formation rules establishes progressive refinement in
the symbolic structure, enabling the individual to
discriminate further among situational cues and among
behavioral cues. In accordance with several theories,
notably in the context of developmental psychology,
it is thus assumed that differentiation processes
will proceed along with increasing age. In addition
to increasing discrimination, particular preferences
with regard to behavioral goals as well as with regard to the proper behavioral means to attain those
goals will be transferred.

*5.1.3.2 The experience assumption*
    *Repeated experience with behavior in the same*
*environment (practice) leads to processes of inte-*
*gration, causing the symbolic behavioral structure to*
*simplify, in sofar as it is pertinent to that parti-*
*cular environment.*
    Experience presupposes the availability in
the individual of information, because the context of
information is required for increase and modification
of competence to occur. Primarily, the effects of experience are pertinent to the behavioral means to be
used to transform a particular situation. However,
eventually shifts may be expected to take place in
the goal structure of behavior as well. Through experience the individual will gradually increase his
knowledge concerning the legitimacy of particular
goals, leading to experiential corrections of
behavioral legitimacy. As a consequence his processes of directed thinking (as they are based on
utility as well as legitimacy) will be affected, finally leading to a change in his decisions regarding
behavioral goals.

*5.1.3.3 The S.T.-conditioning assumption*
    *State transition mechanisms, functioning in*
*reaction to disequilibrium, tend to be coupled with*
*the situation concepts  with which they have occur-*
*red initially.*
    The maximizing assumption is of no particular
consequence for the symbolic behavior structure as
such, but it does have implications for the coupling
of the symbolic structure with the S.T.-structure.
We have assumed S.T.-mechanisms to become connected
with situation concepts according to the principles
of classical conditioning. One of the consequences
of this assumption is, that in a particular situation
the individual not only has available a preferent
transformation rule, but a preferent S.T.-mechanism
as well, in case the transformation does not lead to
control

*5.1.3.4 The disruption generalization assumption*
    *Disruption mechanisms are coupled via proces-*
*ses of generalization with elements of the symbolic*
*behavioral structure, the cues of which show resem-*
*blance to characteristics of the environment, in*
*which the disruption has occurred initially.*
    Disruption is basically seen as a one man's
activity, in which the individual comes to revise his

behavioral structure on the basis of particular phenomena in the actual $S_x$ or $R_x$. Therefore, disruption
will result in strong individualization. The individual will create a subjective $S_y'$, or a unique $R_y'$.
The effect of this initial individualizing reaction
will, however, be 'translated' in terms of the superindividual behavioral structure, so that, finally,
disruption mechanisms will be generalized to elements
of the original symbolic behavioral structure as well.
As a result of these processes of generalization the
symbolic behavior structure will be affected with
respect to situational preference as well as to transformational preference.

Reviewing the assumptions formulated here, it is quite
obvious that they are not independent. Especially important is the fact that definite relations exist between the process assumptions on the one hand and the
product assumptions on the other. In line with the
principles formulated earlier, personality products
are conceived as the results of personality processes. A major conclusion to be drawn is that personality in this conception is not to be seen as a static
given but as a dynamic concept continuously developing and changing as time goes by. The developmental
aspect as determined by the process assumptions constitutes personality as a complicated whole in which
elements and relations between elements are constantly developing.
       However, the picture becomes fantastically com-
plex once it is realized that not only processes determine products, but the reverse may occur as well.
In the previous chapter two instances of this statement have been briefly touched upon. As was pointed
out there, increasing practice with a particular situation not only furthers integration in the *products* of
personality, but presumably also has its effects on
the *processes* occurring subsequently in the same situation. The precise nature of these effects is not
yet quite clear but it looks as if S.T.-mechanisms
gradually change from feedback type to feedforward
type mechanisms. A second example of the influence
of products upon processes was mentioned when the
effects of increasing competence upon S.T.-level preference were indicated. Neither on that occasion did
the picture become quite clear, but once more it was
suspected that learning is effective with respect to
S.T.-preference in a particular situation. The issue

seems very important because it might well give access to particular types of 'process learning', going
far beyond the usual aims of learning through educational processes. However, due to the ambiguities
mentioned we will not pursue this issue any further
at the moment.

In summary of the assumptions stated, it may be
concluded that together they constitute a rough outline of an interactionistic  theory of personality.
The theory includes a conception of the situation, a
conception of the function of behavior, as well as a
conception of the way in which organism and environment reciprocally affect each other. While far from
being complete as yet, the theory is much more explicit, as compared with existing interactionistic formulations, with regard to the statement that 'neither
the situation as such nor the organism in itself, but,
instead, a continuous process of interaction between
the two is seen to underlie behavior' (cf. Chapter I).
The interaction process has been analyzed into a number of component processes, for each of which it is
pointed out how it determines the course of behavior.
Thus, the theory is not merely an interactionistic
theory, but a process theory as well.

Central to the formulation as a whole are two
core concepts, embodied in two core assumptions, i.e.
the first system assumption and the first process assumption. They are the concepts of 'open system' and
'control'. Thus, probably the best way to indicate the
theory would be to speak  of the 'open-system control
theory'. For the sake of brevity, however, we shall
henceforth refer to it as the *open-system theory of
personality*.

In several respects the theory is distinct from
earlier formulations. It comprises a particular combination of the aspects of equilibrium and transformation, of symbolic and sensomotor functioning, of
stimulus and response aspects, that is altogether different from existing theoretical positions. Thus, for
instance, Mischel's (1973) cognitive social learning
theory includes several systems for cognition, evaluation, planning and expectation. However, since the
theory is formulated only at the cognitive level, it
can never serve for a description of the actual interaction between individual and environment.

An essential aspect of the present formulation is
the distinction between three levels of functioning:
a cognitive-symbolic level, a sensomotor-operational
level and, in between, a control level. This distinction is considered necessary to realistically desig-

nate the relationships between the individual and the
world. Among these three levels, the control level is
crucial to embody reciprocal causation, the core concept of interactionistic theorizing.

## 5.2 *Individuality*

The strategy that has been adopted here to construct a theory of personality has some special consequences with respect to the conception of individuality. The assumptions stated in the previous section
were ultimately based on the conception of psychological adaptation developed in Chapter II and elaborated in the subsequent chapters. The theory comprises
a personality structure described in general terms,
that will become individualized only by continual
confrontations between organism and environment. The
processes occurring during these confrontations are
assumed to have consequences with respect to the products constituting the more permanent structural aspects of personality. It is further assumed that all
product assumptions basically have individualizing
effects upon personality.

To get a proper understanding of the nature of
these effects it is important to ascertain first
how precisely we should conceive of individuality. A
well-known statement says that personality should be
viewed as individual by nature. But that statement
would gain considerably in significance if, in addition, a clear explanation were provided with respect
to the definition of the individuality concept.
Stated in its most general form, the individuality of
personality would not be denied by a single personality theorist. The trouble is, however, that within that
concept several degrees of individuality may be distinguished, and it is around these degrees that all
disagreement centers. For the present, they may be
conceived as arranged according to one dimension
characterized by the contrasting concepts nomothetic
and idiographic (Allport, 1937). Other concepts frequently used in this context are indicated with the
terms subjective, unique, and idiosyncratic. We shall
deal with those concepts later. For convenience let us
turn to the nomothetic approach first.

Probably the clearest example of this approach
may be found in Cattell's trait theory. According to
that theory individuality is demonstrated by the values (scores) that individuals obtain on  a large number of traits. Together those trait values determine
an individual's actions in particular situations. As

has been pointed out before, Cattell assumes particular traits to possess fixed predictive validities
with respect to behavior in a given situation. In other words, individuality is demonstrated merely in
trait values (scores) but not in the way traits are
applied in a given situation. The point is demonstrated clearly in the specification equation, in which
trait scores are represented as *individual* parameters,
but trait regression weights are represented as *general* parameters.

Obviously, with respect to the latter issue
Cattell's position is at variance with interactionism
because it is too deterministic. It neither leaves
room for the individual to react to the psychological
meaning the situation has for him, nor for processes
of feedback to occur in order to create a further
specification of the situation. More pronounced forms
of individualization appear to be necessary to fit
interactionistic theory construction. The question is:
which form?

As mentioned earlier there are at least three
possible answers to that question, namely uniqueness,
subjectivity or idiosyncrasy. In an attempt to clarify
and further delimit these concepts, use will be made
here of descriptions of personality theories supplied
by Hjelle and Ziegler (1976), who have analyzed several well-known theories with respect to the issue of
subjectivity versus objectivity.

*Uniqueness* is usually associated with Allport's
trait theory, in which the uniqueness of personality
is strongly emphasized. To Allport, a person's individuality goes so far that it becomes manifest in the
structural units that constitute personality. Allport
makes a distinction between general and individual
traits and considers the latter to be of utmost importance for the description of the individual. Personal dispositions or morphogenic traits determine individual behavior in addition to common traits, but
they pre-eminently determine differences in behavior
*between* individuals. Incidentally, this does *not* imply
that individuals differ in the way they experience
the world around them: in Allport's conception uniqueness does not imply subjectivity. Uniqueness consists
in behavioral dispositions, not in experiential qualities. Uniqueness and subjectivity come closely together in the so-called *proprium*, determining the areas
of life experienced by the individual as especially
his own. Nevertheless, according to Hjelle and Ziegler,
subjectivity is not even there to be considered a key

concept for the understanding of personality.

Quite another picture is presented by the cognitive-phenomenological personality theories. In Kelly's personal construct theory, for instance, the world of the individual is almost entirely subjective. However the individual constructs external events, he will always remain the prisoner of his *subjective* construct system. Objective reality is always filtered by the constructive apparatus: reality is what a person constructs to be reality. The world may change only in so far as the individual is prepared to construct changes.

Roger's self theory is dominated by the subjectivity assumption as well as Kelly's. According to him, each individual lives in a rich, continuously changing private world in the center of which he finds himself. The world is perceived in his terms and the same terms determine his reactions. An individual's conception of a particular event is not only determined by permanent individual dispositions in the sense of Allport, but depends on temporary factors as moods, previous events and plans as well. Human actions can be understood only if we attempt to look *inside* the person and try to see the world from his point of view.

Different from the above position is that of Freud, who indeed acknowledged the 'private world' of the individual, but did not consider it to be the basis of personality. Uniqueness and subjectivity are determined ultimately by objective issues like parental behavior, hereditary givens and social norms. Personality, in Freud's view, develops on the basis of physiological growth and, in addition, the frustrations, conflicts and threats, causing tensions to occur in the organism. Individuality should finally be seen as the resultant of biological powers in the id and the ego's rationality. On that basis an individual combination of objective forces is accomplished, without uniqueness in terms of individual dispositions or subjectivity in terms of individual meanings turning the scale. Freud's position regarding individuality can neither be qualified as subjective nor as unique, it is *idiosyncratic*. That term may be described according to Wolman's (1973) definition of idiosyncrasy as 'A characteristic peculiar to an individual that can be attributed to any general psychological factor'.

To summarize this discussion on individuality it may be stated that nomothetic individuality - weak individuality - is restricted to individual values or

scores in otherwise general elements of personality.
On the other hand, uniqueness and subjectivity - both
forms of strong individuality - are connected with
individualization of personality elements themselves.
The third form, idiosyncrasy, takes an intermediate
position. It is in agreement with the nomothetic position  in that personality elements are conceived
as general elements. But it is in disagreement with
that position in assuming that *relationships between
elements* are subject to individualization. Thus, for
instance, the regression weights in Cattell's specification equation would not be assumed to be equal
over individuals. In table 4 the claims of the different positions are briefly summarized.

| *Individuality* | Elements | Relations between elements | Element values |
|---|---|---|---|
| Nomothetic | General | General | Individual |
| Idiosyncratic | General | Individual | Individual |
| Idiographic | Individual | Individual | Individual |

Table 4. *Individualization typology*

The subjectivity as well as the uniqueness position are both considered to be idiographic ways of the
orizing about personality. Both positions take strongly individualized personality into account. The difference among them may be clarified with the aid of
the symbolic behavior structure or SRS-matrix as developed here. The subjectivity position would claim
different situation  concepts ($S_y$) for each individual, so in our terminology each individual would have available his own private $S_y$-structure. The uniqueness position, on the other hand, would claim different behavioral dispositions for each individual,
which in the present terminology would imply individual sets of transformation rules ($R_y$). Idiosyncrasy
is a moderate form of individualization, referring
to the mere presence or absence in the individual
structure of general $S_y$'s and $R_y$'s, as well as to the
individualized relationships between particular $S_y$'s

on the one hand and $R_y$'s on the other.

To locate the present theory in the context of individualization is rather complicated. It should be kept in mind, first, that in any interactionistic theory two systems are important, viz. the organismic system and the environmental system. Whether a theorist comes to formulate a nomothetic, idiographic or any other form of personality theory depends on a number of additional considerations, connected with the assumptions he is prepared to make regarding the two systems. Two issues appear to be specially relevant in this context i.e. the *generality* issue and the *dominance* issue. If one of the two systems is assumed to function according to general laws and the other on a private incidental basis, it may be stated that:

a. If the more general system dominates the other, the organism will function according to a nomothetic model, no matter whether the organism or the environment dominates.
b. If the least general system dominates, the organism will function according to an idiographic model, again no matter which system dominates.

The position taken here with respect to both issues is quite clear, but that does not immediately solve the problem of individuality. With regard to the generality issue, we did not conform to the current idea that the individual has to resort to private means in order to behave adaptively in a general and lawful world. Earlier we had assumed the individual's behavior to be mainly based on general - notably intersubjective - means, whereas we have been reluctant to make any strong assumption regarding the true nature of the environment. This means that the dominance issue becomes crucial for our position with respect to the nature of individuality. However, on that issue we have taken an intermediate stand in assuming continuity to be located at the control level. The major implication of that position is that personality is defined here in terms of general elements that are connected on an individual basis. That means that the open system theory is basically *idiosyncratic*, rather than nomothetic or idiographic.

To illustrate this conclusion in more detail we may have a closer look at the effects of the product assumptions made earlier. Each of these assumptions produces the effect of individualizing the personality structure. Thus, for instance, assumption 5.1.3.1

concerns an increasing differentiation of the SRS-
structure. In the course of development the individual will increasingly have at his disposal a system
of situation distinctions on the basis of discriminative cues. He will also have available an increasing
set of response distinctions in terms of alternative
transformation rules, to be discriminated on the basis of elementary changes occurring successively during transformational activities. The permanent character of these developments as well as their generality make us conceive of differentiation as a *general
process of growth*.

It must, however, be realized that differentiation will not become manifest equally strongly in all
areas of the symbolic behavior structure. Dependent
on the 'relevance' of certain areas for the individual (or his milieu) differentiation may be expected to
occur strongly in some areas and be entirely absent in
others. Therefore, we assume that the general *process*
of differentiation will lead to specific *products* of
differentiation within each individual. Earlier we
had defined the structure in which differentiation
takes place  as superindividual, so we should speak
here of *specific* products to be attributed to *general* factors. Differentiation thus leads to idiosyncratic personality structures.

Assumption 5.1.3.2, the experience assumption,
refers to the processes of integration occurring in
the structure of behavior as a consequence of repeated confrontations with the same situation. The studies (cited in section 4.1) on which support for this
assumption was based, are all of an essentially nomothetic character. Individual differences are assumed to exist only with respect to the level of skill-
acquisition each individual has reached; however,the
learning process as such is supposed to be of a general nature. This view has been adopted here, so we
assume skill training to be a *general process of
growth*. Since, however, the areas (situations) in
which skill training occurs will show an enormous
variety in daily life, we must assume that the experience assumption leads to idiosyncratic developments
in the symbolic structures of the individual.

Differentiation and integration together determine the general competence  which is at the individual's disposal at any given moment. Competence basically indicates and provides the means and ends of
adaptive behavior, and it thus constitutes the basis
for individual behavior to gain control over the en-

vironment. But in view of the fact that no two situations are perfectly equal, that the circumstances never repeat themselves exactly, general competence is
frequently insufficient as a condition to maintain
control. Over and above this the individual has the
possibility to maximize competence by means of special processes directed at change in the states of a
number of subsystems. We assume that in everyday life
these processes will function on a continuous basis
and that they will cease to function only after prolonged exposure, to perfectly monotonous and redun-
dant environments. Maximizing, again, functions by
means of general mechanisms that are being applied in
specific situations.

Product assumption 5.1.3.3 refers to the results
of the application of S.T.-mechanisms in such situations. That assumption leads to the expectation of individual couplings to be established between general
situation concepts ($S_y$) and general S.T.-mechanisms,
so that once again an idiosyncratic moment is added
to the structure of personality. Extrapolated to the
total structure this implies that for each $S_y$ in his
SRS-structure an individual has an individually preferent S.T.-mechanism to be applied in case of disequilibrium within that $S_y$.

In case the S.T.-mechanisms do not provide sa-
tisfactory results, disruption processes may start
functioning to minimize noncontrol in the future.
These processes are assumed to function on a very discontinuous basis, and to leave behind deep traces in
the individual's symbolic structures. The nature and
the extent of these effects may be inferred from the
different assumptions of the open system theory. According to that theory personality does *not* develop
spontaneously as a consequence of individual biological or spiritual powers, but is conceived as the result of the system of relations with the world which
the individual engages in and maintains. In such a
context, strong individualization can only be understood on the basis of a special kind of confrontation
of the individual and a unique environment.

The uniqueness of the environment is recognized
in the relationship individual - environment by the
occurrence of a permanent disturbance of equilibrium.
The disruption reaction that consequently takes place causes $S_x$- and/or $R_x$-elements to be included in
the individual's symbolic behavior structure. At this

point, it might be concluded that the development just
mentioned will cause strong individualization to occur in the structure of personality either in the
form of subjectivity or uniqueness. However, for the
present, one single confrontation as described is not
assumed to lead to such far-reaching consequences.
Granted the event in question was very traumatic in
the sense that the individual's disruption reaction
was strong, the permanent effects upon personality
will usually be diminished. After the event has occurred, information processing activities will be
started within the individual to 'translate' the traumatic event in terms of the existing structure.

To speculate a bit further about these processing activities we may look at behavior in a strongly
threatening situation. Initially, a situation like
that will cause fear, which as we saw in the previous chapter, will lead to some sort of random sampling
of $S_x$-elements (cues) to be included in the existing
$S_y$-structure. As a consequence, the individual will
henceforth show a heightened sensitivity to threat
cues. Presumably, those cues will figure in the symbolic structure in a number of divergent $S_y$'s, so
that consequently those $S_y$'s will from then on be u-
tilized with more than the usual caution. On that basis a process of stimulus generalization may be assumed to occur in the system, resulting in *avoidance*
behavior in a number of situations corresponding more
or less to the original traumatic $S_x$.

However, if the individual is not confronted
with that $S_x$ a second time, we must assume that the
consequences of the traumatic experience will be restricted to the effects mentioned. Processes of information exchange and thinking will serve to restore
the elements of the $S_y$-structure in their original
shape. The residual of the traumatic experience will
finally consist of a certain amount of idiosyncrasy
of the personality structure but it will not lead to
a stronger form of individualization.

The argument concerning a threatening situation
may be applied analogously to a situation in which
the individual becomes helpless. *Extinction* of $R_x$ as
a result of disruption will be generalized by way of
processes of response generalization to those $R_y$'s
that have elements in common with the $R_x$. The same

type of reasoning can finally be applied to the consequences of frustration. If a particular intended
goal fails to be achieved and disruption occurs, the
original $S_{y_2}$ will be replaced in the symbolic structure by new $S_{y_2}$'s having elements in common with the
result that was obtained ($S_{x_2}$). Thus *distraction* as a
consequence of frustration finally amounts to a shift
in the goal structure of the matrix in terms of existing elements, whereas the original strong individualization reaction disappears.

To summarize then, it is assumed here that panic reactions, either in the form of fear, helplessness or frustration will have scattered disruptive
effects, finally leading to a shift of the individual's preference regarding the existing symbolic elements $S_{y_1}$, $R_y$ or $S_{y_2}$.

With respect to the primary disruptive effects,
an additional comment may be made. Earlier we have
assumed an intersubjective basis to exist  to determine the amount of agreement or disagreement between
symbolic elements by means of cue similarity. On that
basis it is possible to more or less exactly determine the nature of the original disruptive condition,
by systematically scanning the effects of the disruption upon a larger number of symbolic elements. In
clinical practice a principle like that is applied in
the determination of anxiety hierarchies in phobic
patients.

The final effects of panic states can, according
to the position taken here, usually be interpreted in
terms of existing symbolic elements, the relations
among which are changed and individualized by means
of panic. So the conclusion must be  that the pertinent product assumption (5.1.3.4) leads to an increase in *idiosyncrasy*, as do the other product assumptions. However, a restriction should be made regarding this conclusion, in that it hinges on the assumption that the original strong individualization
effects of panic will gradually disappear. In some
circumstances this is not to be expected, especially
if the individual is repeatedly confronted with the
same traumatic condition to which he keeps reacting
with panic over and over again. In such a case a permanent change must be expected that goes beyond mere
idiosyncrasy: permanent subjectivity or permanent
uniqueness will enter the symbolic structure and
start to govern subsequent behavior.

In and of itself this does not necessarily constitute a problem, but one of the consequences will
be that parts of the symbolic structure are thus deprived of communication with the speech community.
The individual has to face his adaptation problems all
alone and if he does not manage to solve them, severe
disturbances may arise, eventually leading to psychopathology. It is important to point out here that
within the context of the open system theory individuality is conceived as idiosyncrasy. Stronger forms of
individuality do not lend themselves directly to description in terms of the theory: they may at best be
illuminated 'against the background' of it. Later, in
section 5.4, we will come back to this issue.

The preceding pages have made it clear that under each of the product assumptions individuality is
established as the result of interactions between individual and environment. Therefore the question becomes relevant of how far innate individual characteristics may determine the result of those interactions. Put otherwise, the question is whether innate
powers in the organism have steering effects upon the
*nature* of individualization to be brought about in
personality development. Although decisive evidence
on this issue is lacking, we expect innate personality constants to be active primarily in the processes
mentioned under assumptions 5.1.2.4 and 5.1.2.5: the
maximizing and minimizing assumptions. With respect
to the effects of S.T.-mechanisms and disruption mechanisms we have taken an interactionistic position,
in the sense that specific couplings with situation
concepts are assumed to exist. But that does not alter the fact that differences resulting from the individual learning history  might in part be determined by an innate general preference or base rate of
those mechanisms. One argument to support that statement is the fact that those mechanisms are supposed
to be largely regulated by physiological processes.

Empirical evidence on the issue may be derived
from research with animals specially bred to excel in
very specific task situations, as, for instance, Tryon's (1942) $S_1$- and $S_3$-strains that were maximally
different in maze-brightness. Under the assumption
that a task like maze learning makes specific demands
with respect to the adaptive mechanisms of the animal, one might start looking for systematic differences regarding those mechanisms. A number of studies
has been directed at this issue. Thus, for instance,
Krech (1932) found that maze-bright and maze-dull

rats differed in the amount of purposeful 'hypothesis'-behavior. Searle (1949) noted differences in to-
lerance of ambiguity. Vossen (1966) found differences
in the tendency to explore. Obviously, some relationship exists between those findings and the mechanisms
distinguished here, so the possibility of some kind
of inheritable 'preference' in relation to adaptive
S.T.-mechanisms should be kept open.

The question whether the preference for particular disruption mechanisms is due to heredity is perhaps at least as important, but seems even harder to
answer in the absence of research in that area. Within the present context the most plausible outcome of
such research would not be the identification of a
general panic type, but rather a differential preference for particular disruptive states to occur.

5.3  *Assessment and prediction: personality as a stra-
     tegic-tactical coalition*

Traditionally, personality theories comprise a
number of relevant assumptions systematically related to each other, as well as a set of empirical definitions pertinent to personality structure and
functioning. Some important assumptions of the open
system theory have been set out and elaborated with
respect to their structural effects upon individual
functioning. What is still lacking is the formulation
of empirical or operational definitions to make the
theory accessible for empirical research and testing
experiments. Within the present context, it would obviously be best to try and measure the effects of all
product assumptions directly and separately. Thus,
the amount of differentiation and integration of each
separate part of the symbolic structure would be established as well as the distinct effects of S.T.-con-
ditioning and disruption generalization upon each element of that structure.

However, personality is conceived as a complex
whole of idiosyncratic relationships, that has been
established as an amalgamation of the successive effects of a number of basic processes. To disentangle
all separate causes and effects of those processes is
completely impossible. In order to try and unravel at
least the effects, an artifice has to be resorted to.
A closer study of the product assumptions shows that
the effects of the assumptions apparently have some
mutual overlaps. On that basis it should be possible
to look for the combined effects of more than one product assumption, in order to attempt and direct mea-

surement procedures to such shared areas of personality. An approach like this could lead to operational definitions doing justice to each of the product assumptions, albeit in an *indirect* way.

An additional requirement is a practical one. To enhance utility of the theory for practical purposes, the empirical definitions should be chosen in such a way as to allow for connections with concrete situations to be made. As has been pointed out earlier, the individual is assumed to take an active and structuring position with respect to the environment. While dealing with the environment, the individual utilizes directives and mechanisms aimed at maintaining and enlarging control over the environment. It seems only logical to define the personality system empirically by systematically mapping out those directives a mechanisms in connection with a number of situations.

As a first suggestion it is proposed here to partition empirical definitions of the personality system into two different groups of definitions. The first group is connected with the product assumptions 5.1.3.1, 5.1.3.2 and 5.1.3.4: the differentiation assumption, the experience assumption and the disruption-generalization assumption. The reason for dealing with these three assumptions together is that they are supposed to have joint effects upon the system. Assumptions 5.1.3.1 and 5.1.3.2 are connected with discriminations and generalizations of the elements of the symbolic structure. They pertain to the question of which elements are distinghuished within the individual's sets of $S_y$'s and $R_y$'s respectively. The structure as a whole serves to connect and to disconnect situation definitions and transformation rules.

In addition, the symbolic structure indicates which $S_y$'s are preferred as well as which means are preferably used to obtain the preferent $S_y$'s. At this point the contribution of assumption 5.1.3.4 must be emphasized as well. The effects of this assumption are partly demonstrated as alterations of the individual's preference for particular initial situations, transformations and final situations. Thus, the symbolic structure established as a joint product of the three assumptions mentioned  may be defined as an individual indicator of behavioral *opportunities*, as well as of behavioral *preferences* on the basis of a survey of situations and transformations.

The second group of empirical definitions is especially connected with assumption 5.1.3.3, the S.T.-

conditioning assumption. Contrary to the three assumptions mentioned, this assumption does not pertain to the symbolic structure as a whole or to large areas of that structure, but rather to small segments, notably to separate rows, columns and cells of the matrix. Behavioral *preference* is not primarily what is involved here, but rather the *course* of behavior once an initial behavioral choice has been made. S.T.-mechanisms play a major part in the establishment of links between organism and environment and in maintaining control as well as restoring control in states of disequilibrium. Thus, these mechanisms may cause major deviations to occur in the course of behavior as compared with a line of action as preferred initially.

The first group of empirical definitions refers to *what* the individual wants and does, whereas the most important question with respect to the second group is, *how* the actions are carried out to maintain control. The first group of definitions refers to the *simultaneous* weighing of options, the second group refers to the *successive* determination of the direction of actions within chosen options. These formulations with respect to the two groups of operational definitions show a strong resemblance to what is generally conceived as the *strategic* and the *tactical* point of view. Therefore, it is proposed here to further define the measurement procedures of personality variables in the framework of the open system theory in terms of strategic and tactical aspects of behavior.

In the context of theory of games a strategy is defined as a set of personal rules for playing the game (Von Neumann & Morgenstern, 1944). Cronbach and Gleser (1957) have described strategy as a set of conditional probabilities determining the chance of an event Y, given an antecedent event X. Miller *et al.* (1960) have defined strategy and tactics as the molar versus the molecular elements in the organization of behavior. A more detailed definition may be found in Clausewitz (1974), who gave both concepts currency originally in 1832 within the context of warfare. In Clausewitz' view, tactics refer to the organization of activities within a limited field of objects, whereas strategy refers to an unlimited field of possibilities. Tactical activities occur successively, strategy on the other hand utilizes the available potential simultaneously.

The difference between the two concepts is clearly demonstrated by Clausewitz on the basis of the

reserve held in readiness during a battle. Tactical
reserves serve the purpose of prolonging a battle for
some time in case it would otherwise be lost. Strategic reserves on the contrary are created as a weapon
against unexpected developments: the amount of strategic reserve is a direct function of the amount of
uncertainty existing initially with respect to the
course of the battle. Transposed into behavioral
terms strategy refers to broad behavioral opportunities as well as to behavioral preferences existing
before the actual execution of behavior is started,
whereas tactics refer to smaller mini-decisions for
adjusting behavior during behavioral execution.

Strategy is obviously connected with individual
discriminations and generalizations as well as individual preferences. With regard to his environment
the individual has available behavioral information
on the basis of his culture as well as his private
experience. That information may be conceived as a
set of conditional probabilities referring to the occurrence of particular consequent situations on the
basis of particular antecedent situations as well as
particular transformations applied to those situations. The matrix containing that information supposedly determines the individual's strategy, in that it
offers insight into the possibilities and impossibi-
lities of certain activities and permits weighted
comparison of several activities in processes of directed thinking. It is proposed, then, to take the
view that the *individual SRS-matrix represents the
strategic behavioral aspect*.

The individual SRS-matrix is not to be confused
with the exploitative system (table 2) although obviously there are points of similarity. The individual SRS-matrix is conceived as an idiosyncratic structure, i.e. a structure the elements of which may be
defined in general terms, whereas the relations between the elements are viewed as individualized. The
margins of the matrix are occupied by situations as
distinguished by culture. These situations are ordered on the basis of the amount of agreement existing
among the cues used to define each of them: the more
correspondence between the cues, the closer together
situations are.

In the body of the matrix two types of information are represented: preference values and transformation rules. The preference values are considered to
be conditional values, indicating the individual preference for transforming an initial situation $S_{y_1}$ into

a final situation $S_{y2}$. These values are conceived to
be joint products of general cultural preference acquired by processes of information transfer, as well
as of individual preference established on the basis
of individual learning processes. The transformation
rules are defined in general terms, whereas their relative positions in a response hierarchy are supposed
to be the product of general cultural information as
well as individual experience.

The tactical aspect of behavior is established
mainly on the basis of S.T.-mechanisms operating within the context of a particular situation. Tactical aspects may be represented in terms of the SRS-matrix as
well as strategic aspects because they are assumed to
be effective in connection with symbolic elements.
They can be represented as a vector running parallel
to the $S_{y1}$-vector in the margin of the matrix. Tactical aspects of behavior may of course be studied in
their own right. However, if one wishes to use them
for the prediction of overt behavior in concrete situations, they must be connected with the strategic
aspects. The very idea that tactics may influence a
previously determined strategy  is a point of view
that was already expounded by Clausewitz. But that
influence is far from unrestrained.

The impact of tactics may be demonstrated by considering the alterations occurring in a strategy on
the basis of each of the S.T.-mechanisms. Hence we
shall once again have to bring in the S.T.-structure
as represented in table 3. On the basis of that table
it may be concluded that the impact of tactics is a
function of the phase in which the S.T.-mechanism o-
perates in terms of the U.C.-structure: 'earlier'
mechanisms have more radical effects than 'later' mechanisms. Another conclusion that can be drawn is
that *primary* strategic alterations will occur only as
a consequence of S.T.-mechanisms operating directly
upon symbolic elements, viz. reflection, uncoupling
and redirection. The other mechanisms (exploration,
substitution and persistence) may alter the strategy
only as a derivative of primary alterations on the
basis of couplings existing with symbolic elements.

A closer inspection of the effects of S.T.-me-
chanisms upon the initial strategy reveals that four
different kinds of shift may occur in the SRS-matrix.
Initially, a single cell of the matrix is involved,
in which a particular $R_y$ is chosen to transform the
$S_{y1}$ in the left margin into the corresponding $S_{y2}$ in

the top margin. A first alteration takes place if the $S_{y_1}$ is replaced by a new $S_{y_1}$', thus causing a *vertical shift* to occur with respect to the pertinent cell. If, on the other hand, $S_{y_2}$ is replaced by a new $S_{y_2}$', a *horizontal shift* will become manifest. If both $S_{y_1}$ and $S_{y_2}$ are replaced, the *shift* will be *diagonal*. And, finally, the alteration may be restricted to the original cell, when the $R_y$ is merely *replaced* by another $R_y$ without any alteration occurring regarding $S_{y_1}$ or $S_{y_2}$. In terms of the four possible alterations the effects of each of the S.T.-mechanisms may be derived from table 3, taking the distinction between primary alterations and derived alterations into account. The results are brought together in table 5.

*Strategic shift*

| S.T.-mechanism | Vertical | Within cell | Horizontal | Diagonal | None |
|---|---|---|---|---|---|
| Reflection | x | 0 | 0 | 0 | – |
| Exploration | – | 0 | 0 | – | x |
| Uncoupling | – | x | 0 | – | – |
| Substitution | – | – | 0 | – | x |
| Redirection | – | – | x | – | – |
| Persistence | – | – | – | – | x |

Table 5. *Strategic shifts as a consequence of several S.T.-mechanisms*

x = Primary alteration
0 = Derived alteration
– = No alteration

It becomes clear, then, that there are some striking differences with respect to the 'predictive validity' of each of the mechanisms. Thus, under persistence the initial strategy will remain essentially unchanged and under redirection a horizontal shift will occur in the matrix. Under uncoupling, however, a within cell shift *will* occur, but in addition a horizontal shift *may* occur as well. Under substitution a horizontal shift *may* occur. Under reflection a vertical shift *will* occur initially, but

all other shifts *may* consequently take place. And,
finally, under exploration a within cell shift *may*
occur as well as a horizontal shift, but neither *must*.

   To demonstrate in a very concrete way how the
S.T.-mechanisms function and what their strategic effects may be, two examples will be worked out in some
detail. The first example refers to a man who is driving his car to another town, in order to attend a
meeting. On his way the engine of his car suddenly
cuts out and refuses to start again. The question is
what our man will do:
1. Try and get a lift to be at the meeting in good
   time.
2. Get help to have his car repaired.
3. Keep starting the car long enough to get it running again.
4. Walk to the nearest town to catch the train.
5. Try and repair the car himself.

   The purpose of this example is to show that all
actions mentioned may originate from *the same strategy*, provided that the strategy is 'modulated' by
*different S.T.-mechanisms*. Let us assume the strategy to take the form as presented in table 6.

$S_{y_2}$

|  | Late at meeting | At meeting on time | Back home |
|---|---|---|---|
| Car is out of order |  | Get lift | Have car repaired |
| Drive to meeting | Take train | Start car ――――――― Get lift ――――――― Repair car | Have car repaired ――――― Take train |

$S_{y_1}$ (row group label)

Table 6. *Strategy in a break-down*
         *situation*

The initial situation is the same in all cases, namely 'by car, driving to a meeting'. The final situation is equally the same in all cases, viz. 'be at
the meeting on time'. The activity our man is involved
in at the time of the break-down is called 'driving'.
   After the car has stopped, a state of disequili-

brium is assumed to occur and several S.T.-mechanisms
may serve to restore equilibrium. In the case of *persistence* repeated attempts will be made to start the
car. Under *substitution* other elements will be inserted in the same general plan, such as pulling out the
choke, jamming down the accelerator, waiting some time before a new starting attempt, and so on. Under
*uncoupling* this kind of behavior is abandoned in favor of other possibilities for getting to the meeting
time, for instance try and get a lift. As can be noted in table 6 that activity is located in the same
cell as the initial behavior. If *exploration* is the
S.T.-mechanism set to work, the engine may be checked
to provide additional cues that may serve as a basis
for behavior. Starting from that new information the
man may either repair the car himself and try to be
at the meeting on time yet ($S_{y_2}$ is maintained: within cell shift), or have the car repaired and give up
the meeting to go home ($S_{y_2}$ is altered: horizontal
shift).

Under *redirection* the driver just assumes that
the situation cannot be changed ($S_{y_1}$ is maintained),
he will divert his original goal into 'being late at
the meeting' ($S_{y_2}$ is altered: horizontal shift) and
will take the train. *Reflection*, finally, results in
a re-appraisal of the initial situation: the driver
comes to realize that his car has broken down and
that he will have to get a lift to be at the meeting
on time (vertical shift). The example shows that an
impending loss of control may be averted in several
ways by means of each of a number of S.T.-mechanisms.

The situation selected for the example refers
to a mechanical defect, but in the domain of interpersonal behavior combining the effects of strategy
and tactics may be illuminating as well. Let us sup-
pose for instance that two married couples Smith and
Jones spend their holidays in France. They have been
using Smith's car. On the evening before the last day
they are all together in a very pleasant atmosphere.
Suddenly Smith announces that he wants to spend his
last day in France visiting the Louvre in order to
look at the famous paintings in all peace and quiet.
His wife is willing to join him, but it's a different
matter with the Joneses. They are all set to spend
the last day of their vacation in the open air and go
swimming. After Smith's proposal that they visit the
museum some friction arises, finally escalating into
an impending quarrel. What is Smith going to do?

1. Leave their lodging and let things drift (escape).
2. Repeat his proposal in order to reach a better understanding (reformulate).
3. Acquiesce in the Joneses'wishes (conform).
4. Propose a visit to the museum in the morning followed by an afternoon swim, which implies that
   both plans will come to nothing (compromise).
5. Explain his own motives extensively and ask for
   background information regarding the Joneses'plans,
   in order to come to a joint decision (confrontation).
6. State that he and his wife will go to the museum
   anyway, so that the others will have to go to their
   destination all by themselves (coercion).
(The six reactions as distinguished here, have been
 adopted from a study by Caminada, 1978).
     Once more, a general strategy is assumed to
exist, represented in table 7.

$$S_{y_2}$$

|  |  | Visit museum + go swimming | Visit museum to-gether | Do any-thing to-gether | Visit museum alone |
|---|---|---|---|---|---|
| $S_{y_1}$ | On holi-day with friends | Compro-mise | propose ------ reformu-late ------ confront | confront ------ conform | Escape |
|  | Acquain-tances taken along |  | coercion |  |  |

Table 7. *Strategy in a conflict situation*

The initial situation $(S_{y_1})$ is supposed to be equal
in all cases, viz. 'spending holidays with friends'.
The final situation $(S_{y_2})$ is described as 'visiting
the museum together' and the transformation rule is
defined as 'proposing to go to the museum'.

After the proposal is not warmly received, Smith might *persist* and repeat his proposal, thus essential- ly not altering his strategy. He might also *substitu- te* and reformulate his proposal again leaving his strategy unaltered. If *uncoupling* occurs, the origi- nal $R_y$ will be replaced by an $R_y$ from the same cell, in this case confrontation. Under *redirection* a hori- zontal shift will occur, resulting for instance in a compromise proposal directed at a new $S_{y_2}$ (visit the museum *and* go swimming). *Reflection* would cause a vertical shift to occur: $S_{y_1}$ is replaced and Smith resorts to coercion. Under *exploration* a horizontal shift might take place, leading for instance to con- frontation, or to escape from the conflict situation.

In this example a particular S.T.-mechanism has been intentionally provided with several response op- portunities, to make it perfectly clear that the strategic-tactical approach does not generally lead to unequivocal predictions. The prediction model is basically of a probabilistic nature, so that it leads to predictions merely in terms of *response probabili- ties*.

An important issue in the context of empirical defi- nition is the assessment of a person's strategy and tactics in a more general sense. One of the major questions to be answered in that context is concerned with the methods to be used to gather the information. This question has to be answered by the theory itself, although in personality theorizing this has been the exception rather than the rule.

Ever since Campbell and Fiske (1959), thinking about methods of data collection in personality re- search has been going through an important phase of growth and re-appraisal. Early investigators usually started out from the assumption that different me- thods of data collection should basically lead to the same knowledge about the individual. Thus, for in- stance, it had been presupposed for a long time that data, gathered with respect to the same individuals by means of ratings and self-ratings, should converge and essentially lead to the same result. However, it has gradually become clear that this requirement is un realistic since it is based on too narrow a concepti- on of personality as an object of knowledge (cf. e.g. Hettema, 1979).

The problem of method variance has been further emphasized in the work of Fiske (1971), who no longer conceives of method variance as sheer error variance, but advocates attaching a specific meaning to each method, in connection with the personality theory in the content of which the method is being utilized. In this connection, instead of methods of data collection, Fiske prefers to speak of *modes*. When gathering information on persons one may utilize several modes, such as self-ratings, descriptions of direct experience, performance measures, ratings, behavior observations and physiological measures.

The problem is, now, how to decide which mode should be used in the context of which theory? This question may well be one of the most important questions to be asked by contemporary personality investigators. To answer that question is generally far from simple. In a very global sense the research strategy to be employed here may be adopted from the strategies devised some decades ago to investigate questions concerning construct validity. However, a large difference exists, since instead of a measure we are talking about a mode here, and instead of a concept we are talking about a theory.

A recent study by the present author has been directed at the question which of two modes - ratings or self-ratings - is best suited to represent the concepts of a particular theory, in this case, trait theory. In that study, two criteria were assumed to be particularly relevant for the trait measurement model: internal consistency and external consistency of the measures. These two criteria were especially emphasized in a comparative study of the trait character of rating and self-rating scales. The data were borrowed from studies directed at the construction of personality questionnaires in the Netherlands during the last seven years (the studies added up to 30 rating scales and 51 self-rating scales). The analysis of these data led to some puzzling results: internal consistency was clearly superior in rating scales, but external consistency was generally higher in self-rating scales! On the basis of additional evidence it was concluded that rating scales did agree better with the trait measurement model as compared to self-rating scales, although the latter showed higher external consistencies.

Subsequently an attempt was made to outline the theoretical framework in which self-ratings should preferably be used. It was concluded that self-ratings primarily refer to the *intentions* of the self-rater, rather than to his *judgments*. The self-rater presumably exposes the actions he would intend and the results he would prefer, instead of giving a rationalistic account of his 'real behavior'. This interpretation of self-rating behavior provides a nice explanation for phenomena that are ususally found in self-rating research, as, for instance, social desirability and the subject's tendency to complain. In the study mentioned both phenomena are explained as the expressions of intentionality (rather than reality) supposedly dominating the answers in self-rating procedures (Hettema, 1979).

This interpretation of self-rating behavior is particularly relevant in the present context, because it indicates which mode should preferably be utilized to measure the strategic aspects of behavior. As has been pointed out before, the individual strategy is based on the exploitative system, i.e. a culturally determined matrix referring to the partitioning and transformation of the environment. In addition it has become clear that the transfer of elements of that system to individual members of the community is dominated by linguistic activities. Furthermore it has been indicated how semantic memory may be conceived as an intersubjective reference system for individual behavior. Thus, within the context of the present theory, the obvious thing to do is to determine the strategic aspect of an individual's behavior by means of language. The mode that comes to mind first, then, is the self-rating mode, through which the individual may indicate which transformation rules he would prefer in which situations as well as which alterations he would like to achieve.

Our analysis of self-rating behavior has lent support to this approach, in that self-ratings appeared to emphasize intentional aspects of behavior even if they are constructed to measure traits. Thus we are led to the proposition to determine an individual's strategy by means of the *mode of self-rating*. More specifically, it is proposed to construct a strategic questionnaire of a special format, roughly corresponding to the exploitative system represented in table 2. To be of some generality the questionnaire has to be based on a taxonomy of situations to be located in the margins, as well as on a taxonomy of transformation rules to be placed in the body of the matrix. After such provisions have been made, it may become possible to determine the strategy by asking the individual to indicate his preference for particular goal situations as well as for particular transformation rules to be used to attain those situations.

With respect to the tactical aspects of behavior self-ratings are not considered to be the adequate mode to establish those aspects. Tactical aspects refer to inner states and inner processes, of which it has been pointed out (in section 3.2.) that they are presumably not accessible to introspection and that they cannot be transferred by verbal means.

Attempts, within an interactionistic context, to transfer those states by verbal means anyway, have led to the development of so-called S-R questionnaires of anxiety (Endler, c.s., 1962) and of hostility (Endler, c.s., 1968). Although these studies must be considered of major relevance for the development of the interactionistic position as such, it has never been explicitly ascertained that inner states as reported in those questionnaires have manifested themselves outside the questionnaire domain as well. A recent study by van Heck (1979) has been directed at this issue, and has cast considerable doubt on the connection between verbally reported and 'real' states.

It is proposed here to select *psychophysiological measures* as the mode to measure tactical aspects of behavior. In Chapter IV several arguments have been put forward on which this preference may be founded. Notably, recent research in the area of psychophysiology has indicated that it should be possible, after careful research has been completed, to unequivocally assess the operation of S.T.-mechanisms determining the tactical aspects of behavior.

In order to assess an individual's tactics it is essential to select the stimulus material in such a way that reliable and valid measurement is permitted. From the descriptions in Chapter IV concerning the operation of S.T.-mechanisms, it follows that they become manifest merely in states of disequilibrium in *specific situations*. Effects like this may not be expected to occur from verbal descriptions of the situation. As a research tool it is proposed here to use films in which the cues of particular $S_y$'s are represented as accurately as possible. On the basis of a number of studies (cf. Levi, 1972) it has been ascertained that film as a medium is particularly suited to evoke states as meant here.

Within the present context, testing a predictive system based on the individual strategy and individual tactics should be done in real-life situations. A special problem in such a procedure concerns the establishment of the criterion. In agreement with a number of statements made earlier, it is obvious that *behavior observation* is the mode to be used here. In this context observations should be guided by special observational schedules to be established on the basis of the taxonomy of transformation rules as referred to earlier. Furthermore use could be made of the situation taxonomy mentioned, to establish behavioral effects in terms of $S_{y_2}$

Personality assessment by means of behavioral strategies and tactics leads to special forms of psychodiagnostics that must be considered to be much more complicated than psychodiagnostics in the context of psychometric or psychodynamic theorizing. Situation-free assessment is impossible within the framework developed here: any statement concerning individual behavior is conditional.

On the other hand, specific problems concerning placement or treatment do not generally require the individual's entire strategy to be assessed. Usually the assessment of a submatrix will suffice, in which only those situations and behaviors are represented that may be considered relevant in the framework of the pertinent problems.

However, even if these restrictions are taken into account, the diagnostic procedure will always show a larger amount of complexity. If, for example, one only wishes to predict an individual's behavior in a well-defined situation ($S_{y_1}$), a number of possible final situations ($S_{y_2}$) will always have to be involved. Furthermore, a number of initial situations, located taxonomically close to $S_{y_1}$, will always have to be considered. These situations may become relevant as well, as soon as tactical alterations occur in the organization of behavior.

According to the open-system theory behavior has to be viewed as an ongoing stream of activities, proceeding internally as well as externally, including many alterations, shifts with respect to goals as well as means, anchored in a number of situations, figuring now as initial situations, now as final situations. This complexity appears to be adequately tackled only if computer facilities are being used in the diagnostic process. Messick (1972) has pointed out that the computer is especially useful if complex personality models are involved, assuming a dynamic integration of continuously changing probabilistic powers to occur. The general structure of a computer model to  simulate personality may be derived from

the assumptions of the open system theory. Individual
parameters in such a model may be obtained by means
of individual assessment procedures as outlined.

A great advantage of this type of personality
assessment is the fact that it allows for immediate
connections to be established with several kinds of
treatment. Once an individualized computer program
has been developed, it may be fed with divergent
treatments in order to trace the most probable result
under each of them. To be able to do that, treatments
have to be carefully analyzed and translated in terms
of situational cues. The input of the personality system thus consists of situations, situational elements
or sequences of situations, to be processed by the
computer program on an individual basis in terms of
idiosyncratic strategic and tactical mechanisms.

## 5.4  *Psychological adaptation and mental health*

The situation concept as used here is defined at
an intersubjective level, that is to say, we have started from the assumption that situations may be defined in intersubjective terms. However, that does not
imply that all situations are equally important for
every individual. A major feature of an interactionistic theory of personality is the fact that individuals are assumed to establish *idiosyncratic relations*
with situations. From an individual point of view,
situations may thus be categorized according to the
specific relations that are being maintained with
those situations. Such categorizations will demonstrate, then, that individuals are severely restricted
with respect to the number of situations that play a
major role in everyday life conditions.

The individual's radius of action is limited in
the sense that a few situations will occur very often,
whereas a large number of situations will hardly e-
ver be met. Among the former, situations connected
with family life, particular social contacts as well
as work conditions will usually feature prominently.
In these situations a vivid exchange of information
between individual and environment will be accomplished, resulting in a highly differentiated set of behaviors that are affected by minute alterations in
the environmental conditions. The huge amount of experience  gathered by the individual in these situations will undoubtedly lead to a high degree of integration of different situational aspects as well
as elements of behavior. The individual will 'routi-

nize' to a high degree and show an increasing amount
of behavioral efficiency and skill, allowing him to
maintain smooth and uninterrupted relations with these situations,

As well as with this type of situation, every
individual is familiar with a number of situations
causing trouble each time they are met, so that the
quiet of routine will not easily come about. These situations may be found in the area of chronic conditions of life, demanding continuous attention and effort, and to be mastered only if adaptation is continuously maximized by means of S.T.-me-
chanisms. For example, in this context, one might
think of conditions like low level of income, chro-
nically ill or invalid relatives, a study just matching one's powers, an all-demanding job, a trying
relationship with one's next of kin, and so on.

Another group of situations is explicitly avoided either on account of threatening danger, of expected trouble and frustrations, or of the fact that
one is not adequately equipped to meet those situations. The individual might have had bad experiences
with that type of situation so that he has come to
avoid them. He might also have seen his behavior
rewarded negatively in such situations in the past,
and simply does not know how to behave next time. Man
learns and draws conclusions from his experiences. On
that score his radius of action must be assumed to
show retrenchment besides and opposite to expansion,
with the result that his environment as well as his
behavior are continuously further bounded.

A large number of situations is located completely outside the individual's horizon. He might have
gathered some information concerning those situations
from the media or from hearsay, or otherwise, but
he will neither ever meet such situations nor ever
look for them. Thus, those situations will neither
open up new opportunities nor cause any problems with
respect to the individual's psychological adaptation.

Thus far we have dealt with situations that are
either quite familiar or irrelevant with respect to
the individual. But there are other situations that
are especially important because they can be assumed
to cause most of the problems with respect to adaptation. We are referring to *new* situations and to
situations that are *suddenly changed*. In both cases
problems are to be expected since the situations call
on forms of adaptation of a completely different order
from the ones practised till then.

When entering a *new* situation, the individual

will initially show a preference for the S.T.-mecha-
nisms of reflection and exploration to maintain control. These mechanisms are particularly suited to
provide new information through feedback. The individual will usually assume an attitude of expectancy
until the moment is reached for establishing an initial control compromise. Only then is he in a position to perform actions in an attempt to gain control
over the situation. If successful, he may proceed to
expand his control until, finally, the situation is
mastered well enough to look for new information to
be assimilated, and so on. This sequence of activities reveals that in new situations information is to
be gathered before the individual is able to start
processes of directed action. In order to serve as a
basis for directed action, the information has to be
connected with the information already available in
the individual's symbolic structures.

If this condition does not prevail there is a
discrepancy between situational information and environmental control. An important setting in which
such discrepancies presumably occur frequently is the
educational process in the classroom. Pupils are
bound to run into severe adaptational problems,if they
are confronted continuously with knowledge that does
not match the control activities they are used to in
daily life. Mere feedback concerning the correct reproduction of knowledge (outcome feedback) does not
appear to be sufficient to support control. As Hammond and Summers (1972) have shown, the presentation
of information followed by outcome feedback does increase knowledge, but at the same time control regarding the *application* of knowledge is decreased. Knowledge and control appear to go together only if additional information is provided concerning the properties of the task to be performed. Only then is it possible for the pupil to start processes of directed
thinking that are, as we have seen before, essential
for the execution of directed activities and thus for
control.

In education it is not enough to provide feedback. In addition the student should be provided with,
and be urged to use, feedforward activities, in order to
check on the efficacy of his newly acquired knowledge with respect to control. The student who is continually being deprived of this opportunity  will gradually lose confidence and may eventually fall into a
state of panic. As a consequence disruption will occur, leading to processes of either avoidance, extinction or distraction. In such a case the complaint usu-

ally voiced with respect to the student is that he
shows a lack of interest and motivation. However,
what is really going on according to the present theory, is that a relationship has failed to be established between student and learning environment, which
is basically a problem of *adaptation*. The final result of this failure is that the student is being deprived of a considerable amount of cultural information that he might otherwise have used to further
support his psychological adaptation.

From the nature of the failing process it is
quite obvious that it is most likely to occur in students who did have general informational deficiencies
from the start, i.e. socio-culturally deprived students. In educational practice, one of the things to
be done seems to be to provide ample opportunity for
the pupils to carry out their own directed activities
in the framework of the teaching-learning process. A
significant fact in this connection is the present
author's (Hettema, 1972) finding that, among the many
aspects that may be distinguished in teacher behavior,
only one aspect was rejected unanimously by the students, i.e. preventing the students from performing
their own directed activities.

It is assumed here that the phenomena as pointed out in the context of classroom learning will be
of a more general nature, so that in many new situations the relationship between individual and environment will not be established properly. As a result,
many situations will resist attempts to bring them
under control, thus restricting the individual's effective life space.

Even more dramatic developments are to be expected if highly familiar situations are *suddenly changed* with respect to essential aspects, especially if
the individual does not have the opportunity to prepare himself for the alteration to occur. As examples
one might consider the sudden death of close relatives, sudden divorce, serious accidents, dismissal, or
compulsory job transfer. In cases like these, the ap-
peal to adaptation is even stronger as compared with
the confrontationwith new or strange situations. In
his familiar environment the individual had already
established an adaptive relationship on the basis of
many confrontations, involving all the processes of
psychological adaptation, and leading to highly struc-
tured products in terms of differentiation, experience and S.T.-conditioning. If a system like that is
jeopardized on the basis of sudden external alterations, the individual is compelled to introduce major

alterations in the system as well, upon pain of permanent loss of control to occur in that situation.

Being confronted with the altered situation the
individual will soon discover that his usual approach
fails and that other activities are called for. Initially, he may attempt to solve his problem by the use
of tactical S.T.-mechanisms. But if the situational
alteration is considerable, tactical mechanisms will
not provide the right answer and will repeatedly fail
to re-establish control. Finally panic will occur,
leading to specific disruptions of the SRS-matrix, so
that the original strategy is replaced by a new one.
The new strategy may appear to be effective to restore equilibrium and control, either by means of a-
voidance of the situation, by extinction of behaviors
preferred initially, or by distraction from the goals
that had been pursued originally.

However, the problems will mount even higher if
disruption reactions do not lead to a proper solution.
For instance, if the individual has established a
strong tendency to avoid the harmful situation but is
forced by external powers to re-enter it over and
over again. Or, if the individual has the strong tendency *not* to show a particular kind of behavior, but
is forced from outside to enact that behavior each
time he is in the pertinent situation. Or, finally,
if he has turned away from the goals he had initially striven for, but is forced to pursue them again.
Strange as all this may sound, conditions preventing
individuals from disruptive reactions presumably occur very frequently, thus keeping the individual
from establishing new strategies to advance long-term
adaptation.

All situations that show little variablity and
flexibility, that are powerful in the sense of Mischel and that are not easily transformed into new situations, essentially qualify to produce the effects
mentioned. What comes to mind first on seeing this
description is situations like being interned in
jails or in concentration camps, being admitted to
mental institutions, and so on. However, deprivation
of liberty in a physical sense is not at all necessary to create blind-alley conditions.

Wherever the regulation of human existence is
raised to a high level, those living in that condition
always run the risk of getting into adaptational problems on the account mentioned. For instance, many
situations that are hard to live with may be escaped
from and subsequently avoided to solve all the problems that will inevitably occur in those situations.

But in many cultures escape and avoidance behavior
are not encouraged and as a matter of fact are seldom considered acceptable. To escape severe problems in family life, in working conditions or even
social life by flight is generally condemned morally
and considered contrary to social norms as well as to
societal obligations.

If an individual has tried very hard to behave
according to generally accepted rules, but has come
to realize that things just do not work out that way,
he may abandon his initial strategy and call on 'un-
usual' means. But again, society will hasten tell
him that his behavior is incompatible with company
standards, social norms, standards of cooperation,
and the like.

And, finally, if someone lowers his goal standards because he is not capable of attaining them anyway, he will be quickly reminded that the goals in
his job, his school or even his leisure time are to
be lived up to anyhow.

In summary, society is not particularly tolerant
of the outcomes of disruption mechanisms, which is
understandable since they often constitute a menace
to cultural norms and regulations. In the present
context it means that individuals are frequently prevented from using disruptive mechanisms to foster
long term adaptation.

In cases like that, when there is no way out, severe disturbances must be expected to occur. If an
individual is forced to go on the way he did before
the panic reaction took place, states of prolonged
disruption may occur, that will interfere crushingly
with normal adaptive behavior. A state of permanent long-term adaptation will be established, causing any form of short-term adaptation to become impossible. The individual will continually find himself in a state of strong excitement, usually indicated as a state of *crisis*.

Apart from interfering with behavioral efficiency at the moment of the crisis, it will also cause
long-term effects to be established that may have de-
vastating effects upon personality development. If
the crisis is not somehow averted, it should be assumed on the basis of the theory developed here (assumption 5.1.3.4.)that a process of progressive individualization will be started that, if lasting long enough,
will inundate large parts of the original SRS-matrix. As long as the individual remains involved with
activities in situations where the disruption star-

ted, it must be assumed on the basis of the experience assumption (assumption 5.1.3.2), that processes of integration will occur with respect to strongly individualized elements of the SRS-matrix. These
processes may finally result in the formation of systematic delusions in a way that is usually indicated
as a psychotic condition.

An essential aspect of that condition is the
fact that the individual will gradually move out of
the reach of the speech community and will consequently become more and more resistent to verbal treatment. We are in agreement with Hebb's (1949) statement that psychic disorders of this kind may be characterized either as conditions of chronic emotional
disruption, or as permanent modifications of thinking
on the basis of disruptions in the past (p. 255). The
nature of those thinking modifications is conceived
here as the effect of strong individualization of e-
lements (rather than relationships *between* elements)
in the symbolic behavior structure, either in the
form of extreme subjectivity or in the form of an
extreme uniqueness of that structure. Strong individualization will finally lead to the rejection of
culturally determined patterns that have been used
in the past, but that have failed to provide control
at significant moments of the individual's existence.

Thus, it may be pointed out that the control
principle (assumption 5.1.2.1) constitutes the basis
for pathological forms of behavior as well as for
'normal' behavior. However, the occurrence of pathological behavior is based on a fundamental discrepancy between the control assumption (5.1.2.1) and the
information assumption (5.1.2.2). In view of the
priorities stated, in such a case the individual will
turn away from the community to support his adaptation, and start to develop his own strongly individualized system. As was indicated before, such a development may eventually lead to problems of adaptation in a more general sense, on the basis of deprivation of societal support in dealing with adaptational problems.

According to the present position, the concept
of optimal adaptation should be defined as the degree to which an individual manages to control the
environmental conditions he lives in. More concretely, optimal adaptation refers to the individual's
opportunities to transform his environment, the situations in which he finds himself, into directions
that he prefers. On the other hand, to the extent

that the individual becomes involved in situations
that are inevitable as well as untransformable, his
mental health will increasingly be imperiled.

Any treatment of disturbances of mental health,
occurring on such a basis, should primarily be directed at the recuperation of the *relationships* that the
individual maintains with the situations in question.
To that aim, use should be made of interactional
patterns naturally occurring between individual and
environment, to lead to adaptive behaviors finally
removing the disturbance. In that respect any treatment should be seen as an attempt to develop personality directedly.

Although we have no intention to add one more
treatment to the vast number of treatments existing
already in the realms of education and psychotherapy,
some principles may be indicated to contribute to
thinking in that area. For instance, on the issue of
verbal treatment versus performance treatment (in e-
ducation: lecturing vs. practice; in the clinic: verbal vs. behavioral therapy) it may be stated that the
former may only have consequences with respect to a
person's *strategy*, whereas the latter may be effective primarily with respect to his *tactics*. The question which type of treatment is best  can only be answered from a clear insight into the nature of the
disturbed relationship between individual and environment. Therefore any type of treatment should be
based on assessment procedures, providing information
concerning strategic and tactical conditions existing at the onset of treatment, and, preferably, an
estimation of these conditions during the disturbance.

Treatment itself should be tailor-made, in that
it is closely connected with the specific disturbance. The structure of treatment may be derived on the
basis of the phases that are supposed to be distin-
guishable in the occurrence of the disturbance itself. Thus, for instance, if the disturbance has included phases of differentiation, disruption and integration it might be attempted to evoke the same phases in an order considered to be optimally effective
on theoretical grounds. Thus, treatment in the context of the open-system theory may be tied on to several aspects of personality, it is basically multi-
functional and it adheres to sequential rules.

Obviously, this outline is far from being complete. Much research will be needed so as to enable a
treatment recipe in a more definite sense to be given.

Meanwhile, it seems worthwhile that a perspective may
be derived from the theory, to eventually base treatment on information and knowledge concerning adaptive
processes, occurring normally in everyday life. Mental
health is not defined here in terms of superior
intelligence or strength of the nervous system. The
core of that concept must be sought in the way individuals create and maintain fruitful relations with
their environment for the benefit of their vital
functions. In that perspective it is important to
carefully *select* situations to establish relations
with, as well as to carefully *reject* situations that
are unpromising. If relational frictions become manifest - and according to the present view, they usually
will - it is important to avoid overreactions as well
as underreactions. However, if a situation is considered
to be of utmost importance, no hesitations should keep
the individual from acting in any way possible to
restore the relationship. That he then has a great
many means at his disposal does not need to be emphasized any further.

*Footnote*

(1) '...the real basis of human personality is the
    whole of his societal connections with the world
    in agreement with his nature, but the connections
    that are *accomplished:* they are accomplished
    through his action, more specifically, through
    the whole of his multiple actions'. (translation
    by the author).

REFERENCES

1. Abelson, R.P. Computer simulation of "hot" cognition. In S.S. Tomkins & S. Messick (Eds.), *Computer simulation of personality*. New York: Wiley, 1963.
2. Allport, G.W. *Personality: A psychological interpretation*. New York: Holt, 1937.
3. Allport, G.W. What units shall we employ? In G. Lindzey (Ed.), *The assessment of motives*. New York: Rinehart, 1958.
4. Allport, G.W. Traits revisited. *American psychologist*, 1966, *21*, 1-10.
5. Allport, G.W. *The person in psychology. Selected essays*. Boston: Beacon, 1968.
6. Allport, G.W. & Odbert, H.S. Trait-names: A psycho-lexical study. *Psychological monographs*, 1936, *47*, 211.
7. Arnold, M.B. Brain function in emotions: A phaenomenological analysis. In Black (Ed.), *Physiological correlates of emotions*. New York, 1970.
8. Ashby, W.R. *Design for a brain*. London: Chapman & Hall, 1952.
9. Ashby, W.R. *An introduction to cybernetics*. New York: Wiley, 1956.
10. Aulich, D.K. *Effects of fear on exploratory behavior in the rat*. Ph.D. thesis. Nijmegen, 1978.
11. Ayala, F.J. The concept of biological progress. In F.J. Ayala & T. Dobzhansky (Eds.), *Studies in the philosophy of biology*. London: McMillan, 1974.
12. Bacon, S.J. Arousal and the range of cue utilization. *Journal of experimental psychology*, 1974, *102*, 1, 81-87.
13. Baddeley, A.D. Selective attention and performance in dangerous environments. *British*

*journal of psychology,* 1972, *63,* 4, 537-546.

14. Bandura, A. (Ed.)  *Psychological modeling.* Chicago: Aldine-Atherton, 1971.

15. Barker, R.G.   On the nature of the environment. *Journal of social issues,* 1963, *19,* 17-38.

16. Barker, R.G., Dembo, T. & Lewin, K.   Frustration and regression. *University of Iowa studie in child welfare,* 1941, *18,* 1.

17. Beier, E.G.   The effect of induced anxiety on flexibility of intellectual functioning. *Psychological monographs,* 1951, *55,* 9.

18. Berkun, M., Bialek, H., Kern, R. & Yagi, K.   Experimental studies of psychological stress in man. *Psychological monographs,* 1962, *76,* 1-39.

19. Berlyne, D.E.  *Conflict, arousal and curiosity.* New York: McGraw-Hill, 1960

20. Berlyne, D.E.  *Structure and direction in thinking.* New York: Wiley, 1965.

21. Bertalanffy, L. von   Theoretical models in biology and psychology. *Journal of personality,* 1951, *20,* 24-38.

22. Björkman, M. Feedforward and feedback as determiners of knowledge and policy: Notes on a neglected issue. *Scandinavian journal of psychology,* 1972, *13,* 158-167.

23. Boas, F. (Ed.)  *Handbook of American Indian languages.* Bureau of American ethnology, 1911, bulletin no. 40, 1, 1-83.

24. Bottomore, T.B.  *Karl Marx: Selected writings in sociology and social philosophy.* New York: McGraw-Hill, 1964.

25. Bowlby, J.  *Attachment and loss.* I Attachment. Pelican books, 1971.

26. Brady, J.V.   Emotion and sensitivity of psychoendoctrine systems. In D.C. Glass (Ed.), *Neurophysiology and emotion.* New York: Russell-Sage, 1967.

27. Brenner, Ch.  *Grundzüge der psychoanalyse.* Fischer Bücher, 1967.

28. Bresson, F.   Adaptation, équilibre et modèles tirés de la théorie des jeux. In F. Bresson (Ed.), *Les processus d'adaptation.* Paris: Presses Universitaires de France, 1967.

29. Bromly, D.B.  *Personality description in ordinary language.* London: Wiley, 1977.

30. Bruner, J.S. & Tagiuri, R.   The perception of
    people. In G. Lindzey, *Handbook of social
    psychology*, 2. Cambridge (Mass.): Addi-
    son-Wesley, 1954.
31. Brunswik, E.   Organismic achievement and environ-
    mental probability. *Psychological review*,
    1943, *50*, 255-272.
32. Brunswik, E.   *Perception and the representative
    design of psychological experiments*. U-
    niversity of California press, 1947.
33. Brunswik, E.   The conceptual framework of psycho-
    logy. In *International encyclopedia of
    unified science*, I, 10, 1952.
34. Brunswik, E.   "Ratiomorphic" models of perception
    and thinking. *Proceedings 14th interna-
    tional congress psychology*, Montreal,
    1954.
35. Bunderson, C.V.   *Transfer of mental abilities at
    different stages of practice in the so-
    lution of concept problems*. Research
    bulletin, 67-20. Princeton: Educational
    testing service, 1967.
36. Caminada, H.P.G.M.   Assertiviteit en conflicthan-
    tering. *Interimrapport KH Tilburg*, 1978.
37. Campbell, D.T.   On the conflicts between biologi-
    cal and social evolution and between
    psychology and moral tradition. *Ameri-
    can psychologist*, 1975, *30*, 12, 1103-
    1126.
38. Campbell, D.T. & Fiske, D.W.   Convergent and dis-
    criminant validation by the multitrait-
    multimethod matrix. *Psychological bul-
    letin*, 1959, *56*, 2, 81-105.
39. Campbell, D., Sanderson, R.E. & Laverty, S.G.
    Characteristics of a conditioned respon-
    se in human subjects during extinction
    trials following a single traumatic con-
    ditioning trial. *Journal of abnormal and
    social psychology*, 1964, *68*, 627-639.
40. Cannon, W.B.   *The wisdom of the body* (2nd ed.).
    New York: Norton, 1939.
41. Carr, H.A. & Kingsbury, F.A.   The concept of trait.
    *Psychological review*, 1938, *45*, 497-524.
42. Caspari, E.   Genetic basis of behavior. In A. Roe
    & G.G. Simpson, *Behavior and evolution*.
    New Haven: Yale university press, 1969
    (5e ed.).
43. Cattell, R.B.   Personality and motivation theory
    based on structural measurement. In J.
    L. McCary (Ed.), *Psychology of pers͠*

*lity*. New York: Grove press, 1956.

44. Child, J.L. & Waterhouse J.K.   Frustration and the quality of performance I: A critique of the Barker, Dembo and Lewin experiment. *Psychological review*, 1952, *59*, 351-362.

45. Chomsky, N.   *Aspects of the theory of syntax*. Cambridge (Mass.): MIT press, 1965.

46. Clausewitz, C.   *On war*. Penguin book. Pellican Classics, 1974.

47. Colby, K.M.   Computer simulation of a neurotic process. In S.S. Tomkins & S. Messick (Eds.), *Computer simulation of personality*. New York: Wiley, 1963.

48. Collins, A.M. & Quillian, M.R.   Retrieval time from semantic memory. *Journal of verbal learning and verbal behavior*, 1969, *8*, 240-247.

49. Cowen, E.L.   The influence of varying degrees of stress on problem-solving rigidity. *Journal of abnormal and social psychology*, 1952, *47*, 512-519.

50. Cronbach, L.J.   The two disciplines of scientific psychology. *American psychologist*, 1957, *12*, 671-684.

51. Cronbach, L.J. & Gleser, G.C.   *Psychological tests and personnel decisions*. Urbana: University of Illinois press, 1957.

52. Cross, R.W. la, Litman, F., Ogilvie, D.N. & White, B.L.   *The preschool project*. Monograph no. 9 Harvard university publications office, 1965.

53. Davis, R.C.,   The domain of homeostasis. *Psychological review*, 1958, *65*, 8-13.

54. Davis, R.D. & Cullen, J.H.   Disorganisation of perception in neurosis and psychosis. *American journal of psychology*, 1958, *1*, 229-237.

55. Dempsey, E.W.   Homeostasis. In S.S. Stevens (Ed.), *Handbook of experimental psychology*. New York: Wiley, 1951.

56. Dobzhansky, T.   Chance and creativity in evolution. In F.J. Ayala & T. Dobzhansky (Eds.), *Studies in the philosophy of biology*. London: McMillan, 1974.

57. Dobzhansky, T., Ayala, F.J., Stebbins, G.L. & Valentine, J.W. *Evolution*. San Francisco: Freeman, 1977.

58. Dollard, J. & Miller, N.E.   *Personality and psy-*

*chotherapy: An analysis in terms of
learning, thinking and culture.* New York:
McGraw-Hill, 1950.
59. Dufrenne, M. *La personalité de base. Un concept
sociologique.* Paris: Press Universitaires de France, 1953.
60. Easterbrook, J.A.   The effect of emotion on cue
utilization and the organization of behavior. *Psychological review,* 1959, *66,* 3,
183-201.
61. Edwards, W.   The theory of decision making. *Psychological bulletin,* 1954, *51,* 380-418.
62. Egbert, L., Battit, G., Welch, C. & Bartlett, M.
Reduction of post-operative pain by en-
couragement and instruction of patients.
*New England journal of medicine,* 1964,
*270,* 825-827.
63. Endler, N.S. & Hunt, J. McV.   SR-inventories of
hostility and comparisons of the proportions of variance from persons, responses and situations for hostility and
anxiousness. *Journal of personality and
social psychology,* 1968, *9,* 309-315.
64. Endler, N.S., Hunt, J. McV. & Rosenstein, A.J.
An SR-inventory of anxiousness, *Psychological monographs,* 1962, *76,* 17.
65. Endler, N.S. & Magnusson, D. *Interactional psychology and personality.* New York: Wiley,
1976.
66. Epstein, S. & Fenz, W.D.   Steepness of approach
and avoidance gradients in humans as a
function of experience: Theory and experiment. *Journal of experimental psychology,* 1965, *70,* 1-12.
67. Ferguson, G.A.   On transfer and the abilities of
man. *Canadian journal of psychology,*
1956, *10,* 121-131.
68. Fiske, D.W.   *Measuring the concepts of personality.* Chicago: Aldine press, 1971.
69. Fleishman, E.A. & Hempel, W.E. jr.   Change in
factor structure of a complex psychomotor test as a function of practice. *Psychometrika,* 1954, *19,* 3, 239-252.
70. Fleishman, E.A. & Hempel, W.E. jr.   The relation
between abilities and improvement with
practice in a visual discrimination task.
*Journal of experimental psychology,* 1955,
*49,* 301-310.
71. Frankenhaeuser, M.   Experimental approaches to the

study of catecholamines and emotion. In
L. Levi (Ed.), *Emotions. Their parameters and measurement.* New York: Raven,
1975.

72. Frederiksen, C.H.  Abilities, transfer and information retrieval in verbal learning.
*Multivariate behavioral research mono-
graph* 69-2, 1969.

73. French, J.W.  The relationship of problem-solving
styles to the factor composition of
tests. *Educational and psychological
measurement*, 1965, *25*, 9-28.

74. Freud, S.  *Complete psychological works.* I. Pre-
psychoanalytic publications and unpublis-
hed drafts. London: Hogarth press, 1966.

75. Freud, S., Totem & Taboo  *Standard edition* V 13.
London: Hogarth press, 1955.

76. Fruchter, B. & Fleishman, E.A.  A simplicial design for the analysis of correlational
learning data. *Multivariate behavior research*, 1967, *1*, 83-88.

77. Fullan, M. & Loubser, J.J.  Education and adaptive capacity. *Sociology of education*,
1972, *45*, 271-287.

78. Gage, N.L. & Cronbach, L.J.  Conceptual and methodological problems in interpersonal perception. *Psychological review*, 1955, *62*,
411-422.

79. Geer, J.P. van de  *A psychological study of problem solving.* Ph.D. thesis, Leiden, 1957.

80. Gill, M.M. (Ed.)  *The collected papers of David
Rapaport.* New York: Basic books, 1967.

81. Goffman, E.  *Interaction ritual.* New York: Anchor
books, 1967.

82. Grossman, S.P., Peters, R.H., Freedman, P.E. &
Willer, H.I. Behavioral effects of cho-
linergic  stimulation of the thalamic
reticular formation. *Journal of comparative and physiological psychology*, 1965,
*59*, 57-65.

83. Guilford, J.P.  *Personality.* New York: McGraw-
Hill, 1959.

84. Hall, C.S. & Lindzey, G.  *Theories of personality.*
New York: Wiley, 1957 and 1970.

85. Hamburg, D.A., Coelho, G.V. & Adams, J.E.  Coping
and adaptation. Steps toward a synthesis
of biological and social perceptions. In
G.V. Coelho, D.A. Hamburg & J.E. Adams
(Eds.), *Coping and adaptation.* New York:
Basic books, 1974.

86. Hammond, K.R.   Probabilistic functionalism: Egon
        Brunswik's integration of the history,
        theory and method of psychology. In K.R.
        Hammond (Ed.), *The psychology of Egon
        Brunswik*. New York: Holt, 1966.
87. Hammond, K.R. & Brehmer, B.   Quasi-rationality and
        distrust: implications for interactional
        conflict. In L. Rappoport & D.A. Summers,
        *Human judgment and social interaction*.
        New York: Holt, 1978.
88. Hammond, K.R. & Summers, D.A.   Cognitive control.
        *Psychological review*, 1972, *79*, 158-167.
89. Harlow, H.   The evolution of learning. In A. Roe
        & G.G. Simpson, *Behavior and evolution*.
        New Haven: Yale university press, 1969
        (5e ed.).
90. Hebb, D.O.   *Organization of behavior. A neuropsy-
        chological theory*. New York: Wiley, 1949.
91. Hebb, D.O.   On the nature of fear. In D.K. Cand-
        land (Ed.), *Emotion; bodily change*.
        Princeton: van Nostrand, 1962.
92. Heck, G.L.M. van   *Traits and behavior*. Ph.D. the-
        sis Tilburg, 1979 (in press).
93. Heck, G.L.M. van & Van der Leeuw, E.   Situatie en
        dispositie als variantie-komponenten in
        zelfbeoordeling en beoordeling van de
        ander. *Gedrag*, 1975, *4/5*, 202-214.
94. Helson, H.   *Adaptation level theory*. New York:
        Harper and Row, 1964.
95. Hettema, P.J.   Trekken, processen en persoonlijk-
        heidstests. *Nederlands tijdschrift voor
        de psychologie*, 1967, *22*, 10, 618-641.
96. Hettema, P.J.   Cognitive abilities as process
        variables. *Journal of personality and so-
        cial psychology*, 1968, *10*, 4, 461-471.
97. Hettema, P.J.   *Doceerstijlen*. Nijmegen: Nijmeegs
        instituut voor onderwijs research, 1972.
98. Hettema, P.J.   *Verschillen tussen mensen*.
        Inaugural, Tilburg, 1972.
99. Hettema, P.J.   Persoonlijkheid en sociaal gedrag.
        In J. Jaspars & R. van der Vlist, *Sociale
        psychologie in Nederland*, 1979 (in press).
100. Hettema, P.J.   *The utilization of cue redundancy
        in judgment in a natural setting*, 1979
        (in preparation).
101. Hilgard, E.R.   Human motives and the concept of
        the self. *American psychologist* 1949,
        *4*, 374-382.
102. Hinde, R.A.   *Animal behavior. A synthesis of etho-
        logy and comparative psychology*. New

York: McGraw-Hill, 1970.

103. Hjelle, L.A. & Ziegler, D.J. *Personality theories: Basic assumptions, research and applications*. New York: McGraw-Hill, 1976.

104. Humboldt, W. von *Über die Verschiedenheit des menschlichen Sprachbaues und ihrem Einfluss auf die geistigen Entwicklung des Menschengeschlechts*. Berlin, 1936.

105. Hundleby, J.D., Pawlik, K. & Cattell, R.B. *Personality factors in objective test devices*. San Diego: Knapp, 1965.

106. Hunt, J. McV. *Intelligence and experience*. New York: Ronald, 1961.

107. Hunt, J. McV. Traditional personality theory in the light of recent evidence. *American Scientist*, 1965, *53*, 80-96.

108. Huxley, J.S. Cultural process and evolution. In A. Roe & G.G. Simpson (Eds.), *Behavior and evolution*. New Haven: Yale university press, 1969.

109. Janis, I.L. Problems related to the control of fear in combat. In S. Stouffer *et al., The American soldier*. 2. Princeton: Princeton university press, 1949.

110. Janis, I.L. *Psychological stress*. New York: Wiley, 1958.

111. Janis, I.L., Mahl, G.F., Kagan, J. & Holt, R.R. *Personality. Dynamics, development and assessment*. New York: Harcourt, Brace and World, 1969.

112. Jung, C.G. *Collected works*. Bollingen series. 5 Symbols of transformation. New York: Routledge-Kegan Paul, 1956.

113. Kardiner, A. *The individual and his society*. New York, 1939.

114. Kardiner, A. *The psychological frontiers of society*. New York, 1945.

115. Katz, J.J. *Semantic theory*. New York: Harper-Row, 1972.

116. Kelly, G.A. *The psychology of personal constructs* New York: Norton, 1955.

117. Kety, S.S. Psychoendocrine systems and emotion: biological aspects. In D.C. Glass (Ed,), *Neurophysiology and emotion*. New York: Russell-Sage, 1967.

118. Klabbers, J.H.G. *Simulatie van een mens-machine systeem*. Ph.D. thesis, Nijmegen, 1972.

119. Klages, L. *The science of character*. London: Allen & Unwin, 1932.

120. Kluckhohn, C. & Kelly, W.H.    The concept of cul-
        ture. In R. Linton (Ed.), *The science of
        man in the world crisis*. New York: Colum-
        bia university press, 1945.
121. Kluckhohn, C. & Murray, H.    Personality formati-
        on: The determinants. In C. Kluckhohn,
        H. Murray & D.M. Schneider, *Personality
        in nature, society and culture*. (2nd ed.).
        New York: Knopf, 1971.
122. Kouwer, B.J.    *Existentiële psychologie*. Meppel:
        Boom, 1973.
123. Krech, D., Rosenzweig, M.R. & Bennett, E.L.    Di-
        mensions of discrimination and level of
        cholinesterase activity in the cerebral
        cortex of the rat. *Journal of comparati-
        ve and physiological psychology*, 1956,
        *49*, 261-268.
124. Krech, D., Rosenzweig, M.R. & Bennett, E.L.    Re-
        lations between brain chemistry and pro-
        blem solving, among rats raised in enri-
        ched and impoverished environments.
        *Journal of comparative and physiological
        psychology*, 1962, *55*, 801-807.
125. Krechevsky, I.    Hypotheses in rats. *Psychologi-
        cal review*, 1932, *39*, 516-532.
126. Lazarus, R.S.    *Psychological stress and the co-
        ping process*. New York: McGraw-Hill,
        1966.
127. Leontiev, A.N.    *Probleme der Entwicklung des
        Psychischen*. Frankfurt am Main: Athenäum
        Fischer Taschenbuch Verlag, 1973.
128. Leontiev, A.N.    *Tätigkeit, Bewusstsein, Persön-
        lichkeit*. Stuttgart: Klett, 1977.
129. Levi, L. (Ed.)    *Stress and distress in response
        to psychosocial stimuli*. New York: Per-
        gamon, 1972,
130. Levy-Brühl, L.    *Les fonctions mentales dans les
        sociétés inferieures*. Paris: Alcan, 1912.
131. Loehlin, J.C.    *Computer models of personality*.
        New York: Random House, 1968.
132. Lorenz, K.    *Evolution and modification of behavi-
        or*. University of Chicago press, 1965.
133. Lorenzer, A.    Symbol, Interaktion und Praxis. In
        A. Lorenzer (*et al.*), *Psychoanalyse als
        Sozialwissenschaft*. Frankfurt am Main:
        Edition Suhrkamp 454, 1971.
134. Lorenzer, A.    *Kritik des psychoanalytischen Sym-
        bolbegriffs*. Frankfurt am Main: Edition
        Suhrkamp 393, 1972.

135. Machiavelli, N.  *The Prince*. Penguin classics, 1974.

136. Maier, N.R.F.  Frustration theory: restatement and extension. *Psychological review,* 1956, *63,* 370-388.

137. Malinowsky, B.  *Sex and repression in savage society*. New York: Harcourt, Brace, 1927.

138. Mandler, G.  The interruption of behavior. In D. Levine (Ed.), *Nebraska symposium on motivation*. Lincoln: University of Nebraska press, 1964.

139. Mandler, G.  *Mind and emotions*. New York: Wiley, 1975.

140. Mayr, E.  Taxonomic categories in fossil hominids In *Cold Spring harbor symposia on quantitative biology.* V 15. Origin and evolution of man, 1950.

141. McHugh, P.  *Defining the situation. The organization of meaning in social interaction*. New York: Bobbs-Merrill, 1968.

142. Mead, G.H.  *Mind, self and society*. Chicago: University of Chicago press, 1934.

143. Mechanic, D.  Social structure and personal adaptation: Some neglected dimensions. In G.V. Coelho, D.A. Hamburg & J.A. Adams (Eds.), *Coping and adaptation*. New York: Basic books, 1974.

144. Menyuk, P.  *Sentences children use*. Cambridge (Mass.): MIT-press, 1969.

145. Mesarovic, M.D.   A mathematical theory of general systems. In G.J. Klir (Ed.), *Trends in general systems theory*. New York: Wiley, 1972.

146. Messick, S.  Beyond structure: In search of functional models of psychological process. *Psychometrika,* 1972, *37,* 4, 357-375.

147. Meyer, F.  Le concept d'adaptation. In F. Bresson (Ed.), *Les processus d'adaptation*. Paris: Presses universitaires de France, 1967.

148. Miller, G.A. & Johnson Laird, P.N.  *Language and perception*. Cambridge (Mass,): Cambridge university press, 1976.

149. Miller, G.A. & McNeill, D.  Psycholinguistics. In G. Lindzey & E. Aronson, *Handbook of social psychology,* VIII. Cambridge (Mass.): Addison-Wesley, 1969, 666-794.

150. Miller, G.A., Galanter, E. & Pribram, K.H. *Plans and the structure of behavior*. New

York: Holt, 1960.

151. Mischel, W. *Personality and assessment.* New
     York: Wiley, 1968.

152. Mischel, W. Toward a cognitive social learning
     reconceptualization of personality.
     *Psychological review,* 1973, *80,* 4, 252-
     283.

153. Montgomery, K.C. & Monkman, J.A. The relation
     between fear and exploratory behavior.
     *Journal of comparative and physiological
     psychology,* 1955, *48,* 132-136.

154. Moser, U., Zeppelin, I. von & Schneider, W.
     Computer simulation of neurotic defense
     processes. *Behavioral science,* 1970, *15,*
     194-202.

155. Murdock, G.P. The common denominator of cultu-
     re. In R. Linton (Ed.), *The science of
     man in the world crisis.* New York: Co-
     lumbia university press, 1945.

156. Neumann, J. von & Morgenstern, O. *Theory of ga-
     mes and economic behavior.* Princeton:
     Princeton university press, 1944.

157. Newell, A. & Simon, H.A. *Human problem solving.*
     Englewood Cliffs: Prentice Hall, 1972.

158. Nisbett, R.E. & DeCamp Wilson, T. Telling more
     than we can know: Verbal reports on men-
     tal processes. *Psychological review,*
     1977, *84,* 3, 231-259.

159. Nissen, H.W. Axes of behavioral comparison. In
     A. Roe & G.G. Simpson, *Behavior and evo-
     lution.* New Haven: Yale university press,
     1969.

160. Norman, D.A. Learning and remembering: A tuto-
     rial preview. In A. Kornblum (Ed.), *At-
     tention and performance IV.* New York:
     Academic press, 1978.

161. Orchard, R.A. On an approach to general systems
     theory. In G.J. Klir (Ed.), *Trends in gene-
     ral systems theory.* New York: Wiley, 1972.

162. Osgood, Ch.E. *Method and theory in experimental
     psychology.* New York: Oxford university
     press, 1953.

163. Osler, S.F. Intellectual performance as a func-
     tion of two types of psychological
     stress. *Journal of experimental psycholo-
     gy,* 1954, *47,* 115-121.

164. Pally, S. Cognitive rigidity as a function of
     threat. *Journal of Personality,* 1954,
     *23,* 346-355.

165. Pavlow, I.P.  *Selected works*. Ed. by J. Gibbons
     1950.
166. Pervin, L.A.  Performance and satisfaction as a
     function of individual-environment fit.
     *Psychological bulletin*, 1968, *59*, 56-58.
167. Petersen, D.R.  Scope and generality of verbally
     defined personality factors. *Psychologi-
     cal review*, 1965, *72*, 48-59.
168. Peursen, C.A. van, Bertels, C.P. & Nauta, D. *In-
     formatie*. Utrecht: Aula boeken, 1968.
169. Piaget, J.  *Play, dreams and imitation of the
     child*. New York: Norton, 1951.
170. Piaget, J.  La portée psychologique et épistémo-
     logique des essais neohulliens de D. Ber-
     lyne. In *Etudes d'épistémologie généti-
     que*. Paris: Presses Universitaires de
     France, 1960.
171. Piaget, J.  Intelligence et adaptation biologique.
     In F. Bresson (Ed.), *Les processus d'a-
     daptation*. Paris: Presses universitaires
     de France, 1967.
172. Powers, W.T.  *Behavior: The control of percep-
     tion*. Chicago: Aldine, 1973.
173. Pribram, K.H.  Emotion: Steps toward a neuro-
     psychological theory. In D.C. Glass (Ed.),
     *Neurophysiology and emotion*. New York:
     Russell-Sage, 1967.
174. Pribram, K.H.  Comparative neurology and the evo-
     lution of behavior. In A. Roe and G.G.
     Simpson, *Behavior and evolution*. New Ha-
     ven: Yale university press, 1969.
175. Pribram, K.H.  *Languages of the brain: Experi-
     mental paradoxes and principles in neuro-
     physiology*. Englewood Cliffs: Prentice-
     Hall, 1971.
176. Pribram, K.H. & McGuiness, D.  Arousal, activa-
     tion and effort in the control of atten-
     tion. *Psychological review*, 1975, *82*, 2,
     116-149.
177. Putnoky, J.  Are cognitive processes regulated
     only by feedback systems? *Studia psycho-
     logica*, 1973, *15*, 1, 65-71.
178. Rapoport, A.  The uses of mathematical isomor-
     phism in general systems theory. In G.J.
     Klir (Ed.), *Trends in general systems
     theory*  New York: Wiley, 1972.
179. Rappoport, L. & Summers, D.A.  *Human judgment and
     social interaction*. New York: Holt, 1973.
180. Reynolds, V. *The biology of human action.* Lon-

don: Freeman, 1976.
181. Roe, A. & Simpson, G.G. *Behavior and evolution.*
Introduction. New Haven: Yale university
press, 1969.
182. Rotter, J.B. *Social learning and clinical psychology.* New York: Prentice-Hall, 1954.
183. Rotter, J.B. Generalized expectancies for internal versus external control of reinforcement. *Psychological monographs, 1966,
80, 1,* whole no. 609.
184. Sapir, E. *Culture, language and personality.*
Berkeley: University of California press,
1970.
185. Sarason, I.G. *Personality: an objective approach.*
2nd ed. New York: Wiley, 1972.
186. Saussure, F. de *Cours de linguistique générale.*
Paris, 1916.
187. Searle, L.V. The organization of hereditary maze-brightness and maze-dullness. *Genetic
psychology monograph, 1949, 39, 279-325.*
188. Sechrest, L. Personality. *Annual review of psychology, 1976, 1-27.*
189. Secord, P.F. Social psychology in search of a
paradigm. *Personality and social psychology bulletin, 1977, 3, 41-50.*
190. Seligman, M.E.P., Maier, S.F. & Solomon, R.L.
Unpredictable and uncontrolled aversive
events. In F.R. Brush (Ed.), *Aversive
conditioning and learning.* New York: Academic press, 1969.
191. Shands, H.C. An outline of the process of recovery from severe trauma. *American medical
association archives of neurology and
psychiatry, 1955.*
192. Shapiro, D. & Crider, A. Psychophysiological approaches in social psychology. In G.
Lindzey & E. Aronson, *The handbook of
social psychology, 2nd ed. III,* Reading:
Addison-Wesley, 1969.
193. Shotter, J. Men, the manmakers: George Kelly and
the psychology of personal contructs. In
D. Bannister (Ed.), *Perspectives in personal construct theory.* London: Academic
press, 1970.
194. Simpson, G.G. *The meaning of evolution.* New Haven: Yale University press, 1949.
195. Simpson, G.G. *This view of life.* New York: Harcourt, Brace and World, 1964.
196. Simpson, G.G. Behavior and evolution. In A. Roe

& G.G. Simpson, *Behavior and evolution*. New Haven: Yale university press, 1969.

197. Simpson, G.G.   The study of evolution: Methods and present status of theory. In A. Roe & G.G. Simpson (Eds.), *Behavior and evolution*. New Haven: Yale university press, 1969.

198. Skinner, B.F.   The phylogeny and ontogeny of behavior. *Science*, 1966, 1205-1213.

199. Skinner, B.F.   *Contingencies of reinforcement: A theoretical analysis*. New York: Meredith, 1969.

200. Skinner, B.F.   *Beyond freedom and dignity*. Pelican books, 1973.

201. Slovic, P. & Lichtenstein, S.   Comparison of Bayesian and regression approaches to the study of information processing in judgment. In L. Rappoport & D.A. Summers, *Human judgment and social interaction*. New York: Holt, 1973.

202. Sokolov, E.N.   Neuronal models and the orienting reflex. In M.A.B. Brazier (Ed.), *The central nervous system and behavior*. New York: Josiah Macy jr. foundation, 1960.

203. Spitz, R.A.   Aggression and adaptation. *Archives of general psychiatry*, 1971, *23*, 2, 107-118.

204. Stagner, R.   Homeostasis as a unifying concept in personality theory. *Psychological review*, 1951, *58*, 5-17.

205. Stebbins, G.L.   Adaptive shifts and evolutionary novelty: A compositionist approach. In F.J. Ayala & T. Dobzhansky (Eds.), *Studies in the philosophy of biology*. London: McMillan, 1974.

206. Stephenson, W.   *The study of behavior*. Chicago: University of Chicago press, 1953.

207. Stern, W.   *Allgemeine Psychologie auf personalistischen Grundlage*. Den Haag, 1935.

208. Thorpe, W.H.   Ethology and the coding problem in germ cell and brain. *Zeitschrift für Tierpsychologie*, 1963, *20*, 529-552.

209. Tinbergen, N.   *The study of instinct*. Oxford: Oxford university press, 1969.

210. Tolman, E.C. & Brunswik, E.   The organism and the causal texture of the environment. *Psychological review*, 1935, *42*, 43-77.

211. Tolson, W.W., Mason, J.W., Sachar., E.J., Hamburg, D.A., Handlan, J.H. & Fishman, J.R.   Uri-

nary catecholamine response associated
with hospital admission in normal human
subjects. *Journal of psychosomatic research,* 1965, *8,* 365-372.

212. Tryon, R.C.   Individual differences. In F.A. Moss
(Ed.), *Comparative psychology.* New York:
Prentice-Hall, 1942.

213. Vossen, J.M.H.  *Exploratief gedrag en leergedrag
bij de rat.* Amsterdam: Swets, 1966.

214. Vygotsky, L.J.  *Thought and language.* Cambridge
(Mass.): MIT press, 1962.

215. Waddington, C.H.  *The ethical animal.* London:
Allen Unwin, 1960.

216. Wagner, A.R.  Conditioned frustration as a learned drive. *Journal of experimental psychology,* 1963, *66,* 142-148.

217. Wallace, J.  An abilities conception of personality: Some implications for personality
measurement. *American psychologist,*
1966, *21,* 132-138.

218. White, R.W.  Motivation reconsidered: The concept
of competence. *Psychological review,*
1959, *66,* 5, 297-333.

219. Whorf, B.L.  *Language, thought and reality.* Cambridge (Mass.) : MIT, 1956.

220. Williams, R.J.  *Biochemical individuality.* New
York: Wiley, 1956.

221. Wittgenstein, L.  *Philosophical investigations.*
English edition. Oxford: Blackwell, 1968.

222. Wolman, B.B.  *Dictionnary of behavioral science.*
London: McMillan, 1973.

223. Yerkes, R.M. & Dodson, J.D.  The relation of
strength of stimulus to rigidity of habit formation. *Journal of comparative
and neurological psychology,* 1908, *18,*
459-482.